Dundee United
Who's Who

Dundee United
Who's Who

PAT KELLY

JOHN DONALD PUBLISHERS LTD
EDINBURGH

ISBN 0 85976 502 4

British Library Cataloguing in Publication Data

A catalogue record for this book is available
from the British Library.

Typesetting and prepress origination by Brinnoven, Livingston.
Printed and bound in Great Britain by Bell & Bain Ltd, Glasgow.

CONTENTS

FOREWORD BY LORRAINE KELLY

Dundee, the City of Discovery, holds many special memories for me. It was the city where I married Steve, and it's the home of my favourite football team Dundee United.

When I was a reporter for TV-AM, I used to spend most of my weekends in the city, and when Dundee United were at home I would be standing there in all weathers cheering them on.

Will we ever forget the international-quality players; Dave Narey, Paul Sturrock, Paul Hegarty, Maurice Malpas and so many others?

One of my favourite Tannadice memories was in 1987 when the side reached the final of the EUFA Cup. For me the result was immaterial, and I will never forget the emotions of the United fans that night. They so sporting that they cheered the winning side. The fans were a credit to Dundee United and the Scottish nation.

Dundee United are a team with a strong historical background. They were relatively poor in financial terms, but now they can hold their heads high for they are up there with the 'greats', in a new look stadium and with an abundance of talented players.

The former manager and now chairman, Jim McLean, and his fellow directors past and present must take credit for what has been achieved over the past few years, and no doubt the side will go forward and win a few more trophies for the fans.

When I was asked to write for the *Who's Who*, I gladly accepted. Being one of United's biggest fans, I enjoyed reading about the players past and present.

Personally, I think that the *Dundee United Who's Who* is a very useful guide for anyone who has a genuine interest in the club.

I sincerely hope that you enjoy reading it too.

Best Wishes
Lorraine

ACKNOWLEDGEMENTS

I would like to personally thank all the people who have helped me complete this book.

First, my son Patrick who I dedicate this book to, my wife Lynne for all her encouragement. Tony Saunders for all his advice, my brother-in-law Fred Menzies for the books and other expert knowledge on the club, Dundee United Chairman Jim McLean, Bill Littlejohn and the United Board. Former Club Manager Tommy McLean, Maurice Malpas and the United players. John Rudd, Jim Lambie, Bill Donald, Terry Noon, Billy Anderson, Margaret McLeod, Margaret Farrell, Sandy Wilkie, Ally Bally, Ian Reilly, Grant and Maurice Speedie, Dave Bussey, Helen and Pauline in the United Shop. To Dundee City Council and the Library Staff Eileen Moran, Deirdre Sweeney, Edna Cable, Ida Glendinning, Carol Lamb and Carol Smith. Dave and Gwen MacDougall. Jean Martin. Bill Campbell and the Dundee United Commercial Department. Gillian Mason at Dundee United. Dave Martin and George Martin at Foto Press.

Also written for my late niece Stacey Menzies and the late Jim Mannion who both died at such a young age.

INTRODUCTION

When I began to research old newspapers and books I soon began to realise that Dundee United was a club steeped in history. I never fully appreciated the changes that have taken place at Tannadice over the years. Wonderful varieties of characters are now written into the club's history. After thinking long and hard I embarked on this project of writing about the people who have made the club what it is today. However, if I have omitted any name from this book, I can only apologise. There were many players who played for the club, especially during the war years, and others have had trials or played for the reserves, who may have been missed. Unfortunately, my sources could not be 100 per cent accurate but I did my best to include all the names that I could find.

From a historical point of view, considering the early financial difficulties together with the humble and relatively poor financial beginnings and the way the club has struggled through the financial quagmire, it really is amazing to see Tannadice Park today. When Pat Reilly and others first formed Dundee Hibs in 1909, who would have dreamed that the club would still have been in existence in the 1990s, albeit with a different name.

From manager Jimmy Brownlie to United's most successful manager, and now club chairman, Jim McLean, all deserve credit for their contribution to the club. And we must not forget the board of directors, past and present, for their off-the-park achievements. Without their financial input, the club would have ended many years ago. Names such as George and Johnston Grant, George Fox, Jimmy Littlejohn and Ernest Robertson may mean little to the younger supporters, but their input as directors and chairpersons has been immense.

From the early days some may remember one of United's top goal scorers, 'Hurricane Hutch', who, with his immense talent and skill set many fans into a frenzy with his outstanding style of play. And how can we ever forget the delightful talents of player, and now manager, Paul Sturrock, when he entertained the Tannadice faithful. Not forgetting Kenny Cameron, Doug

Smith, Dennis Gillespie, right through to the rock solid defence of Paul Hegarty and Dave Narey – all gifted and talented players. Each and every player has helped to entertain the fans in his own imitable way.

During the 1960s and 1970s changes began to ring out at Tannadice. Jerry Kerr began to revive the United fortunes when the club won promotion from Division Two into Division One in season 1959-60. Under the direction of Jerry Kerr, United remained in Division One throughout that decade. In December 1971, Jim McLean took over and his history of achievements is well documented in this book.

It was not until the McLean era that the Tannadice faithful tasted any real major success. Their first real honour for the club was in 1979 when they lifted the Scottish League Cup after beating Aberdeen 3-0 at Dens Park after a 0-0 draw played out at Hampden Park on a cold December Saturday afternoon. This was achieved under the managership of Jim McLean, and there was more to follow. The following season they were back in the final again. This time the opponents were city rivals Dundee. The score was 3-0; and the rest, as they say, is history.

Throughout the years, Dundee United has gone through many major upheavals, from major ground improvements, to changes at managerial levels. It all makes up the unique United history.

One thing that cannot be ignored is the fact that Dundee United supporters are the finest in Europe. One only has to look back to EUFA Cup Final of 1987 to prove that. Defeated 2-1, the United fans were held in high esteem throughout the world for their sportsmanship.

Certainly there have been disappointments; but a club will always have lean years. Again, this all part of history, and Dundee United has always triumphed in the end. That should never be forgotten.

The project is now completed, and the book, *Dundee United Who's Who*, is for you – the fans. I sincerely hope that you will use it as a reference source, and at the same time you will enjoy its content, recalling at a glance the major improvements and achievements of United's past and present system.

Pat Kelly

– 1 –
THE PLAYERS

Charlie Adam, was 27 years of age when he signed for United on 20 March 1989 from Brechin City. The reported fee was in the region of £35,000. He played his first game for the club on 21 March 1989 in a reserve match against Motherwell. Charlie then made his first team debut on 1 April 1989 against Aberdeen at Pittodrie. Aberdeen ran out 1-0 winners that day.

G. Adams, was a player with Dundee Hibs. In season 1921-22 he made 16 league appearances for the club.

Bob Adamson, signed to United in August 1941 as a War guest. As a player, he had previously been with Hearts and Dundee. Bob made his United debut on 16 August 1941 in the North-Eastern League against St Bernard's. United ran out 4-1 winners that day.

James Adamson, was 17 years old when he signed for United on 12 August 1944. James made his debut for the club the same day against East Fife at Tannadice. The young lad had attended Harris Academy and played for junior side Dundee Violet.

Thomas Adamson, born in 1910, and signed for the club in 1937 from Lochee Harp. During his spell with United he played in 30 competitive fixtures and scored two goals. In 1938 he joined Forfar, but returned to Tannadice on 2 November 1939 as a War guest. Thomas made his return debut with United on 4 November 1939 against Cowdenbeath. He was also in the squad that lost 1-0 to Rangers in the 1940 War Cup Final. In July 1940 he was in the RAF.

Derek Addison, born in 1955, and signed by manager Jim McLean, in 1973, from Lochee United. The player was also a former S-signing with Hibernian. Derek made his first team debut on 12 January 1974 in a game against Hibernian. United lost that day 3-1. In January 1981 Dundee United turned down a bid of £50,000 from Hibernian. However, they eventually sold him to Hearts on 18 September 1981 in a deal that included Billy Pettigrew also heading for Tynecastle. The media said that the fee was in the region of £180,000. Hearts struggled to meet the payments for both players, and United had to wait until May 1983 before they received the final instalment of £12,500. Dundee United were far from happy at the delay in payment, and demanded that Hearts should also pay interest on lost revenue. To add insult to injury, Hearts had already transferred Addison to another club the previous year. On 23 June 1982 Hearts transferred Addison to St Johnstone for a fee in the region of £60,000. St Johnstone appointed him player-coach on 21 June 1985.

Jock Adie, signed by manager Tommy Gray on 22 August 1958. Jock made his first team debut on 23 August 1958 against St Johnstone at Tannadice. While he was with the club, he featured in five competitive games.

Archie Aikman, signed by manager Reggie Smith on 4 February 1955. Archie made his United debut on 5 February 1955 against Brechin at Glebe Park, and he scored the club's winning goal.

The player made his Tannadice debut on 12 February 1955 against Cowdenbeath. United freed him in April 1957. While he was with United, he played in 55 games and scored 17 goals.

Colin Ainslie, was a product of Hill O' Beath Swifts. United freed Colin on 10th January 1985, who then joined Oakley Juniors.

David Allan, signed by Jerry Kerr on 8 August 1963 from Edinburgh Athletic. At the time of signing, David was 16 years old and had played in a trial game for the club two days before he signed. The club freed David in May 1965.

Julian Alsford, born in Poole on 24 December 1972, and signed by manager Tommy McLean on 26 March 1998 for a reported fee of £50,000 paid to Chester City. Also signed on the same day was his Chester club-mate Iain Jenkins. Julian made his United debut on 28 March 1998 against Motherwell at Fir Park. The player made his home debut on 7 April 1998 in the 2-2 draw with Dunfermline.

Alec Anderson, signed for United on 18 August 1954 and had previously played for St Johnstone, Forfar, and Southampton. Alec made his first team debut on 21 August 1954 against Brechin City at Glebe Park. While he was with the club, he featured in four competitive matches.

Doug Anderson, signed by manager Jimmy Brownlie during season 1935-36. While he was at the club, he made 27 league appearances and scored six goals. After he left United, Doug signed for Hibs and made his debut for them on 26 September 1936 against Clyde. Hibs later freed Doug in April 1937.

Mikael Andersson, signed by manager Tommy McLean on 3 November 1997. The 24-year-old Scandinavian had been playing for Orbero at the time of signing. He played in a reserve match against Hibernian on 5 November 1997 at Tannadice. United reserves won 5-1 with Mikael grabbing one of the goals. Mikael made his first team debut on 9 November 1997 when he came off the subs bench in a game against Aberdeen. United won 5-0 and the following day Aberdeen sacked their manager Roy Aitken.

Gordon Archibald, was 19 years old when he signed a provisional form for the club in January 1977. The goalkeeper played for Brechin Vics. Gordon played his first game for United in a reserve match on 29 January 1977 against Clydebank.

Vincent Arkins, came from Dublin, and signed by manager Jim McLean on 4 December 1987. The 17-year-old became a full-time player on the 7 December 1987. He made his debut in a tangerine shirt the same day in a Youth Cup Tie against Hearts at Tannadice. Vinnie signed for St Johnstone on 26 November 1991 from Shamrock Rovers for a fee of £55,000.

Paul Armstrong, played in a trial match between United and Queen's Park on 4 August 1990.

Sandy Arnold, signed by manager Willie MacFadyen in August 1952 from Fife club Dundonald Bluebell. Sandy made his first team debut on 16 August 1952 against Ayr United at Somerset Park. Three years earlier in 1949 he was playing for Hibs. United freed the player in April 1957. While he was with United, he featured in 71 competitive games.

Jimmy Baigan, called up by the club on 29 July 1963 and made his debut for United on 27 September 1963. This was in a reserve game played at Tannadice against Dunfermline.

James Baillie, signed by manager Willie Reid on 5 November 1931. James previously played for Fulham in season 1930-31 and then went onto Cardiff City. He made his United first team debut on 7 November 1931 against Falkirk. While he was with United, he featured in five first team games.

Jock Bain, played in several trial games for United during season 1929-30. The player was eventually signed by manager Jimmy Brownlie and made 11 appearances for the club in that season. In August 1931 he signed for Brechin City.

John Bain, signed to United by manager Jimmy Brownlie on 1 June 1927 from Dunfermline Athletic. He had also played for Inverkeithing Juniors. John made his United debut on 13 August 1927 in the 4-2 win over Bathgate at Tannadice. While he was with United, he featured in 36 league games.

Peter Bain, signed by manager Jimmy Brownlie on 28 March 1936 on a free transfer from Partick Thistle. Peter made his first team debut for United on 8 August 1936 in the 4-2 win over King's Park. He parted company with United on 7 November 1936 by mutual consent. While he was with United, he appeared in ten league games and scored three goals for the club.

Ian Ballantyne, was 20 years old when he signed for the club on 1 May 1979 from Queen's Park. The media reported the fee as £12,000. Ian had scored 19 goals with Queen's Park in season 1978-79. United also included Ian in a pool of players that toured Japan in 1979. Dundee United transferred the player to Raith Rovers in 1980. Raith in turn released him on 12 May 1983.

Gordon Bannerman, signed to Dundee Hibs by manager Pat Reilly on 15 April 1914 from St Johnstone. His previous clubs included Forfar Athletic. Gordon made his club debut on 18 April 1914 against his former club Forfar. This game ended in a 2-1 victory for Dundee Hibs in the Northern-League game. He made his Tannadice debut on 22 April 1914. This match was against Forfar. Again Hibs ran out winners that day 2-0.

Tom Bannister, played for Dundee Hibs in the 1920s. In season 1921-22 he made 36 league appearances for the club.

Eamonn Bannon, born in 1958, and signed for Hearts in 1976 from Links Boys Club. He signed for Dundee United from Chelsea on 31 October 1979 for a reputed fee of £165,000. The player made his United debut the same night in a match against Raith Rovers. Eamonn scored his first goal for the club on 3 November 1979 in a game against Aberdeen. The score that day was United 3 Aberdeen 0. Bannon soon became a favourite with the crowd and stayed with United for nine years. He played in the Scottish Cup final in 1988, which incidentally was his last game with the club. On 13 July 1988 he signed again for Hearts for a reported fee of £225,000, and he spent five seasons with them. In 1996 he became manager of Falkirk, only to lose his job after a disagreement with the club chairman. His post lasted all of six months. On 20 December 1996 the Falkirk directors sacked him after they were fined £25,000. The Scottish League had fined them, and told them that they had to replay the First Division match against St Mirren. The reason was that Eamonn had included John Clark as a trialist. There was a mixup over him playing in this game. The League Committee stated that this player should not have been playing. They then handed out this punishment to Falkirk. Incidentally, John scored in the game. Eamonn's former clubs included Hearts, Chelsea, and a spell as coach with Hibernian.

Frank Barclay, signed by manager Reggie Smith in August 1955 from Nottingham Forest. The player made his United debut in a B. Division game against Brechin City at Glebe Park on 24 August 1955.

Jeffrey Barker, played for Aston Villa and signed for United as a War guest on 27 August 1942. Jeffrey made his United debut on 29 August 1942 against Dunfermline at Tannadice. However, shortly after this game they moved him to another district with the Forces.

George Barr, was a scout for United in the Glasgow area in the 1920s. He sued the club for what he claimed were unpaid wages and expenses of £142 between 1925 and 1929. At that time manager Jimmy Brownlie and club-chairman William Hutchison had engaged him. Both men by this time had departed from the club so it was a difficult case to answer. Neither side could put together a reasonable legal argument. However, they eventually settled the case out of court.

John Barr, signed for United on 14 November 1947 by manager Willie MacFadyen. John had previously played for Third Lanark and Queen's Park Rangers. The player made his United debut on 15 November 1947 in a C-Division game against East Stirling. John made his first team debut on 13 December 1947 in a 3-3 draw against Ayr United.

George Barron, played in a trial match for United on 24 November 1945 against Albion Rovers at Tannadice. The club signed George on 30 November 1945 from Mugiemoss. George left United in

December 1946 and played his last match for the club on 16 November 1946.

James Bateman, signed by manager Jimmy Brownlie on 13 May 1930 from Dundee Violet. While he was with United, he turned out four times for the club.

Bobby Bauld, signed for United by manager Jimmy Brownlie on 30 October 1923 from Raith Rovers. Bobby had been with Raith for three years prior to signing for the club, and before that he was with Glencraig Celtic. He made his club debut on 3 November 1923 against St Bernard's at Tannadice, and scored one of the goals in the game. While he was with the club, he played in 134 games and scored 27 goals. In July 1927 United transferred him to Bradford City, and in January 1933 he was still turning out for them.

Arthur Baxter, played for Dundee, and was a member of United's side in the Scottish Regional Cup Final side of 1944. His career began with Portsmouth, then Falkirk, and then signed to Dundee. At the end of season 1938-39, he signed for Barnsley. Arthur died in action in September 1944.

Stuart Baxter, released by United in November 1975. Stuart had joined the club from Preston in 1975. He returned to England after turning down an offer to go to Australia.

Eric Bayolsen, played centre-forward for United's reserves against Dundee reserves on 15 September 1967. The Scandinavian was working in Dundee at the time, and had been showing up well in practice matches. However, the club freed the player in April 1968.

R. Beattie, signed for United in August 1938 from Motherwell. The player made his United debut on 13 August 1938 in the 5-4 win over Montrose at Links Park. While he was at Tannadice, he played in 21 league games and scored six goals.

Dave Beaumont, was 15 years old and a pupil at Kirkcaldy High School when he signed an S-form with the club on 15 November 1978. In 1982 Dave was a full-time student studying Civil Engineering at Dundee College of Technology. On 20 January 1989, Dave signed for Luton Town. The reported fee was £150,000.

Bebbeining, of Birmingham City, guested for Dundee Hibs during the First World War. His first game for the club was on 19 August 1916 and the side ran out winners 5-1 that day against Lochgelly

United. They played this match at Tannadice in the Eastern-League.

Stuart Beedie, signed a provisional contract with Montrose on 27 February 1979 from Lewis United. Beedie joined St Johnstone from Montrose in June 1981 for £20,000. The player signed for United on 25 May 1984 from St Johnstone. The reported fee was £90,000. Along with Billy Kirkwood he signed for Hibernian in May 1986. Eventually Hibs transferred Beedie to Dunfermline where he teamed up with Billy Kirkwood and John Holt whom they transferred from United in September 1987. In the close season of 1989-90, he signed for Dundee. Again he was teamed up with Billy Kirkwood and John Holt. In 1993 he was playing for East Fife.

Danny Bell, signed to the club in 1954 after Dumbarton had released him. Danny made his first team debut on 14 August 1954 against Ayr United at Tannadice. In season 1954-55, he made seven appearances in United colours and scored one goal.

Jim Bell, signed to United in November 1959 by manager Jerry Kerr. Jim made his first team debut on 21 November 1959 in the 2-1 win over Alloa at Tannadice. While he was with United, he featured in four first team games.

Arman Benneker, signed by manager Billy Kirkwood on 9 August 1996. The 27-year-old centre-half played for Dutch side MVV Maastricht. Arman made his first team debut on 10 August 1996, against Motherwell.

Colvin Bennett, joined United on 8 August 1930 and made his United debut on 9 August 1930 against Armadale. While he was with United, he played in 50 first team games and scored 17 goals. Colvin signed for Montrose on 25 July 1932.

David Benzie, signed for United on 29 August 1963 from Drumchapel Amateurs. At the time of signing he was playing in an International Tournament in Italy.

W. Benzie, signed for the club in August 1938 from Morton. The player made his United debut on 13 August 1938 in the 5-4 win over Montrose at Links Park. While he was with the club, he made 29 league appearances and score 15 goals.

Mogens Berg, born in 1944, and signed by Jerry Kerr on 10 December 1964. He made his first team debut on 12 December

1964 in the 3-1 defeat by Rangers at Tannadice, before a crowd of 18,000. Mogens played his last game for United on 27 April 1968 against Stirling Albion. The final score that day was 2-2. Shortly afterwards he returned to Denmark. Berg then returned to his old club B 1909. In 1977 he was working as a compositor with a local newspaper in Denmark.

Doug Berrie, was born in Calcutta, and signed for the club by manager Willie MacFadyen on 30 May 1946 from Stobswell juniors. Doug played with the junior club not long after the family returned to Dundee from India. He had played with them for three years before signing for United. While he was at Tannadice he played in 188 first team games. Doug was freed in May 1953 and signed for Forfar in July 1953. On 30 April 1964 he was freed from the Station Park side.

Jim Bett, signed by manager Billy Kirkwood on 29 August 1995. His previous clubs included Lokeren, Rangers, and Aberdeen. Jim was released by Hearts two weeks prior to signing for United. The player made his debut the same night as he signed against Motherwell at Tannadice. The club freed him on 21st May 1996.

T. Bibby, signed for Dundee Hibs in April 1922. The player had previously played for Blackburn Rovers. He made his club debut on 8 April 1922 against Dunfermline at Tannadice. In season 1921-22 he played in three league games for the club.

H. Black, signed by Dundee Hibs manager Pat Reilly during the close season of 1912. While he was with the club, he made six appearances during season 1912-13.

Joe Black, was the brother of fellow United player Willie. Joe signed for United shortly after he appeared in a trial game played on 22 October 1938. This match was against Morton, and United won 1-0 that day. He made 15 league appearances, and scored two goals for the club.

R. Black, played for United on 14 August 1937 against St Bernard's at Tannadice. The player made only two appearances in a United shirt.

Willie Black, signed to United on 2 September 1938. Willie made his debut for the club on 3 September 1938 in the 1-0 win over Alloa at Tannadice. In his first season he scored 23 goals for the club, and was an instant success with the supporters. On 17 January 1942 they granted Willie permission to turn out as a War guest for Gateshead. His brother Joe was signed shortly afterwards and played on the left-wing.

Blackwood, played in goal for Dundee Hibs against Armadale on 15 January 1916 in the Eastern-League. The keeper also played for St Johnstone, but guested with Dundee Hibs during the First World War.

Ian Blair, was a 17-year-old amateur who came to United from Aberdeen Recreation. Ian was signed up to the club by Jerry Kerr on 10 March 1962 after he played in a trial match against Stirling Albion at Tannadice. They played this game on the 1 March 1962.

Tom Blair, played in goal for Kilmarnock during season 1919-20, and signed for United on 11 June 1937. The Board had originally appointed him secretary-player-coach. The keeper played one game for the club on 14 August 1937. This was in the opening game of season 1938-39 against St Bernard's at Tannadice. Tom also helped with management duties under director George Greig.

Ger Blok, was a former manager with Holland's Under-21 side. He started coaching the younger player's at Tannadice on 27 November 1989. Ger had signed a short term contract with the club.

Bloomquest, signed on a provisional form for the club by manager Jimmy Brownlie on 2 June 1930.

Allan Boath, made a limited number of appearances with the reserves. Allan also played for Forfar. He featured in the New Zealand squad that took on Scotland in the World Cup June 1982. The player gained his first cap for his country in 1980.

Walter Bojczuk, attended St Michael's Secondary and signed an S-form with the club on 23 September 1969. At the time of signing he was playing with Northfield in the Angus Amateur League.

Tom Boland, played in the first ever Dundee Hibs fixture. They played this match on 18 August 1909 in the 1-1 draw against Edinburgh Hibernian. Pat Reilly later appointed Tom, trainer at the club. Tom also played in the first ever Scottish League game played by Dundee Hibs. They played this game on 20 August 1910 against Leith Athletic at Tannadice. Sadly the club lost 3-2 that day. Tom also played for the side when they won the Carrie Cup on 22 April 1910 after Brechin City was unable to play in the final. The player also played on 25 March 1911 in the Forfarshire Cup Final in the 1-0 win over Arbroath at Dens Park. Tom was also in the side that lost 3-0 to Albion Rovers in the Qualifying Cup Final on 27 December 1913. While he was with Dundee Hibs he featured in 75 league games and scored one goal. In 1914 Tom left the club to fight for the British forces during the First World War.

Roger Boli, signed to the club by manager Tommy McLean on 15 July 1998 from Walsall. The 32-year-old was signed for a reported fee of £250,000. Boli had extensive experience playing in France with Auxerre, Le Harve and Lens. While playing in England during season 1997-98, he scored 26 goals. Roger made his United debut

in a friendly game against St Mirren on 18 July 1998 when he came off the subs bench and scored his first goal for the club. Roger made his Premier League debut for the club on Saturday 1 August 1998 against Kilmarnock at Rugby Park. He scored two goals for the club that afternoon, however, these goals were disallowed. United lost 2-0. His brother Basil played for Rangers in the 1990s.

Gary Bollan, born in Dundee in 1973, and a pupil with Linlathen High School. Gary joined United from Fairfield Boys Club. Bollan found it difficult to command a regular first team place, and suffered from several injuries. Due to his contractual problems with the club, Bollan decided to challenge the matter in court. However, United transferred him to Glasgow Rangers in a joint deal along with Alex Cleland. This took place on 26 January 1995. The media had claimed that they believed the deal to be in the region of £750,000.

On 20 February 1998 he was signed by Paul Sturrock manager of St Johnstone for £100,000.

Jimmy Bone, joined United on 24 February 1988. Jimmy was appointed first team coach with United, and he had been a professional player since 1972. He signed for Norwich City from Partick Thistle, and would later join Celtic. In 1975 he was signed to Arbroath by manager Bert Henderson. In 1978 Alex Ferguson signed him for St Mirren, after a spell there, he joined Hearts. Jimmy returned to Gayfield in 1985 as player-manager. Then at Christmas time 1986, he left Arbroath and teamed up with Alex Smith at St Mirren. In May 1989 Jimmy left United to become manager of Airdrie. Then he became manager of East Fife in October 1996. However, he left the club on 9 December 1997 after the Bayview side had suffered a series of bad defeats.

David Boner, was 19 years old when he was signed by Jerry Kerr on 19 January 1961 from Everton. David joined that club after he left St Mary's School in Bathgate. He made his United debut in a reserve match on 21 January 1961 against Hearts at Tynecastle. His first game was on 18 March 1961 against Rangers at Tannadice. The final score was 1-1. A crowd of 17,000 watched this match. In October 1962, David was playing for Raith Rovers. Manager Jerry Kerr allowed the player to leave the club at the end of the 1962 season. The player was getting married to a girl from Liverpool and he wanted to settle there.

While he was with United, he featured in 21 first team games and scored four goals.

Peter Bonetti, born on 27 September 1941. Chelsea had freed Peter in April 1979 and signed for United on 22 June 1979. Bonetti arrived in Scotland after purchasing a hotel on the island of Mull. The goalkeeper was 37 when he signed having spent his whole career with Chelsea, joining them in April 1959. Peter visited Tannadice with his wife and family on 2 July 1979. Then he made his first team debut on 11 August 1979 in a game against Dundee. Bonetti was brought in by manager Jim McLean following a dispute with first team keeper Hamish McAlpine. Peter played his last Premier Division match on 29 September 1979. United freed the player in April 1980, and Peter announced he was retiring from the game on

4 August 1980. While he was with the club, Peter featured in five first team games.

John Bourke, signed for Dumbarton from amateur club Dumbarton United. While he was playing amateur football, he was actually playing as a goalkeeper. He was signed by Jim McLean on 15 September 1977 for a reported fee of £60,000. The player made his debut on 17 September 1977 in a league game against Clydebank. United won 3-0. His home debut was at Tannadice on 24 September 1977 in a game against Motherwell. The score that day was United 3 Motherwell 2. While at Dumbarton, Bourke gained the reputation of being a high scoring player. However, this was certainly not the case after he signed for United. After playing 26 competitive matches, Bourke had scored only five goals for the club. A year later, Bourke walked out of Tannadice following a dispute. Manager McLean was happy to sell the player for £40,000 to Kilmarnock on 3 October 1978. After he left Kilmarnock, John then signed for Dumbarton again. John later signed for Brechin City on 13 November 1986, with a small fee being involved. He was placed on their transfer list on 19 February 1988.

Dave Bowman, born in Tunbridge Wells on 10 March 1964. The fiery player signed for United in 1986 from Coventry City. Dave played his first game for United on 2 August 1986 in a Forfarshire Cup game against Dundee at Dens. His nickname is 'Psycho' for his hard style of play. Bowman soon made his name in Scottish football for his aggressive tackling. In season 1995-96, the United management offered him a Testimonial in recognition of his fine skills and club loyalty. This match was played on 6 August 1995 against Dundee. His former clubs also included Hearts. Bowman has also been capped at Scottish Under-21 level and at Full Cap level. At the end of season 1998, Dave left United and signed for Raith Rovers.

John Boyd, signed by manager Willie MacFadyen on 14 August 1947 from Dunipace Juniors. John made his goal-keeping first team debut for the club on 16 August 1947 against Leith Athletic at Tannadice. United freed him in May 1949 and he later signed for Albion Rovers. On 4 May 1950, Albion Rovers freed him.

Ian Boyer, was a former Nottingham Forest player and appointed to the United coaching staff on 31 July 1991. Ian had previously been manager of Hereford United.

Billy Boyle, played for junior side Osborne, and had featured in the game played on 18 September 1954 against St Johnstone at Muirton Park.

Tom Bradley, scored the winning goal for Dundee Hibs in the Forfarshire Cup Final against Dundee A on 24 April 1920. However, the game had to be replayed after Dundee complained that Hibs had played David Gibb, an ineligible player, who had previously played in a cup game with his former club. Also, on the team-lines Gibb's name had been omitted, and in its place was the name Anderson. The match was replayed on 1 May 1920 and Hibs won 1-0.

L. Braidford, turned out for Dundee Hibs in the 1920s. In season 1921-22 he played in 35 league games and scored six goals.

Brady, joined Dundee Hibs from Lochgelly United. He was in the first ever side to wear the green colours of Dundee Hibs. On Wednesday 18 August 1909 the club stepped onto Tannadice for the first time. The goalkeeper also played in the side when they won the Carrie Cup on 22 April 1910. Dundee Hibs won the cup by default, after Brechin City failed to fulfil their fixtures.

Bradley, signed to Dundee Hibs by manager Pat Reilly on 18 August 1919 from Dundee. The player made his club debut on 23 August 1919 in the 2-1 win over Montrose in the Eastern-League.

Norman Brand, signed for United on 9 February 1940. Norman had played for junior side Stobswell, and his first senior club was Queen of the South. From there he signed for Nottingham Forest before heading off to play in Ireland. Over there he played for Larne and Ballymena. The 27-year-old was included in the United squad that met St Johnstone at Muirton Park on 9 February 1940. He was on leave from the Army when he turned out for United on 14 March 1942 against St Bernard's in Edinburgh.

John Brannon, made his United debut as a War guest on 20 February 1943 against Hearts. At that time the halfback was in the Marines, and in the early days of the Second World War he guested with Manchester United. John later returned to Dundee United and made his first team debut on 30 April 1947 in a Forfarshire Cup Semi-Final game against Forfar. United freed him in May 1949.

Henry Brant, signed by manager Willie Reid on 20 August 1931 from Bury for a reported fee of £300 pounds. The player made his

United debut on 22 August 1931 against Partick Thistle at Tannadice. Dundee United freed Harry in April 1933. While he was with the club, he played in 56 first team games and scored 20 times.

Billy Bremner, signed by manager Jerry Kerr on 27 September 1967. The Aberdonian had played well in his trial matches, and was signed as a full-timer at Tannadice.

The player made his first team debut on 16 August 1969 in the 1-0 win over St Mirren at Love Street. (Not to be confused with the former Leeds United and Scotland captain.)

Craig Brewster, born in Dundee in 1966, and the striker signed in 1993 from Raith Rovers for a reported fee of £250,000. As a youngster Brewster had been an S-signing with United playing regularly in the Youth Team. However, manager Jim McLean did not offer him a full-time contract first time round. Craig signed for Raith Rover's during the close season of 1991-92 from Forfar. Both clubs could not settle their differences as to how much the player was worth financially. A tribunal eventually decided the fee and it was fixed at £57,000. Craig signed to United on 5 August 1993 for a reported £200,000. The player made his club debut on 7 August 1993 in a Premier League game against Aberdeen at Tannadice. It was through Brewster's goal that United won their first ever Scottish Cup Final in 1994 against Rangers. On 19 July 1996 he signed for Greek side Ionikos. United did not receive a fee for the player as he left under the Bosman ruling when his contract expired.

Frank Bridgefoot, the goalkeeper signed to the club by manager Jimmy Brownlie in April 1924 from junior side Forfar Celtic. His first game for the club was as a trialist on 15 March 1924 against Bo'ness. His first game as a signed player was on 5 April 1924 in a 2-1 victory over Albion Rovers. From 1924-25 he played 42 league games for the club.

Jimmy Briggs I, played for Dundee Violet, and signed for Birmingham City on 14 April 1933. During the close season of 1934-35, Jimmy was training with United, and played in a trial match on 8 August 1934.

Jimmy Briggs II, born in 1937, and signed for the club in June 1955 from St Mary's Youth Club. He was the son of 'Toddler' Briggs, a nickname his dad had picked up during his junior playing days. Jimmy made his United debut on 24 August 1955 in a B. Division game against Brechin City at Glebe Park. The player made his first team debut on 14 September 1955 against Forfar at Tannadice. After 15 seasons with the club, manager Jerry Kerr released him in April 1970. Then he signed for Montrose in September 1970. By November he was having discussions with Highland League club Keith. In the 1980s Jimmy was working in the Timex factory in Dundee.

Ian Britton, had been with Chelsea since leaving school in 1969. The Dundonian signed for United on 11 August 1982 and made his debut the same night in a game against Southampton. Ian scored his first goal on 21 August 1982 in a match against Raith at Tannadice. United ran out winners that day 5-1. Ian was released by United on 24 October 1983. Within days he was signed up for Arbroath. Then he signed for Blackpool, before leaving for Burnley.

Eric Brodie I, stepped up from Blairgowrie juniors to Forfar Athletic in 1958. However, in 1957 he was capped at junior level for Scotland in a game against Ireland Juniors.

Eric was signed by manager Jerry Kerr on 3 November 1961. He made his first team debut for United on 18 November 1961 against Motherwell at Fir Park. The home side won 2-1 that day. After he left United, he was transferred to Shrewsbury Town in June 1963. From there they transferred him to Chester. Then later to Tranmere Rovers on 2 September 1969.

Eric Brodie II, manager Jerry Kerr provisionally signed the centre-half at the beginning of the 1962-63 season. They had signed the player from Fife juvenile side Methil Star. Eric was given a free transfer from the club in May 1965.

Alec Brown, was born in Fife, and signed in September 1958 from Lochgelly Albert. Alec played in goal for the club in the 1960s and was a member of the United side that won promotion to the First Division in 1960. The club freed the keeper during the close season of 1962. He made his United debut on 27 September 1959 against Stenhousemuir at Tannadice.

Henry Brown, left Dundee Hibs and joined St Johnstone during the First World War. However, he again turned out for Dundee Hibs on 10 November 1917 in the 1-1 draw with Dundee in the Loftus Cup.

Ian Brown, signed from Lochee Renton by manager Jerry Kerr. Ian made his first team debut on 20 April 1968 against Dunfermline at Tannadice.

Jacky Brown, signed to United on 14 May 1935. Jacky had previously played for Brechin City, Montrose, and his junior side was Crieff-based Vale of Earn. Jacky made his first team debut for United on 10 August 1935 against St Bernard's at Tannadice. They granted him a free transfer from United on 16 December 1936. While he was with United, he featured in 14 first team games and scored two goals. On 27 January 1937 he signed for Forfar and made his debut for them on 6 February 1937 against Leith Athletic at Station Park.

James Brown, from Kirkcaldy United, and had the distinction of scoring the first ever goal for Dundee Hibs. This occurred on 18 August 1909 in the 1-1 draw against Edinburgh Hibernian. James received a gold medal as a reward for the first ever competitive goal. He was also a member of the side that won the Carrie Cup on 22 April 1910 after Brechin City could not play in the final.

Jimmy Brown, signed to United in April 1957 by manager Tommy Gray from Glencraig Colliery. While he was with United, he featured in 23 first team games and scored six goals. He spent one season with United before returning to the junior ranks with Thornton Hibs. Jimmy then joined East Fife in season 1960-61, but was released.

John Brown, signed for United in August 1932 from Crossgates Primrose. John made his first team debut on 3 September 1932 against Alloa. In his first season at Tannadice, John appeared for the club on 30 occasions, and scored ten goals. During season 1933-34 he made 32 league appearances and scored nine goals. On 12 July 1934 John signed for Cowdenbeath.

Ken Brown, was called up by the club on 29 July 1963 by manager Jerry Kerr. United freed the player in May 1965.

Kenny Brown, signed by manager Jim McLean on an S-form from St Columba's Boys Club in April 1974. Kenny was a pupil at Lawside Academy at the time of signing.

W. Brown, played in the Dundee Hibs side that lost 3-0 to Albion Rovers in the 1913 Qualifying Cup Final. He made five appearances for Dundee Hibs during season 1913-14.

Chic Brownlee, played for United as a guest during the Second World War. On 5 August 1944 he played in a trial game for Arbroath. At the time Chic was playing for Brechin City. Then they transferred him to Arbroath on 11 August 1944. Chic was signed by United manager Willie MacFadyen on 1 November 1952. The keeper was freed by the club the previous season, but returned for another spell with United. However, he was freed again by the club in May 1953.

Bruce, of Brechin Hearts, played his first game for Dundee Hibs on 20 February 1915 against Brechin City at Nursery Park. Dundee Hibs won that day 5-0. The goalkeeper made his Tannadice debut on 6 March 1915 in the 3-1 win over Dundee A in the Forfarshire Cup. He also played for the club when they beat Arbroath 2-0 on 27 March 1915 in the Forfarshire Cup Final. The player featured in the first city derby against Dundee on 13 March 1915.

Percy Bryson, signed to Dundee Hibs by manager Pat Reilly on 3 January 1911 from Lochee Harp. He made his club debut on 7 January 1911 in the 1-0 win over Albion Rovers.

Percy made one league appearance for the club during season 1910-11. In season 1911-12 he played in three league matches.

Martin Buchan, played for St Clement's before signing for his first senior side Aberdeen. His first appearance in a United shirt was as a guest in a game against East Fife on 19 January 1946. Martin was signed by manager Willie MacFadyen after this game. While he was with United he played in seven first team games and scored twice. His son Martin also played for Aberdeen and Manchester United, and was capped for Scotland on 34 occasions.

Archie Buchanan, made his first team debut on 13 August 1932 against Hibs at Easter Road. During season 1932-33, Archie made 33 league appearances and scored two goals for the club. He was freed by United in April 1933.

William Buchanan, signed by manager Willie Reid on 31 August 1931 from Carluke Rovers. While he was with United, he appeared in 33 competitive matches and scored two goals.

William Burke, joined the Directors board of Dundee Hibs in November 1922.

Alf Burnett, played his first United game as a senior player on 10 April 1943 against Raith Rovers at Tannadice. Alf went on loan to

Barrow in 1946, and was transferred from there to Bradford City on 12 November 1949.

J. Burns, made his debut for Dundee Hibs on 4 November 1911 against St Bernard's in Edinburgh. The player made 12 appearances for Dundee Hibs during season 1911-12.

Rodney Bush, was signed by Jim McLean in October 1973. The South African made his club debut in a 2nd eleven game against Hearts on 10 October 1973. Hearts won that day 4-2, and Bush received his first caution in the game.

Jacky Butchart, played for Y. M. Anchorage, and played as a War guest for United on 28 April 1945. This match was against Hearts at Tannadice and ended 0-0.

Bob,Buyers, played in a United reserve side on 17 December 1949 in a C-Division game against Dunfermline at East End Park.

Peter Cabrelli, signed for Dundee FC on 6 August 1929 from junior side Osborne. However, after he left Dundee, Peter was later transferred from Forfar to Falkirk on 24 December 1934. He signed for United on 9 May 1940 as a War guest. Peter made his United debut on 11 May 1940 against Hibs at Tannadice. Then he went off to play for Raith Rovers. However, Peter returned to United on 29 September 1945 and played that day in a game against Airdrie at Tannadice. The score was a 4-2 victory for United, and he was signed up again after this game.

Andy Cadenhead, was appointed as a scout by Jim McLean on 27 November 1974. In his playing days Andy played for Aberdeen, St Johnstone, and Nairn County. His role for United was to look out for any future prospects in the Aberdeen area.

Kevin Cairns, made his United debut against St Johnstone on 10 September 1960. United won 2-0 at Muirton that day. During his spell with United Kevin turned out on 23 occasions.

Neil Caldwell, signed by Billy Kirkwood on 17 July 1995 from Rangers. They had granted him a free transfer from Ibrox after he made just one first team appearance.

Frank Callaghan, played right-back for the club, and signed in December 1953. Frank made his first team debut for United on New Years Day 1954. This match was against St Johnstone at Muirton Park. Frank made his Tannadice debut on 4 January 1954 against Third Lanark. During his spell with United, Frank featured in 76 first team games and scored twice. Frank was freed by United in April 1957. In April 1962, he was playing for Inverness Clachnacuddin.

Alec Cameron, played in a first team trial match for United on 23 November 1957 against Stirling Albion at Tannadice. Manager Tommy Gray provisionally signed the player on 22 February 1958. During his spell with United, Alec played in 12 first team games and scored on three occasions.

Donald Cameron, signed by Dundee Hibs manager Pat Reilly in October 1912. The goalkeeper made his club debut on 2 November 1912 in the 1-1 draw with Inverness Caley in the Qualifying Cup. Incidentally it took the team eight hours to reach Telford Park in Inverness by train. Dundee Hibs received their share of the gate money that was 13 pounds ten shillings. On 4 June 1913 Donald signed for Cowdenbeath. His first trip back to Dundee was on 7 March 1914. Cowdenbeath lost 3-0 to Dundee Hibs that day. Donald made 19 appearances with Dundee Hibs during season 1912-13.

Jim Cameron I, signed by manager Jerry Kerr on 14 October 1966 from Ashcroft Juniors. Jim made his first team debut on 22 April 1967. The 19-year-old was in the side that drew 2-2 with Partick Thistle at Tannadice. The defender spent seven seasons at Tannadice before signing for Falkirk for a fee of £7,000 on 21 September 1973. In June 1977 Jim signed for Montrose. In April 1978 Montrose gave him a free transfer. Jim later signed for Forfar and given a free transfer from them in January 1981. The player later emigrated to Australia.

Jimmy Cameron II, joined the club from Lochee Harp in December 1928 and played in his first game for the club on 29 December 1928. This match was against Bathgate at Tannadice and United won 6-1. Jim stayed at Tannadice until being freed in May 1931. While he was with United, he played in 70 competitive team games and scored 17 goals. In August 1931 he signed for Third Division side Chester City. Then he went on to play for Shelbourne in November 1931. Then he signed for Celtic in May 1932.

James Cameron III, signed for United on 21 February 1949 from Blairhall Juniors. James made his first team debut on 26 February 1949 against Stirling Albion at Tannadice. While he was with the club, he featured in 12 competitive games.

Kenny Cameron, born in 1942, and joined Dundee FC from Blairgowrie juniors. Kenny made his first team debut for Dundee on 25 August 1962 against United at Dens Park. The player left Dundee and signed for Kilmarnock for £10,000. He was signed by manager Jerry Kerr on the 6 May 1968 from Kilmarnock. The reported fee was £8,000. Kenny made his United debut on 8 May 1968 against Forfar in the Forfarshire Cup game played at Station Park. Kenny Cameron was a regular first team player from 1968 until 1974. While with United, Kenny played in 150 games and scored 82 goals. The player scored 36 goals in season 1968-69, a club record at the time. He left the club in May 1974, and joined Montrose. Later he had a spell at management with the same club. On 1 July 1997, he joined Dundee FC as their Youth Development Officer.

Willie Cameron, became United's trainer in July 1944. On 10 January 1946, Willie left the club. Willie would later take up a similar position across the road at Dens Park.

Alistair Campbell, provisionally signed for the club on 28 December 1965. Manager Jerry Kerr was suitably impressed by the young 17 year old's performance in a trial reserve game. They played this match on 23 December 1965, against Stirling Albion. At the time of signing he was playing outside-left for junior side Jeanfield Swifts. Ally played in his first game since signing, on 6 April 1966, against Celtic reserves at Tannadice. The player was freed by the club in May 1967.

Bill Campbell, became United's new Commercial Manager in July 1996. Bill had previously worked in a similar capacity with St Mirren for four years.

Charlie Campbell I, signed on 5 December 1949 from junior side North End. Charlie made his first team debut on 10 December 1949 against Stirling Albion at Tannadice. The player was freed by the club in May 1953.

Charles Campbell II, signed for United on 31 August 1933 by manager Willie Reid. Before signing for United, Charles played nine senior games with Clyde in season 1932-33. He made his United debut on 2 September 1933 against Dumbarton at Boghead. While he was with United, he featured in 30 competitive games.

Colin Campbell, signed for United on a free transfer from Hibernian.

Ian Campbell, was a trainer with the club in the 1970s.

Malcolm Campbell, signed on as an amateur player with United on 17 December 1936. The player had been playing for Irish side Ballymena.

Malcolm 'Micky' Campbell, signed by manager Jimmy Brownlie in June 1925 from Falkirk. The player made his United debut on 15 August 1925 against Raith Rovers. During his spell at Tannadice the player made 67 appearances and scored 17 goals. Micky played for East Stirling in season 1930-31. On 27 July 1931, Micky was fixed up with Irish side Ballymena.

Tommy Campbell I, signed by manager Jerry Kerr on 3 March 1960, for £2,000 from Albion Rovers. He made his debut on 5 March 1960, against Hamilton at Tannadice. United won 5-1, and Tommy scored three in that game. Tommy had the distinction of scoring the only goal against Berwick Rangers on 30 April 1960. This goal secured United's entry into the First Division. At the time of signing, Tommy was working as a painter and decorator in Glasgow.

While he was with the club, he featured in 19 games and scored 14 goals.

Tommy Campbell II, played for Clackmannan Juniors and joined United on 1 September 1961. Tommy made his debut with United as a trialist in a reserve match on 29 August 1961 against Dunfermline. Manager Jerry Kerr was so suitably impressed that he signed him a couple of days later.

When the club freed Tommy in May 1962, he had never made a first team appearance.

Andy Cant, signed by manager Jimmy Brownlie on 11 September 1924 on a free transfer from Dunfermline. Andrew made his club debut on 13 September 1924 in the 1-1 draw against King's Park. The player made his Tannadice debut on 20 September 1924 in the 1-0 win over East Fife. While he was with the club, he played in eight matches scoring twice.

Andy Cargill, was a former Scottish Youth International player who played in several fringe games. Andy was released by the club on 23 September 1994. After his release he was signed up by Jim Duffy at Dens.

John Cargill, played for Dundee Hibs in the 1920s.

Nicoll Cargill, provisionally signed by manager Reggie Smith in the close season of 1956.

Cargill, of junior side East Craigie played in goal for United on 11 November 1933. The game was against Montrose at Tannadice, and the keeper helped United out after first team regular Chic McIntosh was out through injury.

Walter Carlyle, born in Grangemouth on 23 May 1938, and joined Rangers in July 1958. He had also played junior football with Shettleston United. Walter was signed by Jerry Kerr in March 1960. The player made his debut on 13 August 1960, in a 2-1 victory over Stirling Albion. Then Walter signed for Millwall on Thursday 7 November 1963. While at Tannadice, Walter played in 103 League and Cup games, and scored 45 goals.

John Carnegie, was a Director with the club who died on 4 February 1928 aged 68 years.

J. Boyd Carnegie, co-opted onto the United board as a director, in succession to his late father John in June 1928. His father had been Chairman at the club and his grandfather had also been a director.

Carroll, played in the Dundee Hibs side that won the Carrie Cup on 22 April 1910. The club won the trophy by default after Brechin City was unable to play the tie.

Bobby Carroll, signed for the club in July 1965 by manager Jerry Kerr. Not one of Kerr's better signings, however he did score against his old club Celtic in front of a 25,000 crowd at Tannadice. This game was on the opening day of season which was on 14 August 1965. Bobby was freed by United in May 1967.

Eddie Carroll, signed for United in September 1926 on loan from Aberdeen. The player made his United debut on 4 September 1926 against Kilmarnock at Tannadice. Eddie made 21 appearances in a United shirt and scored 11 goals for the club. He signed for Irish club Dundalk on 7 June 1927.

Frank Carroll, signed by manager Jimmy Brownlie in 1926. While he was at Tannadice he played in three matches for the club.

Paul Cavanagh, joined the club in 1968 and signed to United from Tartan Boys Club. On 3 August 1982, Paul signed for Stirling Albion for £12,500. Paul had been on loan to them since December 1981.

Willie Cavanagh, signed for Dundee Hibs by manager Pat Reilly on 26 March 1914 from Dundee Violet. Willie made his club debut on 4 April 1914 against Vale of Leven at Milburn Park. The game ended in a 2-1 victory for Dundee Hibs. During season 1913-14 he played in three competitive games for the club and scored one goal. In season 1914-15 he made 17 appearances and scored one goal for the club.

Cermack, played for Dundee Hibs in their first ever Scottish League match played on 20 August 1910. They played this game against Leith Athletic. Dundee Hibs lost 3-2 that day.

Charlie Chalmers, played for United in a first team trial match on 22 August 1957 in a 2-2 draw with Alloa.

Robert Chalmers, signed for the club on 25 August 1942. Robert was signed after he had previously played in three games for the club. These were against Rangers, Hearts, and Raith Rovers.

Alexander Chaplin, signed by Dundee Hibs manager Pat Reilly on 25 May 1914. His club debut was on 15 August 1914 against Dunfermline at East End Park. Alexander also featured in the first city derby for Dundee Hibs against Dundee on 13 March 1915. While he was with the club, he appeared in 23 competitive games for Dundee Hibs during season 1914-15. During the First World War Andrew was guesting for Tottenham Hotspur in January 1916.

John Chester, was a former player with Dundee Hibs. In August 1923 he was playing for Beith FC.

James Cheyne, signed for Dundee Hibs by manager Pat Reilly in August 1914. James made his club debut on 29 August 1914 against St Johnstone. His Tannadice debut was on 5 September 1914 against Forfar in the Qualifying Cup. The player featured in the first city derby against Dundee on 13 March 1915. On 27 March 1915 James scored the two goals that won the Forfarshire Cup for the club. They played this match against Arbroath at Dens Park.

J. L. Christie, signed for the club on 2 September 1938 from Perth Craigie, and he had also featured in a couple of games for Brechin City. This was prior to signing to United.

The player made his United debut on 3 September 1938 in the 1-0 win over Alloa at Tannadice. While he was with United, he played in 27 league games. In July 1939 he signed for Forfar Athletic.

Dave Clark, made his United debut on 7 October 1944 against Raith Rovers at Tannadice.

Jocky Clark, signed to the club by manager Jerry Kerr on 26 October 1963 from Nairn County. Jocky made his first team debut on 30 October 1963 in a benefit game against St Johnstone at Muirton Park. He made his home debut for the club on 2 November 1963 in a match against Falkirk. Dundee United won 3-1 that day. The player was freed by United in April 1968. On 22 July 1982 he was appointed coach with Inverness Clachnacuddin. He was the previous coach with Ross County.

John Clark, signed an S-form with United on 30 March 1981. At the time of signing John was a pupil at Musselburgh Grammar School and had been playing for Musselburgh Windsor Boys Club. John signed for Stoke City on 9 February 1994 for £200,000. Their manager at that time was former Hearts manager and Scotland striker Joe Jordan. John actually returned to Tannadice on 6 August 1994. This time he was with his newly signed club Stoke. This game was part of his United testimonial. However his stay with Stoke was short-lived as he signed for Falkirk on 16 September 1994 for £100,000. He made his debut with Falkirk on 24 September 1994. It was ironic that this match was against Dundee United and played at Tannadice. United ran out winners by 1-0. The player was freed from Falkirk in November 1996. John played for United reserves on 9 December 1996 in a game against Kilmarnock reserves. They played this match at North End Park Dundee.

Neil Clark, was 19 years old when he signed a provisional form for United on 28 July 1978. The goalkeeper played for Cuminestown in Aberdeenshire.

Pat Clark, joined Hamilton on 9 February 1994. There was no fee agreed between the clubs. However, after the player had made a number of first team performances, Hamilton agreed to pay United a nominal sum.

Willie Clark, played for United as a War guest on 16 August 1941 against St Bernard's. At that time Willie was in the RAF and was stationed close to Dundee. Willie was also a player with St Johnstone.

Tom Clarkson, signed for the club on 15 July 1937 and had played for Kilmarnock the previous season. Tom had joined them from junior club Troon Athletic. He made his first team United debut on

14 August 1937 against St Bernard's at Tannadice. In his first season with the club Tom played in 24 games and scored 11 goals.

Alex Cleland, born 1970, and joined the club in 1987. Alex made his first team debut at the age of 17. This game was played on 30 April 1988 against Morton. United won that day at Cappielow 4-0.

Three years later he was commanding a regular spot in the first team. Cleland won a Scottish Cup Winners medal with the club in 1994. On 26 January 1995, along with Gary Bollan, he signed a contract with Rangers in a deal estimated at £750,000. According to reports Cleland was worth £500,000. Alex made his first team debut at Ibrox on 4 February 1995. Ironically it was against his old club. United drew 1-1 that day. During the close season of 1998, Alex signed for Everton.

Jimmy Clements, was a former Third Lanark player who played in a trial reserve game for United on 4 October 1958 against Dunfermline at Tannadice.

Archie Coats, signed for Arbroath on 15 May 1946 after he was freed by Third Lanark. Archie was a trainer with United for many years.

Archie Coats, the goalkeeper was the son of the United trainer. He played for junior side Elmwood, and played for Logie School and 6 Boys Brigade. The player made his first team debut for United on 16 March 1957 against Forfar at Station Park. Archie did return to the club later in his career. He resigned in September 1976. Archie was the man in charge of the reserves. He had lived in the city for 42 years and was heading off to spend his retirement in Bangor, County Down.

Jimmy Colgan, was an ex-player with Airdrie, Partick Thistle, Bournemouth, and signed for United in August 1949. Jimmy made his United debut in a C-Division game on 13 August 1949 against Montrose at Tannadice. The player made his first team debut on 20 August 1949 against Arbroath at Gayfield.

John Collins, played for Dundee Hibs in season 1910-11. John featured in the club's first appearance in the Scottish League. They played the game on 20 August 1910 against Leith Athletic and he scored two goals in this game. However, it was not enough to stop Leith winning by 3-2. While he was with the club, he played in 15 league games and scored three goals.

Robert Collins, played for Dundee Arnot, and also turned out for Brechin City. Robert played his first game for United on 3 April 1946 against Queen's Park at Hampden.

Tom Collins, made one appearance for Dundee Hibs during season 1910-11. This was in the first ever Scottish League fixture that Dundee Hibs featured in. They played this match on 20 August 1910 against Leith Athletic. Unfortunately Dundee Hibs lost 3-2 that day.

W. Connolly, played in goal for Dundee Hibs on 6 February 1915 against East Stirlingshire. He was well known in the junior circles around the Glasgow area. The keeper made his Tannadice debut on 13 February 1915 in the 4-1 victory over Vale of Leven.

Jack Court, signed for United on 3 November 1943 as a War guest and had been playing for Cardiff City. At the time of signing he was in the Royal Marines. Jack played his first game in a United shirt on 6 November 1943 against Aberdeen at Pittodrie. The player made his home debut on 20 November 1943 against East Fife. In August 1944 he signed for Arbroath.

Hugh Cochrane, in July 1963 the United inside-forward had received an offer from the English Southern League side Dartford. However, in August 1963 he was offered a trial with Barnsley, and eventually signed for them. They gave Hugh a free transfer from them on 23 May 1964.

Ian Cochrane, signed in March 1980 by manager Jim McLean from Preston North End. He played his first game for United reserves on 11 March 1980 against Forfar.

Ian made very few appearances in a United jersey and was transferred to Morton after spending only six months at Tannadice. In August 1983 he was with Hamilton. The player signed to Cowdenbeath on 2 November 1984.

D. Collington, played right-back for United. On 23 April 1935 he featured in a 3-3 draw with Fraserburgh during United's tour of the Highlands. Manager Jimmy Brownlie was satisfied with his performance and signed him a short time later. The player made his first team debut on 19 August 1935 against St Bernard's at Tannadice. While he was with the club, he made 35 league appearances.

Alex Collins, played for junior side Carnoustie Panmure. Alex played in United's first team on 15 November 1947 against Leith Athletic at Tannadice.

H. Collins, signed by manager Jimmy Brownlie in March 1925 from Partick Thistle. He made his United debut on 7 March 1925 against Alloa. The player made his Tannadice debut on 14 March 1925 in the 1-1 draw with Arbroath. While he was with the club he featured in four games and scored one goal.

Peter Collins, signed by manager Andy McCall on 6 May 1959 on a free from Partick Thistle. Peter had previously played for St Mungo Academy, then had a spell with Arsenal, before signing for Partick in 1949.

Tom Collins, signed for Dundee Hibs by manager Pat Reilly on 17 November 1915 on loan from Tottenham Hotspur. Tom made his club debut on 20 November 1915 in the 2-1 win over East Stirlingshire at Tannadice.

Dave Condie, played for the club on 13 May 1953 in the Forfarshire Cup Final against Brechin at Tannadice.

J. A. Connolly, made his first team debut on 13 August 1932 against Hibs at Easter Road. While he was at Tannadice, the player made eight appearances in a United shirt and scored one goal for the club.

Paddy Connolly, came from Dunfermline and was called up by the club in June 1986. At the age of 18, Paddy signed a long term contract with the club on 10 March 1989. United transferred him to Airdrie in March 1996 for a reported fee of £150,000. The player signed for St Johnstone on 14 March 1998 for £200,000. He made his debut for St Johnstone that afternoon against Hibs. The game ended in a 1-1 draw.

John Connor, signed for United on 1 March 1944 from Queen of the South. He had previously played with Celtic and Airdrie before signing for Plymouth Argyle. From there he was transferred to Swansea City, and then signed for Queen of the South in June 1939. John made his United debut on 4 April 1944 against Rangers at Tannadice.

Willie Cook, signed for Forfar in 1924-25 and played for Dundee the following season. While he was stationed at Arbroath, with the

RAF, he played one game for United as a War guest. They played this game on 8 November 1941 against Raith Rovers at Tannadice. Dundee FC granted Willie permission to turn out for United as a guest. In total Willie played for seven senior sides.

Brian Cooper, was signed by Jim McLean from Brechin City in 1972. Brian made his first team debut at Tynecastle on 10 October 1972 when he came on as a sub. United won that day beating Hearts 2-1. The player made his home debut on 7 March 1973 in a game against Falkirk.

David Cooper, the goalkeeper was signed by manager Jim McLean in 1975 from Glenrothes juniors. David was released by the club at the end of the 1975-76 season. After leaving the club the keeper signed for Alloa in 1976. Then he signed for Cowdenbeath until the end of season 1979-80.

Jacky Copland, born in Paisley on 2 March 1947. Jacky was signed by Jerry Kerr for £10,000 on 17 December 1970 from Stranraer. He made his club debut two days later in a home game against St Mirren, United won 2-1 that day. One week later he scored his first goal for the club in a 1-0 victory over Hibernian. While he was at Tannadice, he appeared in 144 league and cup games and scored 18 goals.

Dave Corbett, signed to United on 23 August 1933 by manager Willie Reid and played with the club until 1936. Dave had been with Ayr United the previous season, and had joined Falkirk from junior side Camelon earlier in his career. His first appearance as an official signed United player was on 26 August 1933 against Forfar at Tannadice. Between 1933 and 1936 Dave played in 81 league games and scored six goals. Dave returned to Tannadice to play as a War guest. This took place on 6 October 1945 against Cowdenbeath.

Cosgrove, was given a trial for Dundee Hibs on 24 January 1920 against Arbroath at Gayfield.

T. Cottingham, signed by manager Jimmy Brownlie in 1923. While he was at Tannadice he played in ten league games. The player was freed by the club on 19 November 1923 and headed off to Carlisle United. In January 1925 he was playing for Bo'ness.

Willie Coull, played for junior side Stobswell before turning senior with Brechin. Willie was transferred to United on 14 December 1939 as a War guest. His first match in United colours was on 16

December 1939. This game was against St Bernard's in the Eastern Division League.

Jack Court, joined the club on a free transfer from Cardiff City on 30 April 1948. Jack played his last game for United on 9 October 1948 against Stenhousemuir. United transferred the player to Dundee for a reported fee of £1,000 on 21 October 1948. Dundee freed Jack two years later in May 1950.

Doug Cowie, joined the club as a coach in May 1966. As a player he was capped 20 times for his country, gaining his first cap in 1953 in a game against England. Doug joined Dundee FC from Aberdeen's St Clement's in 1945. After Dundee freed him on 23 May 1961, he was transferred to Morton on 14 July 1961. He was two seasons with Morton. Then, on 4 May 1964, Doug left Morton to become manager at Raith. However, he did return to Morton as a coach. Later he joined Dundee United, leaving the club on 12 November 1971, but afterwards he did return to the club and took up scouting duties.

Jimmy Coyle, signed by manager Reggie Smith during the close season of 1955. Jimmy made his United debut in a B. Division game against Brechin City at Glebe Park. The player made his home debut for the club on 31 August 1955 against Motherwell. He was freed by United in April 1957. On 19 March 1960, he signed to junior side Carnoustie Panmure.

Johnny Coyle, born 1933, in Dundee. Club manager Willie MacFadyen provisionally signed Coyle in September 1950. The player was called up for the club on 8 February 1951. Johnny made his United debut on 10 February 1951 in a reserve match at Tannadice against East Fife. He had previously played for junior side St Joseph's. At the age of 18 he made his first team debut. Coyle played in 130 games and scored 115 for United. John was transferred to Brechin on 26 November 1952. On 24 June 1955 he returned to the club after he was demobbed from the RAF. During season 1955-56 he played in 43 League and Cup games for United and scored 43 goals. This worked out at an average of a goal a game. Johnny was the club's top scorer for the season.

The player was later transferred to Clyde on 19 December 1957 for a fee of £5,000. While he was with them, he won a Scottish Cup Medal in 1957-58, in the 1-0 win over Hibernian. In 1961, he moved to England and went back to his trade, bricklaying.

Owen Coyle, signed by Billy Kirkwood on 13 October 1995 for a reported fee of £400,000 paid to Bolton Wanderers. Before he joined Bolton, his previous club was Airdrie. Owen made his United debut on 14 October 1995 against St Johnstone at Tannadice. It was a successful debut for the player as he grabbed one of the goals in the 2-1 United victory.

Tommy Coyne, born in 1962, and signed for United on 28 October 1983 by manager Jim McLean from Clydebank. Tommy joined the Bankies from Hillwood Boys Club in 1981. While he was playing for Clydebank, Tommy was working as an apprentice joiner. Tommy signed for United for a fee of £65,000. He played his first full game for United on 12 November 1983. This was a memorable game for Tommy as United beat St Johnstone 7-0. On 13 December 1986 he joined Dundee for a reported fee of £75,000. On 1 March 1989, they transferred him to Celtic for £500,000. In season 1988-89, while still with Dundee, he won the Adidas Bronze Boot Award for his goal achievements. At the time of signing for Celtic, manager Billy McNeill stated: 'He was a player with a big future at the club.' After being transferred to Motherwell, Tommy was later signed by Dundee manager Jocky Scott on 1 July 1998. He made his Premier League debut for Dundee on 1 August 1998 in the 2-0 defeat at the hands of Aberdeen at Dens Park.

Davie Crabb, signed to United from Montrose Vics on 16 September 1959 by manager Jerry Kerr. Davie played in a first team trial game for United on 12 September 1959 in the 4-0 victory over Queen of the South at Tannadice. The left-half made his first team debut on 6 February 1960, against East Stirling. The final score that day was United 6 East Stirling 1. However, the player did make a first team appearance for United on 5 October 1959, but this was in a friendly game between United and Newcastle at Tannadice. The player was freed on 6 February 1961.

Scott Crabbe, signed for the club on 1 October 1992 from Hearts for a reported fee of £215,000. Also included in the deal was winger Alan Preston heading for Tynecastle. Scott made his first team debut on 3 October 1992 against Aberdeen at Pittodrie. United won 1-0. After a long spell out of the game through injury, Scott was eventually transferred to Falkirk.

Bobby Craig I, signed to Dundee Hibs from Celtic in season 1911-12. During that season Bobby played in 20 competitive games and scored four goals for the club. In January 1913 he was transferred to Southend United.

Bobby Craig II, hailed from Glasgow, and made his first team debut for the club on 8 August 1959 in the 2-0 victory over East Stirling at Tannadice. At that time he was working as a shop-fitter with the SCWS. In that season he turned out for the club on two occasions. Bobby had also been a player with Dundee.

Colin Craig, joined the club in 1978 from Celtic Boy's Club. They spotted Craig playing for Menzieshill High School. United included the 16-year-old in the 16-man pool that played Celtic on 14 October 1978. Manager Jim McLean awarded the young player this honour for the hard work that he had been showing while playing in the reserves.

Danny Craig, played for Thornywood United and played in a trial game for Dundee United on 3 August 1946.

David Craig I, signed for the club on 11 July 1994 from East Stirling. The fee was reportedly £30,000. David's career began with Partick Thistle, and then he had a trial with United in May 1994 before signing.

David Craig II, played in a first team trial for the club on 18 April 1959 in a 4-1 win over Morton at Tannadice. United manager Andy McCall signed the player three days later.

Jim Craig, signed for United by manager Willie MacFadyen on 6 February 1948 from Rosslyn Juniors. Jim made his United debut on 14 February 1948 against Cowdenbeath at Tannadice.

Andrew Crawford, signed for Dundee Hibs by manager Pat Reilly on 12 November 1913 from junior side St Joseph's. Andrew made his club debut on 15 November 1913 against Dunfermline at East End Park. During that season he appeared for the club on seven occasions and scored one goal.

In 1914, Andrew left the club to serve in the forces during the First World War.

Jimmy Crawford, signed on loan from Newcastle United on 20 February 1998. The 24-year-old midfield player, who hailed from Dublin, was signed until the end of season 1998. Jimmy played his first match for the club on 4 March 1998. This was in a reserve game between United and St Johnstone.

Dave Cross, signed to the club during the close season of 1954. Dave made his first team debut on 14 August 1954 against Ayr United at Tannadice. The player was released by United in April 1958. While he was with the club he featured in 102 competitive first team games and scored twice.

Frank Crossan, played in a trial first team match for United on 2 May 1955 against Albion Rovers. At that time he was playing for St Mary's Boys Club.

John Crossan, signed for United by Willie MacFadyen on 11 August 1949. John made his United debut in a C-Division game against Montrose at Tannadice on 13 August 1949. The player was released by United on 14 September 1949.

Willie Crothers, played for the club in a trial match on 18 January 1947 against Arbroath at Gayfield. Then he played in another match for the club on 11 January 1947 against Alloa. Willie signed to the club shortly after the last trial. He made his first team debut as a signed player on 12 April 1947 against Stenhousemuir at Tannadice. The player was transferred to Alloa on 9 March 1949, then re-signed for United a short time later. In August 1951 he went for a trial with Irish League side Ards.

Dickie Cruickshank, played in a first team trial game for the club on 27 September 1954. Dickie scored two goals in the game against Third Lanark. Shortly after this trial, Dickie signed for St Johnstone.

George Cruickshank, signed for United on 4 September 1948. George played in a trial match for United the same day against St Johnstone reserves. He made his first team debut on 18 September 1948 against Stenhousemuir. The player was freed by United in April 1954. While he was with United he played in 135 games and scored 19 goals.

John Cruickshank, guested for United from Aberdeen FC. The player made his United debut on 19 January 1946 against East Fife. John made his Tannadice debut on 26 January 1946 against Raith Rovers.

Bob Crumley, played for Dundee, and his brother James also played for Dundee Hibs. Bob signed for Arbroath in October 1913. He made his debut for them on 1 November 1913 against Kirkcaldy United in the Central League. On 17 September 1926 Bob became

United's new trainer. This was after United's Bob Taylor left the club to become the trainer at Huddersfield.

James Crumley, signed to Dundee Hibs in September 1911. He made his club debut on 16 September 1911 against Albion Rovers at Whipplet. The goalkeeper's brother Bob played for Dundee. James was signed to replace regular keeper Bill Monteith who had joined Albion Rovers.Shortly after he was released by the club, James headed off to America in August 1912. He did, however, return to the United Kingdom, and took up the game again. He returned to play in goal for Dundee Hibs during the First World War. Later, he was transferred to Swansea on 22 December 1919.

John Cunningham, signed by manager Jimmy Brownlie on 20 December 1928 from Vale of Leven. Before signing, John had appeared for the club in a trial match against Dumbarton. John made his United debut on 2 January 1929 in the 4-0 win over King's Park at Tannadice. While he was with the club, he turned out on nine occasions.

Harry Curran, signed to United on 19 February 1987 from Dumbarton for a reported fee of £50,000. The fullback joined the Boghead club in 1985 from Eastercraigs Boys Club. He had just turned 20 at the time of signing for United and he made his first team debut at Tannadice on 7 March 1987. This was in a game against Clydebank and ended in a 1-1 draw. In 1989 United transferred him to St Johnstone. On 14 March 1996 they transferred him from Partick to Dunfermline for £25,000. They then transferred Harry to Morton on 12 March 1998. There was no fee involved, and the player signed on with them for two years.

P. Currie, signed for Dundee Hibs by manager Pat Reilly during the close season of 1913 from East Fife. The player made his club debut on 16 August 1913 in the 0-0 draw with St Johnstone. While he was with the club, he made seven appearances for Dundee Hibs during season 1913-14.

Joe Dalling, signed by manager Willie MacFadyen on 2 August 1947 from Tulliallan Juniors. The 21-year-old player was signed up after he had played in a trial match for the club. Joe made his first team debut on 16 August 1947 against Leith Athletic at Tannadice.

Dailly, played for Dundee A. However, he played for Dundee Hibs in their very first fixture. This match was played on 18 August 1909. The game ended in a 1-1 draw against Edinburgh Hibernian.

Christian Dailly, was born in Dundee on 23 October 1973. He was called up by the club during the close season of 1990. In August the same year, he made his debut for the club. Chris had the distinction of being the youngest player ever to play for United at the age of 16. This match was against St Johnstone on 25 August 1990, United won 3-1. Christian also made Scottish football history when he became the youngest player ever to represent his country at Under-21 level. He made his debut on 11 September 1990 against Romania at Easter Road. He was 16 years and 11 months old. Christian went on to play for the Scotland Under-21 side gaining 34 caps. In 1994 he won a Scottish Cup medal with United in the 1-0 over Rangers. During the season 1995-96 manager Billy Kirkwood made Dailly team captain. He was captain for the first time on 29 August 1994 in a game against Motherwell. United transferred him to Derby County for a reported fee of £500,000 on 16 July 1996. He has now fulfilled his ambition to play for the full Scottish squad, and won his first full cap in 1997 against Wales. Scotland coach Craig Brown will surely be eager to watch the young man's progress. Derby County recently transferred him to Blackburn Rovers for a huge fee.

Johnny Darroch, played for Dundee FC before signing for Dundee Hibs. Johnny made his debut for the club on 17 August 1910 against St Johnstone.

Tarun Das, was a student from Calcutta who popped into Tannadice on 25 March 1958 and asked manager Tommy Gray if he could train with the club. The manager decided to try him out in a practice game played on 1 April 1958.

Fergus Davidson, signed to United in 1936. While he was at Tannadice, he played in 18 league games before being allowed to leave.

Jake Davidson, had a spell with junior side Dundee Violet before joining United. After leaving the club he teamed up with his brother Doug who was playing with East Fife.

Norman Davidson, signed by Jerry Kerr on 29 October 1963 from Hamilton Accies for £5,000. The centre-forward previously played for Aberdeen. Norman made his debut on 30 October 1963, in a benefit game against St Johnstone at Muirton Park. He made his home debut on 2 November 1963, against Falkirk. United won that day 3-1. They swapped the player for Partick Thistle's George Smith on 1 February 1964. During his spell at Tannadice he featured in eight games and scored three goals.

Sandy Davie, signed by Jerry Kerr on 9 August 1961 from Butterburn Youth Club. Sandy made his first team debut on 23 April 1962 against Partick Thistle at Firhill. In July 1963, Sandy lost his job as a gardener at NCR after he went on United's tour of South Africa. On 1 October 1966 Sandy celebrated his 100th appearance in League and Cup games. This took place at Tannadice and the opponents that day were Rangers. The club transferred the goalkeeper to Luton Town on 22 October 1968 for a reported fee of £8,000. Then during the close season of 1970, Luton transferred him to Southampton making his debut for them in February 1971. Sandy again signed for Dundee United in 1972, for £8,000, replacing keeper Donald Mackay, whom Jim McLean had just released. He emigrated to New Zealand in 1974, shortly after he had played in goal in the Scottish Cup Final. In New Zealand, Sandy played for North Shore United.

Jake Davidson, played for Dundee Violet before joining United. The player made his first team debut on 10 August 1946 in a B-Division game against Dunfermline. United ran out 3-0 winners that day. Jake was transferred from the club on 11 September 1947, and joined East Fife. While he was at Tannadice he played in ten league games and scored twice.

Norman Davidson, joined the club in October 1963. Norman played in only nine first team games before being transferred to Partick Thistle in January 1964. The player had previously been with Aberdeen and Hearts. On 9 December 1966, Norrie signed for Johannesburg club Boksburg.

Joseph Deans, played for Dunfermline Athletic, and his club allowed him to turn out for United as a War guest in January 1945. Joseph made his United debut on 6 January 1945 against Rangers at Ibrox. His debut was a bit of a disaster for him as Rangers ran out 5-1 winners. The player made his Tannadice debut on 13 January 1945 in a 5-2 win over Raith Rovers.

J. Dempster, joined United in January 1927 from St Johnstone. The player made his United debut on 5 February 1927 in the 4-1 victory over Vale of Leven in the Scottish Cup tie at Tannadice. While he was with United, he turned out on 13 occasions. On 12 May 1927, the goalkeeper signed for Bo'ness.

Willie Denholm, played for junior side Crossgates Primrose. Willie played in a first team trial game on 10 September 1958 against Brechin City at Glebe Park.

Willie Deuchar, signed by manager Jimmy Brownlie on 30 August 1928 from Raith Rovers. Willie made his United debut on 1 September 1928 in the 1-0 win over Dunfermline at Tannadice. While he was with the club he played on 51 occasions and scored one goal.

Chris Devine, signed a contract that would keep him at Tannadice until the year 2000 in May 1998. Manager Tommy McLean was suitably impressed by the youngster's performances in the reserve side, so extended his contract.

Alan Devlin, born in 1955, and signed by manager Jerry Kerr from Tynecastle Boys Club in 1970. Devlin made his first team debut on 9 January 1971, scoring a goal in his first game in the 73rd minute. However, United lost 3-2 to Morton that day. During that season Alan featured in four first team games scoring one goal.

Neil Devlin, signed by manager Jim McLean on 12 November 1990. The 15-year-old who hailed from Ayr had offers from Rangers, Hibs, Motherwell, and Manchester United, before he decided to sign for Dundee United.

Jack Dewar, signed for the club on 20 May 1948 from Hearts, and remained at Tannadice for three seasons.

John Dewar, signed for United from Hearts in March 1948, and returned to Tynecastle two months later. This occurred on 23 April 1948. He did play for United on 20 March 1948 against Raith Rovers at Tannadice.

Dick, was given a trial by Dundee Hibs in the 0-0 draw against East Fife on 11 December 1920. In January 1921 he was signed by the club from Bonnybridge Rose. The player made his debut as a signed player on 8 January 1921 against Stenhousemuir.

Jimmy Dick, played in a first team trial for the club on 16 November 1957 against Berwick Rangers at Shielfield Park. At the time he was playing for junior side St Joseph's.

Kenny Dick I, joined Queen of the South in September 1965, and was a former manager of Brechin City. Dick was appointed a scout by Jim McLean in December 1974. His task was to look out for budding prospects in the Dundee area. Dick resigned from his duties in June 1975 and joined Forfar.

Kenny Dick II, took over from the regular United keeper, Wylie, who had suffered an accident at his work place. Kenny played in the first team on 10 January 1953, in the 3-1 victory over Stenhousemuir at Tannadice. At the time Kenny was playing in goal for junior side Alyth United.

Sidney Dick, signed by manager Jerry Kerr on 20 April 1961 from Arbroath Boys Club. The player was 16 when he joined United and was attending Arbroath High School. He had signed on as an amateur with United. Sidney made his first team debut on 21 December 1963, in a 3-2 victory over Hibs at Easter Road. Sidney was freed by United in May 1967. On 2 October 1967 he signed for Inverness Thistle.

Willie Dickie, played in a first team trial game for the club on 18 April 1959 in the 4-1 win over Morton at Tannadice. Willie made his first team debut on 8 August 1959 against East Stirling at Tannadice. It was a memorable debut for him as United ran out 2-0 winners. Manager Andy McCall later signed the player. After he left United, he went on trial with Forfar, then he signed for East Stirling on 24 September 1960. While he was with United, he featured in nine first team games.

Andy Dickson, joined Dunfermline as assistant trainer after his War service. In 1950 he became the club's trainer, and on 2 August 1955, he became their manager. Andy resigned from them in March 1960. Then he joined United on 10 May 1960. He was a valued and respected member of the training team at Tannadice for many years. Andy was also the club's physiotherapist, and died in May 1991.

Jimmy Dickson I, was club chairman when United purchased Tannadice for £2,500. The first major task that his fellow directors and himself had to deal with was extensive renovation. The total cost was placed in the region of £7,000. The United directors asked the fans to support their ambitious plans. Sadly their requests fell on deaf ears.

Plans for the 3,000 seater grandstand were put on hold. In 1925 Jimmy was also a shareholder with Alloa FC.

Jimmy Dickson II, came to United on Christmas Day 1947. In an exchange deal for George 'Piper' McKay who headed over the road to Dens. Jimmy played for United on 27 December 1947 in the 3-0 win over Alloa at Tannadice. While he was with United, he featured in 37 first team games and scored five goals. On 2 May 1950, he was freed by Queen of the South.

Dinnie, played for Huddersfield, but guested for Dundee Hibs during the First World War. His first game for the club was on 19 August 1916 in the 5-1 win over Lochgelly United in the Eastern-League.

Helen Docherty, joined Dundee United's marketing department in 1995 as shop manager of the club shop in Victoria Road Dundee.

J. Docherty, from Forfar Athletic, played in the first ever Dundee Hibs fixture. They played this match on 18 August 1909 in the 1-1 draw against Edinburgh Hibernian. During season 1910-11 he made two appearances for Dundee Hibs. He played with the side when they won the Carrie Cup on 22 April 1910. Dundee Hibs won the cup after Brechin City could not play in the final.

Jim Docherty, signed for the club on 18 October 1979. The player moved from Stirling Albion to Chelsea for a fee of £50,000. Jim made his United debut on 20 October 1979 when he came on as a sub in the Dundee derby game. United later transferred Jim to Hearts in January 1980.

Pat Docherty, played for Dundee FC in the season 1933-34. In the late 1930s he joined United and in season 1937-38 he turned out for the club on four occasions.

Billy Dodds, joined United from Aberdeen in September 1998 and scored a hat-trick in his first match against St Johnstone.

Davie Dodds, born in Dundee in 1958, and educated at Dens Road primary. While he was at Logie Secondary School, he was signed as an S-form by Jim McLean from Sporting Club. Davie signed for United in May 1975 and was taken to Spain by the club during their summer tour. He made his club debut at the age of 17. His first team debut was on 18 August 1976 in a game against Arbroath at Gayfield, Davie scored twice. United won that game 3-1. The young player was United's leading scorer in five out of seven seasons. On 28 March 1986 Davie announced that he was leaving United at the end of the season to join Swiss club Neuchatel Xamax. On 2 July 1986 United received a reported £175,000 for the player. However his stay with the Swiss club was brief, and he was soon back in Scotland again. This time he was with Aberdeen. Davie signed for them on 19 September 1986 for £215,000. He made his Pittodrie debut on 4 October 1986 in a 2-2 draw with Motherwell. Three years later, on 30 August 1989, he signed for Rangers for a fee of £100,000. He won a Premier Division medal with them in the same year. Under Ranger's manager Walter Smith, he took up a coaching position with the Ibrox outfit. Dodds held this position until 1997, when he left the club.

J. Doherty, joined Dundee Hibs in December 1912 from Partick Thistle. He played his one and only game for the club on 7 December 1912. This game ended in a 1-1 draw with St Johnstone at Tannadice.

Ernie Doig, joined Kilmarnock in 1948, and signed to United in October 1953. He made his United debut on 10 October 1953 in a second round tie in the Second XI Cup game against Morton at Cappielow. Ernie made his first team debut on 31 October 1953 against Forfar at Station Park.

Graham Doig, joined the club as their physiotherapist in July 1989. Graham had previously been the physiotherapist with West Bromwich Albion.

Jamie Dolan, born in Salsburgh on 22 February 1969, and became a professional player as soon as he left school. The player was signed by manager Tommy McLean on 7 January 1997 in a deal which saw Owen Coyle leave United for Motherwell, and Dolan heading for Tannadice. United also paid a fee of £75,000. Jamie made his first team debut on 11 January 1997 against Dunfermline

at East End Park. United won 3-1. A hard-working ball winner Jamie soon established himself as a regular first team performer On a personal level he would like to win everything in Scotland, and wants to do well at Tannadice. He keeps an open mind about winning a cap for Scotland, but, like most players he would love to turn out as an international player. Jamie says: 'United are a big club and the fans rightly expect a lot from the players. The club set high standards, so you have to work hard on and off the pitch if you want to be successful.' In his spare time he enjoys playing golf and snooker.

John Donald, signed for United on 26 August 1938 from Saltcoats Vics. John made his United debut on 27 August 1938 against Airdrie at Broomfield.

William Donald, announced that he was resigning from the Board of Directors on 12 February 1940. William was a doctor, and had been Chairman for a considerable period.

Andy Donaldson, joined United in August 1949, and made his United debut on 13 August 1949 in a C-Division game against Montrose reserves at Tannadice. In season 1949-50, he made eight appearances in a United shirt before being released.

Brian Donaldson, was 16 years old when he signed for United in August 1982. The young keeper played his first game in United colours on 30 August 1982. This was a friendly match between United and junior side Newburgh.

W. Donaldson, played in one game for Dundee Hibs during season 1911-12.

Barry Donnachie, signed a contract in May 1998 that would keep him at Tannadice until the year 2000. Manager Tommy McLean was suitably impressed by the young player's performances in the reserve side so extended his contract.

Dick Donnelly, played in goal for United's reserves on several occasions. His first game for United was on 15 August 1959 against Queen's Park Strollers at Hampden Park. At that time Dick was also turning out for junior side Carnoustie Panmure. After his spell with United, Dick later signed for East Fife. After retiring from the game, Dick became a sports journalist and is regularly heard on Radio Tay, and he writes for several national newspapers.

J. Donnelly, signed by manager Jimmy Brownlie in September 1936. The player made his United debut on 5 March 1936 against Morton at Cappielow. The player made only three appearances in a United shirt before being freed.

Derek Dooley, turned out for the club in a friendly game at St Andrew's. Derek had become a well-known personality in Dundee for his appearances in half-holiday football. On 21 February 1953 the club sent out a letter to Derek following the amputation of his leg.

David Dorward, was fixed up by manager Jimmy Brownlie from junior side North End. This happened after he played in a trial match for the club on 11 August 1928 against Bathgate. His debut as a signed player was on 15 August 1928, in a Dewar Shield tie against East Stirlingshire at Tannadice. David was transferred from United to Charlton Athletic on 12 May 1930. In December 1931, he signed for Irish side Bray Unknowns. While he was at Tannadice he featured in 45 competitive games and scored once.

John Dorward, signed by United manager Jimmy Brownlie on 7 August 1927 from Logie. The player had previously played in trial matches for United and Dundee. John made his league debut for the club on 13 August 1927 in the 4-2 victory over Bathgate at Tannadice. During season 1927-28 he appeared for United on 36 occasions. In April 1929 he was freed by United.

Finn Dossing, born in 1941, and manager Jerry Kerr signed him to United on 2 December 1964. Finn made his first team debut on 5 December 1964 in the 3-1 defeat against Hearts at Tynecastle. It was a strange debut for the player as he scored United's only goal, and received his first booking in a Scottish match. From the time he joined United in December 1964 until May 1965, he scored 22 goals for the club. Also in that time he had only played in 21 League and Cup games. Finn also scored a goal in an incredible 16 seconds. This happened on 16 October 1965, in a game against Hamilton. His last game for the club was on 21 October 1967 in a game against Partick Thistle. Overall the player played in 102 competitive games and scored 66 goals. Later he returned to Denmark where he opened a clothes retailing business.

Bobby Dougan, signed to the club on his 17th birthday on 14 February 1961 by manager Jerry Kerr. Bobby had the distinction of being United's youngest signed player at that time. In 1963, he was regularly turning out for the reserves.

Ian Douglas, signed by manager Tommy Gray during the close season of 1958 from Banks O' Dee. The player was freed by United on 17 September 1960. Ian was unable to command a first team place each week. The player left the club and tried his luck in the Highland League.

Earle Downie, joined the club from Dundee Violet in September 1949. Earle made his debut as a signed player on 16 September 1949 against Hibs reserves at Tannadice. The player was released by the club in April 1952. While he was playing for United Earle was employed as a bookbinder in the city. He made 68 first team appearances and scored one goal for the club.

Patrick Doyle, joined the committee of Dundee Hibs in March 1909.

Cornelius Duffy, was born in Glasgow, on 5 June 1967. Having played for city rivals, Dundee, this was his second visit to Tannadice. Neil had signed to United in January 1985 but left in

November suffering from homesickness. He later returned from South Africa and came back to United on 5 December 1989. In October 1990 Neil joined Falkirk before signing for Dundee on 1 March 1994. He returned toUnited, signing on 6 August 1996, for a reported fee of £200,000. Neil made his first team debut when he came off the subs' bench in a game against Motherwell on 10 August 1996. The player has suffered from a string of injuries since joining United and plays either in defence or midfield. His father also played professional football with St Johnstone, East Stirling, and Partick Thistle.

Dunbar, the goalkeeper had played for Dundee Arnot, and played for United on 1 October 1938 in the 2-1 win over Kings Park at Tannadice. The regular first team keeper was out through injury, so he took up the vacant position. He also turned out for United as a War guest on several occasions.

D. Duncan, signed for Dundee Hibs in March 1922 from Hearts. The player made his club debut on 4 March 1922 against St Bernard's at Tannadice. During season 1921-22 he appeared in 11 league games for the club.

Jim Duncan, signed by manager Tommy Gray on 8 August 1957. Jim joined Celtic in 1951 and he was freed by them in 1955. Then he signed for St Mirren, and was again freed. The player made his United first team debut on 10 August 1957 against Clyde at Tannadice. They offered Jim a free transfer from United on 13 November 1957. While he was at Tannadice he featured in 11 first team games.

Duncan, played for Lochee Harp and played as a War guest for United on 1 January 1944 against Aberdeen at Pittodrie.

John Duncan, signed to Dundee Hibs by manager Pat Reilly in February 1914. The player made his club debut on 14 February 1914 in the 2-2 draw with Albion Rovers at Tannadice. While he was with the club, he played in four competitive games. On 4 November 1914 he was signed by Vale of Leven.

Tommy Dunlop, signed to United from junior side Osborne. Tommy made his first team debut with United on 10 November 1951 against Kilmarnock at Tannadice. The score was 1-0 to United.

Willie Dunlop, signed by manager Reggie Smith on 12 November 1954, from Falkirk. Both managers had concluded a deal. In the deal was United's George Grant heading for Brockville, and Dunlop coming to Tannadice. The player made his first team debut on 13 November 1954 against Dunfermline at East End Park. During his spell at Tannadice he featured in 20 first team games and scored eight goals.

J. Dunn, signed for Dundee Hibs in December 1910. The player made his club debut on 31 December 1910 against Cowdenbeath. He made two appearances for Dundee Hibs in season 1910-11.

Tommy Dunne, signed by Jerry Kerr in April 1968 from Albion Rovers. Tommy made his first appearance in United colours on 4 May 1968. This was in the Forfarshire Cup Final against Dundee at Dens Park. United won that trophy after beating Dundee 4-3.

Charlie Dunnian, signed by Pat Reilly for Dundee Hibs from Edinburgh Hibs. Charlie made his first appearance for the club in the Consolation Cup game against Cowdenbeath on 25 February 1911. Charlie made his Tannadice debut on 4 March 1911 in the 4-0 victory over Montrose in the Forfarshire Cup. He also played in the Final on 25 March 1911. This match was played at Dens Park and United beat Arbroath 1-0. While he was with the club, he played in three league games and scored four goals.

Andy Dunsmore, signed to the club on 1 March 1949 from Blairhall Juniors. Andy made his first team debut on 12 March 1949 in the 2-2 draw with Hamilton Accies at Tannadice. From seasons 1949-1954 Andy played in 72 league games and scored 16 goals.

Eddie Dunsmore, played for United in the 1940s. Eddie made his United debut on 30 March 1940 against Alloa. After leaving the club, he joined Blairhall Colliery. Then in August 1962 he decided to emigrate to Australia. Eddie had an offer to play for Hakoa.

Tommy Dunsmore, played for Hibs, Luton Town, and Dundee United. In March 1942, he was a War guest for Albion Rovers.

J. Dwyer, played his first game for Dundee Hibs on 30 October 1910 in the 0-0 draw with Brechin City. He made four appearances for Dundee Hibs during season 1910-11.

Jimmy Dyet, signed by manager Willie Reid in December 1931 from Falkirk. The player made his United debut on 19 December 1931 against Hearts at Tynecastle. Jimmy was freed by United in April 1933. While he was with United, he featured in 36 league games and scored 14 goals.

Sieb Dykstra, was born in Kerkrade, Holland, on 26 October 1966. Sieb signed for United from Queens Park Rangers on 4 December 1996, for a fee of £100,000. He made his first team debut on 7 December 1996, against Kilmarnock at Rugby Park – a game which United won 2-0. The big keeper soon became a favourite with the

Tannadice faithful. The Dutchman had loan spells with Bristol City and Wycombe Wanderers before coming to Tannadice. Manager Tommy McLean knew of his reputation as Sieb worked under McLean when he was manager of Motherwell. Former clubs Roda J.C. Kerkrade (Holland), A.Z. Aalkmaar (Holland, on loan), and Hasselt K.S.C. (Belgium, on loan). During season 1997-98 Sieb featured in every first team game – 49 appearances.

Jimmy Easson, had played for Portsmouth, and Fulham, and had been guesting with junior side Carnoustie Panmure during the Second World War. Jimmy guested for United on 6 March 1943 against Hibs at Tannadice. After the War he played for junior side Dennistoun Waverley, before playing in United's first team on 28 February 1953 against Albion Rovers at Tannadice.

Craig Easton, was born in Bellshill, Glasgow on 5 March 1979. Craig made his first team debut on 1 January 1997 when he came off the subs bench in the match against Aberdeen at Tannadice. United won 4-0. His first team game from the start was on 23 August 1997 against Rangers at Ibrox. At the age of 18, the club offered the young Easton an extended contract. The contract was signed on 7 November 1997. Dundee United awarded this to Craig after he showed some excellent skills and performances in the first team. Craig also has several Scottish Under-21 caps to his credit. In August and October 1997, Craig won the Bell's Young Player Award. Craig scored a brilliant goal that took United into the Coca Cola

Cup Semi Finals during the fourth round tie against Aberdeen on 15 October 1997. During his early days at Tannadice you could see the young Easton, along with Steven Thompson, on Friday afternoons, washing manager Tommy McLean's car.

Jim Easton, signed for the club during the close season of 1985. He went on loan to Forfar on 20 March 1985, but returned to Tannadice. On 28 January 1986, he was selected for Canada's pool of 40 players for the World Cup. His family had moved to Vancouver when he was nine. Jim started his playing career with the Tampa Bay Rowdies in the North American League. Before him, Jim's dad had signed for Hibs from Drumchapel. Later he played for Dundee and Queen of the South.

Brian Eddie, signed by manager Jim McLean in April 1972. His previous club was Whitburn Juniors. Eddie made his first team debut on 3 May 1972 against Forfar. While he was with United, he featured in three first team games.

Alec Edmiston, signed for the club on 5 January 1949 from St Andrew's United. He made his debut in the 4-0 home win against Dumbarton on 8 January 1949. Alec was called up for Army service on Thursday 23 August 1951and reported to Fort George. He returned to United after spending over a year in Korea with the Army. Alec returned in goal for United on 22 August 1953 in a 2-2 draw with Morton at Tannadice. During his spell at Tannadice Alec featured in 142 games. Alec was freed by the club in April 1957.

G. W. Edwards, played in a trial match for Dundee Hibs on 8 April 1911 against Forfar Athletic in the Northern League.

Torje Eike, hailed from Norway and became the club's physiotherapist on 22 July 1988. In May 1989 he left Tannadice. In September 1989 he was putting Rolling Stone's star Mick Jagger through his paces in America. Mick was touring there and Torje was making sure that the singer was in top condition.

Elder, signed for United juniors on 9 February 1943. The player made his first appearance in United colours on 12 February 1943 against Aberdeen at Pittodrie.

Jim Elliot, signed by manager Willie MacFadyen in August 1949 and made his United debut in a C-Division game against Dunfermline reserves at Tannadice on 19 August 1949. Jim made his first team debut on 27 August 1949 in a 6-0 victory over Airdrie at Tannadice. While he was with United, he played in six first team games and scored six goals.

Ellmer, played for Notts County and turned out for United as a War guest on 25 April 1942 against East Fife at Tannadice.

James Elrick, signed by Dundee Hibs manager Pat Reilly on 13 June 1912 from Brechin City. He joined Brechin from Dundee junior team North End. James made his debut for Dundee Hibs on 17 August 1912 against East Stirling at Tannadice. While he was with the club, he played in eight competitive matches during season 1912-13.

Sam English, signed as a centre-half from Albion Rovers on 11 November 1952. Sam made his first team debut on 15 November 1952 against Stirling Albion at Tannadice. He played 49 first team games with United, mostly in the right-back position. The club freed Sam in October 1954.

Johannes Edvaldsson, was given a week's trial with the club in December 1974. The 24-year-old Icelandic Internationalist signed for Celtic in July 1975.

I. Evans, made one appearance in a Dundee Hibs shirt in season 1911-12.

John Evans, signed by manager Willie MacFadyen on 27 November 1947. The player had previously played for Dundee and Arbroath. John made his United debut in a C-Division game against Edinburgh Athletic on 29 November 1947 at Tannadice.

Sandy Evans, was freed by the club in April 1957 after he played just one senior game for United.

T. Evans, played in a trial match for Dundee Hibs on 29 April 1911 in the 3-0 win over Forfar Athletic at Tannadice.

Ernie Ewen, resigned from his post as second-team-coach with United on 27 May 1960. He left to join Forfar as trainer-coach at Station Park. Ernie previously played with Dundee and Aberdeen.

Ray Ewen, played for Hall Russell's, and was given a first team trial for United on 11 April 1959 against Albion Rovers.

George Fairbairn, signed to United as a War guest on 13 August 1942 from Fulham, and made his debut on 14 August 1942 against Hearts. The sad announcement of the players death came on 8

March 1943 from United Secretary Mr Cram. George had been killed in action.

Alec Farmer, turned out as a trialist for United on 30 December 1933 against Dumbarton at Tannadice. Alec was turning out for junior side Stobswell at the time.

Donald Farquhar, was club chairman in 1960.

Joe Fascione, was 26 years old when he was signed by Jim McLean on 20 July 1972. Earlier Joe played for Kirkintilloch Rob Roy before signing for Chelsea, being released in July 1969 and then spending two years in South Africa playing for Durban City.

Felton, of Rhoineach Mhor played in goal for United after regular goalkeeper John McHugh was transferred to Portsmouth on 19 November 1930. However, he played only three senior games before leaving.

Charlie Ferguson, turned out for United towards the end of the Second World War. Charlie made his last appearance for the club on 1 September 1945 in the 3-2 victory over Ayr United at Tannadice. In September 1954, he was a scout for Burnley.

David Ferguson, signed to Dundee Hibs by manager Pat Reilly on 9 August 1915 from Forfar Athletic. David made his club debut on 21 August 1915 against East Stirlingshire in the newly formed Eastern League.

Duncan Ferguson, born in 1971, and made his debut for United on 10 November 1990 at Ibrox. The 18-year-old came on as a sub for United in the 59th minute. United ran out winners 2-1 before a crowd of 36,995. Duncan played his first game from the start on 24 November 1990, at Tannadice against Aberdeen. In 1991 he appeared in the Scottish Cup Final, before being substituted at half-time. There were frequent disagreements between Ferguson and manager Jim McLean. In January 1993 the club fined and banished him to the reserves for breaching club rules. Ferguson appealed against the decision and appealed to the Scottish League Management Committee. They dismissed his appeal. However, the matter was resolved between the club and the player on 6 February 1993. The player gave Jim McLean his assurance that he now accepted the club's code of discipline, so that was the end of the affair. Duncan Ferguson was put up for sale by Dundee United on 28 May 1993. Later, on 15 July 1993 Glasgow Rangers stepped in and paid £4 million for him. Rangers eventually allowed him to spend three months on loan to Everton starting on 4 October 1994. Rangers transferred him to Everton on the 13 December 1994 for a fee of £4.3 million. He played in the 1995 FA Cup winning side.

Iain Ferguson, joined Dundee from Fir Park Boys Club and was signed by manager Tommy Gemmell. Ferguson signed for Rangers on 18 May 1984 for a tribunal fee of £200,000. Along with Cammy Fraser, Rangers placed him on the transfer list in September 1985. Ferguson signed for United on 22 August 1986 for a reported fee of £150,000. The player made his Tannadice debut on 23 August 1986 in a 1-0 win against Hearts. In July 1988 he was transferred to Hearts for a reported fee of £90,000. In 1991 he was transferred to Motherwell. By 1994 he was playing for Airdrie. Then he had a spell with Irish club Portadown before signing for Dundee again on 23 August 1996.

Juan Ferrera, signed to the club by manager Ivan Golac on 6 January 1995. The Uruguayan Internationalist was signed for £250,000 from Defensor. Juan made his first team debut on 21 January 1995 when he came of the subs bench in the 6-1 win over Motherwell at Tannadice. The player walked out on the club on 1 August 1995 after manager Billy Kirkwood could not offer him a first team place each week.

Victor Ferrerya, left United on 26 February 1993 and signed for Japanese outfit Mitsubishi for a reported fee of £175,000. This was £50,000 short of what United paid for him.

Ferrier, played in goal for Dundee Hibs on 9 September 1911 against Dundee at Dens Park in the Northern League.

Andrew Finlay, joined United in October 1925, his previous club was Third Lanark. Andrew made his United debut on 17 October 1925 against Queen's Park at Hampden. The player made his home debut on 24 October 1925 in the 3-1 win over Kilmarnock. Andrew made 13 appearances in a United shirt and scored one goal for the club. In March 1927 he was turning out for Hibs.

Andrew Findlay, signed by manager Jimmy Brownlie on 26 December 1929 from St Mirren. He had played with the Paisley outfit for six seasons. Andrew made his United debut on 28 December 1929 against Hamilton at Tannadice. While he was with the club, he featured in nine competitive games.

Bert Findlay, played for Dundee Violet, and made a couple of appearances in United's reserve side during March-April 1948. Bert played his first team game for United on 13 March 1948 against Hamilton.

W. Findlay, made five appearances for Dundee Hibs during season 1911-12.

Peter Fisher, played in a trial match for Dundee Hibs on 14 February 1920 against Arbroath at Tannadice. Peter had previously played for Aberdeen.

Tommy Flannigan, signed to United on 17 September 1968. The 20-year-old had signed from West Calder United. He made his debut in the reserves on 21 September 1968 against Aberdeen reserves at Tannadice.

Bobby Flavell, joined United in October 1983 and played his first game on 24 October 1983 in a reserve match. His first team debut was on 22 November 1983 when he came on as a sub in the match against St Mirren. United freed him on 7 December 1983 and he joined Berwick.

Neil Fleck, signed for the club on 14 September 1951 by manager Willie MacFadyen. He had previously played for Falkirk, Alloa and had also featured in the Llanelly side that played against United in Wales in 1950. Neil played his first game for United on 15 September 1951 in a reserve game against Hibs at Tannadice. The player then made his first team debut on 21 September 1951 against St Johnstone. The team ran out 4-3 winners. During that season he turned out for the club on 11 occasions and scored one goal.

George Fleming, born in 1948. George had his first taste of senior football in 1964 when he joined Hearts from Salvesen's Boys. He was the first United player that manager Jim McLean paid a transfer fee for. The fee was reputed to be around £7,000 back in January 1972. Fleming stayed with the club for around seven years, and he was part of the team that won their first trophy honour, the League Cup in season 1979-80. United transferred George to St Johnstone on 9 July 1980, the fee being less than £10,000. A short time later Fleming took up the post of player-coach with them. On 13 December 1983 he took charge of Arbroath. On 11 January 1985, they sacked George as their manager. While he was with Dundee United, George played in 257 league and cup games and scored 31 goals.

Willie Fleming, born in Alexandria, and played for Celtic and Ayr United before signing for United in August 1934. Willie made his United debut on 25 August 1934 against Third Lanark at Cathkin Park. The player made his Tannadice debut on 1 September 1934 in the 4-0 win over Raith Rovers. He played at full-back, and had been captain of the club for a time. While he was at United, he played in 31 league games.

Brian Flies, played in goal for United's first team on 5 March 1994 against Kilmarnock. The Dutch keeper was on trial with the club at that time. However, he left United two days later.

T. Flood, from Dundee A, played in the first ever Dundee Hibs fixture. They played this match on 18 August 1909 in the 1-1 draw against Edinburgh Hibernian. The player was signed for Dundee Hibs by manager Pat Reilly on 7 October 1914. He made his club debut as a signed player on 10 October 1914 in the 1-0 win over St Bernard's at Tannadice. He played in eight competitive games for Dundee Hibs during season 1914-15.

G. Forbes, signed for Dundee Hibs by manager Pat Reilly on 19 September 1912. The player made his club debut on 21 September 1912 in the 3-1 win over Forfar Athletic in a Qualifying Cup match. The player also featured in the Qualifying Cup Final side that lost 3-0 to Albion Rovers on 27 December 1913. He also featured in the first city derby against Dundee on 13 March 1915, and played 22 games for Dundee Hibs during season 1913-14. In season 1914-15 he made 23 appearances for the club.

Jimmy Forbes, signed by manager Willie MacFadyen on 6 August 1953. Jimmy had joined Rangers in 1948 from Longriggend. In season 1952-53 he went on loan to Dumbarton. The player made his United first team debut on 8 August 1953 against Morton at Cappielow. However, in January 1954 he headed off to the RAF. He signed to Stenhousemuir on 21 May 1957. During his spell with United he played in 67 league games and scored six goals.

Willie Fordyce, played as a War guest with the club.

George Forrester, signed by manager Tommy Gray on 10 February 1958 from Dundee FC. His former clubs included Raith and Sunderland. George made his United first team debut on 22 February 1958 against Dunfermline at Tannadice. On 26 September 1958 he signed for Brechin City.

Alan Forsyth, was signed by Jim McLean in 1976. Forsyth began to make some headway into the first team pool when he played on 7 August 1976 in a game against Aberdeen. United won 1-0 in the Anglo Scottish Cup. In the close season of 1978 he signed for Raith Rovers. While he was with United, he featured in 21 league and cup games.

Donald Foster, played for United reserves on 15 December 1951 against Dundee reserves. The player had previously played for Duntocher Hibs.

George Fox, joined the board at Tannadice in 1955. The director was an accountant and part responsible for introducing Taypools to generate capital into the club. George had also been club chairman twice. After the death of Johnston Grant, George became chairman on 31 August 1984. In 1988 he handed over the reins to Jim McLean. Jim has kept the George Fox and Johnston Grant tradition going for sound financial business acumen. George Fox died in 1993, but his memory will always live on at Tannadice. As a fitting tribute to a man who did so much for the club, the board at Tannadice named the new stand after him.

H. Foy, signed by manager Willie Reid on 14 July 1933. He made his first team debut on 12 August 1933 against East Fife at Tannadice. The player spent only one season with the club and appeared in only four league games.

Lou France, was turning out for United during season 1947-48.

Cammy Fraser, was Jim McLean's first signing when he became manager in 1971. The player had been attending Linlathen High School when he signed an S-form. Manager McLean released him in April 1973. However, Hearts took him from Invergowrie Boys Club in September 1973. Dundee manager Donald Mackay signed him on 11 September 1980 for £61,000. In June 1984 he was signed by Rangers. Along with Iain Ferguson he was placed on the Rangers transfer list in September 1985. On 6 April 1988 he signed a two-year contract with Raith Rovers. Cammy signed to Dundee again on 30 March 1991 on a free transfer from Raith. They later transferred him to Montrose. However, he quit as player-assistant manager on 10 February 1993.

Norman Fraser, played for United in season 1939-40, and was a member of the 1940 War Cup Final side. Norman was called up by the RAF on 6 February 1941. On 29 March 1943 United granted him permission to turn out for Sunderland.

Stewart Fraser, joined United from Banks O' Dee in October 1957 by manager Tommy Gray. Stewart made his first team debut on 12 October 1957 in a game against Brechin City at Glebe Park. This game ended in a 1-1 draw. The player helped United gain promotion to the First Division on 30 April 1960. On 29 October 1960, he made his 50 league appearance for the club. By October 1962, he had made 104. He scored three goals in the 11-0 win over the League of Ireland team at Celtic Park, on 28 November 1962. The club freed Stewart in May 1967 and he went off to work in America. During his spell with United, Stewart played in 193 league and cup games and scored 11 goals.

Hamish French, signed for United in December 1983. However, two days later he asked the club to release him from his contract. The player came back to the club in May 1984 after an invite by manager Jim McLean. Hamish was 19 years old, and had been playing for Highland League outfit Keith. The player was called up for training with the club on 7 July 1987. Hamish made his first league debut for the club on 8 August 1987 at Ibrox in a 1-1 draw against Rangers. Two days later and Hamish suffered a broken leg in a training accident. He returned to first team football on 17 October 1987 in a game against Aberdeen at Tannadice. Later he signed for Dunfermline.

Derek Frye, signed for the club on 10 August 1978 from Stranraer for a reported fee of £15,000. In season 1977-78 he was the Second Division's top scorer with 32 goals. Frye made his United debut in a game against Hibs on 12 August 1978. He came on as a sub in a 0-0 draw with Hibs. Derek scored his first goal for the club on 19 August 1978 in a 1-1 draw against Partick Thistle. Dundee United transferred him on 15 August 1979 to Ayr United for a fee of around £15,000. In 1996 he was manager of Annan Athletic.

George Fyfe, played in the first Scottish League game that featured Dundee Hibs. They played this match on 20 August 1910 against Leith Athletic at Tannadice. Dundee Hibs lost 3-2 that day. George made 27 appearances for Dundee Hibs from season 1910- 1912, and scored one goal.

Gallacher, from Dundee Wanderers captained the first ever Dundee Hibs fixture. They played this match on 18 August 1909. It ended in a 1-1 draw played against Edinburgh Hibernian.

Kevin Gallacher, born in Clydebank in 1966. Kevin was signed from Duntocher Boys and came to United straight from school. He came from a footballing family, and the young player seemed destined for professional status from a young age. In 1983 he joined the club as an apprentice, and two years later made his impressive debut in the UEFA Cup. This tie was between United and Neuchatel Xamax played on 11 December 1985 in Switzerland. One year later he won his first Scottish cap, and his career was still to flourish. On 14 May 1988 Kevin scored United's goal in the Scottish Cup Final, losing to Celtic 2-1. On 25 January 1990, Coventry City signed him for a reputed fee of £950,000. After a medical, Kevin signed a four-year contract with the club. While at Tannadice, Kevin gained five caps for Scotland. Later, on 23 March 1993, he was to sign for Blackburn Rovers in a deal worth £1.5 million. Also included in the deal was striker Roy Wegerie making his way to Coventry City. Kevin's grandfather was the well known player Patsy Gallacher. Patsy retired from football in 1932 after a spell with Forfar.

Patsy Gallacher, played as a War guest for United on 29 November 1941 in the 3-2 victory over East Fife in the North-Eastern League Cup-tie. Before playing for United, Patsy had joined Sunderland, and was capped for Scotland against Ireland in 1935. Patsy had also played for Stoke City joining them in 1938. (Patsy was no relation to the former Celtic player.)

T. Gallacher, joined Dundee Hibs in December 1912. The player made his club debut on 7 December 1912 in the 1-1 draw with St Johnstone at Tannadice. He made nine appearances for Dundee Hibs during season 1912-13 and scored two goals.

Sam Galligan, signed for Dundee Hibs by manager Pat Reilly in May 1913.

David Galloway, signed to the club in October 1982 by manager Jim McLean. United released the 17-year-old player on 12 January 1983.

W. Galloway, played his debut game for Dundee Hibs on 11 November 1911 in the 1-0 win over St Johnstone at Tannadice. The player was signed by manager Pat Reilly from junior side Lochee Harp. While he was with Dundee Hibs he made six appearances during season 1911-12 and scored one goal.

Willie Garden, played in a trial match for United on 7 February 1948. Willie had another trial the following week against Arbroath at Gayfield.

Bobby Gardiner, joined the club in season 1933-34, from junior club Broughty Ex-Service Club, whom he joined from East Craigie. The player made his first team debut for United on 16 December 1933 in the 4-4 draw with Arbroath at Tannadice. Bobby left the club and played for English side Bristol City. In January 1937 he was playing for Darlington. By September 1937 he was playing for Bristol Rovers. Bobby returned to Tannadice as a war guest on 2 October 1939 when Bristol was out of action. Bobby returned from France in August 1947. The former United favourite decided not to renew his contract with the club.

George Gardiner, signed for United during the close season of 1929 from Clydebank. George made his United debut on 10 August 1929 in the 3-3 draw with Clyde at Tannadice. The player was freed by United in April 1933. During his spell at Tannadice he played in 134 games and scored six goals. On 14 July 1933 he signed for Leith Athletic. They later freed George on 2nd May 1934.

John Gardiner, was signed to United during season 1978-79. The young keeper played in goal for the club in Ally Donaldson's Testimonial match on 4 May 1980 at Dens Park. The keeper went on loan to Airdrie on 20 February 1981. Played his first match for them the following day against Aberdeen. He later came back to United after the loan period had ended. On 23 October 1981 he again went on loan this time to Forfar. John signed for Motherwell in 1984.

Pat Gardner, was born in Dunfermline in 1943. Manager Jim McLean signed him from Dunfermline in January 1972. Pat cost the club £8,000, and he had also been a member of Dunfermline's Scottish Cup-winning side of 1968.

He made his first team debut on 29 January 1972 in a game against Morton. United ran out winners that day by 2-1. Pat first joined the senior football ranks when he joined Queen of the South from Belshill in 1963. Then he played two games for Airdrie, then signed for Raith Rovers in September 1964. Raith transferred him to Dunfermline in July 1967 for £20,000. The player was United's top scorer in season 1972-73. In October 1973 Pat left the club and joined Motherwell. On 30 April 1976 he signed for Arbroath. In August 1977 Pat was appointed coach with Airdrie. During his spell at Tannadice, Pat featured in 75 league and cup games and scored 18 goals. After retiring from professional football Pat qualified as a social worker.

Allan Garvie, played in a first team trial game for United on 14 December 1957 against Albion Rovers. Allan had been playing with junior side Perth Celtic. He made his United home debut on 27 December 1957 against Stranraer. The player made nine appearances for United and scored four goals. Allan was freed by United in April 1958.

Steve Garvie, played for Crewe Alexandra, and came to Tannadice on 25 March 1998 for a trial.

Peter Gavigan, was born in Glasgow, and played for United in 1932. His first game for United was on 10 December 1932 against Brechin at Tannadice. While he was with the club, he made 13 league appearances. Peter was freed by United in April 1933. His other clubs included Clacton Orient, Manchester United, Fulham, Dundee, and St Johnstone. Peter died in March 1977 aged 77.

Robert Gemmell, signed by manager Jimmy Brownlie on 8 September 1928 from Hull City.

Charlie George, the ex-Derby and Arsenal player signed a short term contract with United on 10 March 1982. George had problems with his level of fitness, and was a signed and registered player with the club. In January 1983 George still had not played a game for the club, and never did.

David Gibb, played for Dundee Hibs when they won the Forfarshire Cup against Dundee A on 24 April 1920 by 1-0. Dundee FC complained that on the team-lines Gibb's name was down as Anderson, and so they demanded a replay. They were successful with their protest and they played the game on 1 May 1920. Dundee Hibs again won 1-0 and lifted the trophy. David was signed by the club shortly before this game. His brother Edward also played for the club.

Jimmy Gibb, was a groundsman at Tannadice for many years. In October 1976, Jimmy was disgusted when vandals broke into the park and vandalised the pitch with black gloss paint.

Alistair Gibson, signed to United by manager Tommy Gray on 26 June 1957, from Queen of the South. Alistair had spent three seasons with them. He made his United first team debut on 10 August 1957 against Clyde at Tannadice. The wing-half was at Tannadice until May 1959 when United freed him. During his spell with United, Alistair played in 54 games for the club.

Dan Gibson, played for Dundee Hibs. The player made 24 appearances and scored 13 times for the club. On 21 April 1913 he was transferred to Portsmouth.

George Gibson, scored the winning goal for Dundee Hibs in the Forfarshire Cup Final on 1 May 1920 against Dundee A.

Ian Gibson, born in Hamilton in 1956, and signed for United on 16 October 1980 from Partick Thistle by manager Jim McLean. At that time Ian was under the freedom of contract rule when he offered himself to United. The club paid a fee of £75,000 to his former club after the Appeal's Tribunal fixed the price. He made his first team debut on 18 October 1980 in a game against Kilmarnock. Score that day United 0 Killie 1. On 30 December 1982 in a deal that saw Morton player John McNeill going to Tannadice, Ian and Graeme Payne headed for Greenock. He returned to Tannadice on 22 February 1983. Then he went on loan to St Johnstone. In June 1983 he returned to Tannadice. Then St Johnstone offered to buy him, and he signed for them on 19 July 1983 for a fee of £15,000. In December 1984 he was working as a Financial Consultant with Legal and General. Also employed there as a manager was Jim Jeffries, the current Hearts boss. On 18 June 1985 Ian was appointed player-manager of St Johnstone. In May 1987, he had departed the club. However, on 11 May 1987, he signed for Raith Rovers. Later Ian signed for Arbroath and became their manager on 29 May 1990. This was after Arbroath sacked their manager John Young on 21 April 1990. In April 1991, Ian left the club. Ian now turns out for the All-Star XI to raise money for local charities.

Kenneth Gibson, signed for United on 19 July 1944. The player turned out for the club as a War guest the previous season. Kenneth had played for junior side Elmwood.

Martin Gierssen, was 25 years old when Jim McLean invited the player to come to the club in January 1976 from Iceland. This was Jim McLean's third attempt at signing a player from Iceland. The other two were Johannes Edvaldson and Albert Tommasson. However, Gierssen left the club and returned home without any transaction being carried out.

Eddie Gilfeather, signed for the club by manager Jimmy Brownlie in 1923 from Celtic. Eddie made his debut for the club on 29 September 1923 against Vale of Leven at Tannadice. During season 1923-24 he played in 24 league games and scored three goals. In season 1924-25 he appeared in 34 games and scored once. After he left United, he signed for Hibs. During the close season of 1925 he signed for Celtic.

Wayne Gill, signed by manager Tommy McLean on a short term contract on 31 March 1998 from Blackburn Rovers. Wayne made his first team debut on 25 April 1998 against St Johnstone at Tannadice.

Dennis Gillespie, was born in Duntocher, in 1936. Manager Jerry Kerr signed him on 27 August 1959 for a fee of £3,000 paid to Alloa. At the time of his signing Dennis was being paid £4 per week. One of the hardest working players with United, Dennis always enjoyed a friendly rapport with the fans. Dennis made his debut in United colours in a reserve game on 29 August 1959 against Falkirk at Tannadice. He made his first team debut on 5 September 1959 against St Johnstone at Tannadice. The player stayed with the club for 12 years, and later Dundee United rewarded him with a Testimonial game on Monday 7 May 1973. Guest players included Frank Munro (Wolves), Ian Britton (Chelsea), Mel Holden (Preston) and Alan Gilzean (Spurs). More than 11,000 supporters came to show their gratitude to a model professional. Dennis finally ended his career playing with Brechin City. During his spell with United Dennis played in 346 league and cup games and scored 93 goals.

Sam Gilligan, played for Dundee Hibs during the First World War.

Jock Gilmour, played for Dundee FC before a knee injury ended his career there. Jock played in a trial match for United on 7 August 1937 and later signed for United on 9 February 1938. He also played in a cup tie against East Fife played in Methil on 12 February 1938. United were beaten 5-0 that day. While he was at Tannadice he made eight league appearances.

George Gilmour, played in a game for the club on 10 October 1953. This was in the second round of the Second XI Cup against Morton at Tannadice.

Sandy Gilmour, signed to Dundee Hibs by manager Jimmy Brownlie in 1923 from Raith Rovers. Sandy played his first game for Dundee Hibs on 15 August 1923 against St Johnstone. Within a few months of signing, the club changed its name to Dundee United. During season 1923-24 he made 36 league appearances and scored six times for the club. In season 1924-25 he made 32 appearances and scored five goals.

Tommy Gilroy, signed by manager Jimmy Brownlie in December 1925 from Fauldhouse United. Tommy made his United debut on 19 December 1925 in the 2-1 win over Rangers at Tannadice. The player later moved from United to Falkirk in May 1927. While he was with United, he made 26 appearances for the club. Tommy was placed on the transfer list at Brockville on 14 May 1930, the asking price was £200 pounds. On 15 July 1931, Tommy was transferred to Albion Rovers.

Robert Glassey, played a few games for Third Lanark, Mansfield Town, and Liverpool. On 28 January 1942 it was announced that he would turn out for United as a War guest. Robert made his United debut on 21 February 1942 against Dunfermline. The player made his first Tannadice appearance on 27 March 1942 against Raith Rovers. In March 1943 he was playing for Raith Rovers.

Alec Glen, played for United during season 1939-40. Alec had previously played for Raith Rovers.

Edmund Glover, signed for United on 6 January 1932. Edmund had previously signed for United two or three seasons earlier, but returned to junior side Lochee Harp. The player made his first team debut for United on 9 January 1932 against Partick Thistle at Firhill. As a young player he featured in the Dundee High School team.

James Glover, joined the committee of Dundee Hibs in March 1909.

Jim Goldie, was an inside-forward who had the distinction of being manager Jerry Kerr's first signing. Jim signed for the club on 21 July 1959 after he was freed by Falkirk. He had also played for Aston Villa. In March 1962, he was playing for Kilsyth Rangers. Then Luton Town offered to sign him on 31 March 1962 for £500 pounds.

Sergio Heneriques Gomes, was signed by manager Ivan Golac on 20 January 1995 from Portugese club Amora. The media-reported fee as £300,000. Sergio made his debut for the club on 21 January 1995 in a game against Motherwell at Tannadice. United ran out 6-1 winners. The player signed for Kuwait's Sporting Club on 5 December 1995 for an undisclosed fee.

Brian Goodall, joined the club in November 1972 from Lochee Harp. In July 1974, he was included in a United pool that headed for a short tour of the north of Scotland.

Alan Gordon, signed for the club on 31 March 1969. Alan was signed by Jerry Kerr from Hearts for a reported fee of £8,000. Gordon had played for Hearts from 1961 until 1967 when he left for South Africa. He returned in season 1968-69, before joining United. Alec made his United debut on the evening that he signed for the club against Hibs at Tannadice. He would later leave United to sign for Hibs. The player scored his first goal for United on 20 September 1969 in a 2-1 win over Dundee at Dens.Gordon eventually signed for Dundee FC on 14 December 1974 from Hibernian. They reported that the fee was £15,000. On 29 April 1976 Gordon announced that he was retiring from the game. During his spell with United, Alan featured in 78 league and cup games and scored 34 goals.

Alec Gordon, was signed by manager Jerry Kerr on 19 November 1960 from Armadale Thistle. The player made his first team debut on 18 February 1961 in a game against Raith Rovers at Tannadice. Score that day 4-1 United. In 1965 he was playing for Bradford City. On 30 September 1967 he signed for St Johnstone. During his spell with United he featured in 79 matches and scored one goal for the club.

Jim Gordon, played in a United first team trial game against Cowdenbeath on 14 March 1959.

Richard Gough, born in Sweden on 5 April 1962, however, he was brought up in South Africa. Coming from a footballing background, his father was a professional player at Charlton Athletic. Gough's father spotted his son's early potential and informed manager Jim McLean who arranged a trial. He first played in a tangerine shirt on 17 April 1980 in a reserve match against Celtic. Jim McLean was suitably impressed, and Richard signed for United in season 1981-82, shortly after his arrival from South Africa. Gough returned to South Africa in December 1981 because he was homesick. In season 1981-82 his wages were an incredible £350 a week! However Richard did return to Tannadice a short time later, and under Jim McLean's guidance he soon became a highly-rated defender. By now, other big money clubs had taken notice of the talented player. On 30 September 1985 Dundee United turned down a bid of £350,000 from Aston Villa. Then on 18 April 1986, Glasgow Rangers attempted to purchase him for a reported fee of £500,000. However, manager McLean and the board did not want the player to go, and they turned down his request. On 4 August 1986 Richard asked for a transfer. The United directors turned down his bid. However, on 18 August 1986 the club transferred him to Tottenham Hotspur for a fee in the region of £750,000. The media speculation about the player over the past months had taken its toll. Richard Gough had wanted more money from the Tannadice Board. In fact he was looking for £50,000 from the club, even though he still had four years of his contract to run. The board at Tannadice had no option but to sell the player.

In 1986 he received the Scottish Brewers Player of the Year Award. Also included was a trophy and a cheque for £1,000. In September 1987 Gough was back in Scotland, signing for Rangers. The deal was reputedly worth £1.5 million. Ironically he made his Rangers debut against United on 10 October 1987 before a crowd of 18,214 at Tannadice. The score that day was United 1 Rangers 0. By now Richard Gough was playing at international level. On 11 June 1990, Richard gained his 50th Cap for Scotland in a match against Costa Rica. Unfortunately for Richard he limped off with a foot injury. However, his Scotland days were soon to end. This was after he criticised the then Scottish coach Andy Roxburgh in his autobiography. Scotland soon appointed a new Scottish coach Craig Brown, who, like his predecessor, has steadfastly refused to allow Gough to return to international duty. On 8 May 1997 he lifted the Premier League trophy for Rangers for the ninth time. A few days later Gough left Ibrox to play in the States. He signed a contract to join the Kansas City Wizards. Several months later Gough returned to Ibrox again for another spell at the heart of their defence.

J. Govan, played for Dundee Hibs. The player featured in the first city derby against Dundee on 13 March 1915. From seasons' 1910-1915 he played in 49 matches and scored eight goals.

D. 'Chappie' Gowans, signed for Dundee Hibs in August 1912 by manager Pat Reilly from Dundee FC. He made his club debut on 24 August 1912 against Leith Athletic at Logie Green.

While he was with the club, he made 11 appearances during season 1912-13.

Andy Graham, signed for the club on 19 December 1977 from Johnstone Burgh. The goalkeeper became a full time player at Tannadice in January 1978. He was 21 years old when he signed for the club. Andy made his first team debut on 2 May 1978 in a game against Clydebank. However, United lost 2-0 to the relegated

Bankies. On 7 August 1982, Andy played as guest for Aberdeen in Drew Jarvie's Testimonial match. Andy had replaced the injured Jim Leighton. On 12 August 1983, Andy joined Raith on a two-month loan.

Jackie Graham, signed for United on 15 August 1966 from Morton. Both clubs had concluded a swap deal. This saw United player Ian Stewart heading for Cappielow. Jackie made his first United appearance that evening in a reserve game against Dundee at Dens Park. The player made his first team debut on 27 August 1966 against Dundee in the 1-1 draw at Dens. He was freed by the club in April 1969. During his spell with United, Jackie featured in 27 league and cup games and scored on ten occasions.

Johnny Graham, was 19 when he was signed by manager Jerry Kerr on 10 June 1964. His previous club was Third Lanark and the winger signed to them from Strathclyde Juniors. At the time of signing for United, the club had paid a reported £6,000 for his services. The player made his first team debut in the 3-2 victory over Dundee on 8 August 1964, at Dens Park. While he was at Tannadice, he played in 47 games and scored 17 goals. In 1965 he was playing with Falkirk. Also playing in the same team at that time were fellow ex-United player's Jim McManus and Doug Moran. On 11 November 1969 he was transferred from Falkirk to Hibs for a fee of £15,000.

Tommy Graham, was a member of the United side that won promotion to the First Division on 30 April 1960. The side beat Berwick Rangers 1-0 that day. Tommy ended his footballing career playing in England. While he was with United, he featured in 51 league and cup games.

W. Graham, made 18 appearances during season 1910-11 for Dundee Hibs.

George Grant, born in Dundee in 1923 and had played for New Stevenston United. George signed to United from Arbroath in January 1946 by manager Willie MacFadyen. His United debut was on 7 December 1946 against his old club Arbroath at Tannadice. On 3 October 1949, George did something amazing, he scored three goals in three minutes to demolish Hamilton 3-0 in a B-Division game. He scored many goals for the club in the post war era, before embarking on a new career with Falkirk in 1954. United gave him a testimonial for his hard work and dedication. In April 1954 United met Dundee and the proceeds of this match were split two ways –

George receiving half of the funds. The other half went to Dundee's Jimmy Toner. After he left the club he joined Fauldhouse, where he spent 16 years. Then, on 2 June 1962, he was appointed trainer with them. During his spell with United, George played 195 games and scored 32 goals.

George Grant, became a director at Tannadice in 1973. On 23 August 1988, he succeeded George Fox as Club Chairman. Two days later George Grant died, aged 67 years. His brother Johnston had been Chairman for 16 years until he died in 1984.

Johnston Grant, born in 1915. Along with George Fox both men became directors with the club in 1955. Both men offered stability and financial acumen. In 1965 Johnston became vice-chairman of the club, and his financial stewardship paid dividends when the club went through its successful period under Jim McLean. Mr Grant died in July 1984.

Ian Grassick, signed by Hearts in March 1964, and manager Jerry Kerr fixed him up with a months trial with United on 8 January 1965. Ian made his debut in a reserve match played against Hibs at Tannadice on 16 January 1965.

Gray, played for Ayr United, East Fife, and Albion Rovers. He played for United as a trialist on 12 August 1939 against Edinburgh City. Dundee United won that day 3-2.

Andy Gray, born in 1955 and turned professional in May 1973. Manager Jim McLean signed Andy from Clydebank Strollers. Andy made his first team debut against Motherwell on 18 August 1973 when he came on as a sub. His first full first team match was on 29 August 1973 in a League Cup tie against East Fife. He went on to score 40 goals in 96 games for the club. By 1974, the player was creating a name for himself. In August 1974 an offer of £75,000 came in from Nottingham Forest. Manager Jim McLean and the United directors flatly rejected this. On 27 September 1975, after severe media pressure, manager Jim McLean reluctantly sold Gray for £110,000 to Aston Villa. This was the first ever six-figure fee that United had been paid for a player. Five years later he signed for Wolves for a reputed £1.46 million. Gray spent three years there before signing for Everton for a fee of £200,000. There he had his most success, winning the FA Cup, a League Championship, and the European Cup Winners Cup. However, Gray returned to Aston Villa for a short time, before he signed for his favourite side.

Glasgow Rangers manager Graeme Souness offered Gray the chance to sign for the club in September 1988. At the age of 32, he had achieved a lifetime's ambition. He had joined the club that he had supported as a youngster. Andy has 20 International caps, winning his first one in 1976 in a game against Rumania. After retiring from the game, Andy went on to become a highly successful TV commentator with Sky Sports.

Billy Gray, was signed by Jerry Kerr on 16 July 1971 from Morton. Billy had previously spent six years at Cappielow, and then two seasons with St Mirren. While he was with United, he featured in 29 league and cup games and scored one goal for the club.

Dale Gray, born in Edinburgh on 15 February 1978. Dale was turning out for United's reserve side during season 1997-98. His contract with the club was extended in April 1998 to keep him at Tannadice until the year 2000.

Davie Gray, played for Rangers, and made his debut against Moscow Dynamo in a 2-2 draw at Ibrox in 1945. After leaving them he signed for Preston, then Blackburn Rovers, then Dundee. Later, on 13 September 1956, United manager Reggie Smith signed the player for United. Davie made his United first team debut against his old club Dundee on 15 September 1956. United won 2-1at Tannadice. Davie announced that he was quitting the game on 21 March 1958. The club then freed the player in April 1958. On 18 November 1958 he was appointed training supervisor of Forfar Athletic. His brother Tommy played centre-half for Dundee for many years. During his spell at Tannadice, Davie featured in 36 league and cup games.

George Gray, signed by manager Willie Macfadyen in December 1952. The player made his first team debut as a trialist in a game against Dunfermline at East End Park.

Jimmy Green, signed by manager Willie MacFadyen on 10 August 1950 from Queen of the South. Jimmy had also had a spell with Bournemouth before signing for United. The player made his United debut on 12 August 1950 against Dundee at Dens Park.

Alex Grieve, signed by manager Pat Reilly for Dundee Hibs in March 1914. The goalkeeper made his club debut on 4 April 1914 against Vale of Leven at Milburn Park. This game ended in a 2-1 victory for Dundee Hibs. He played in three competitive matches for Dundee Hibs in 1914. During season 1914-15 he played in 22 matches. In January 1915 he left the club and headed off to England.

Dick Grieve, signed by manager Willie MacFadyen during season 1950-51. The player made his United debut in a reserve game against Leith Athletic on 27 January 1951. Dick made his first team debut on 3 February 1951 against Cowdenbeath at Tannadice. Before Dick joined United he was transferred from Rochdale to Wrexham for a considerable fee. After being freed by Wrexham he signed for United.

R. Grieve, signed for United during season 1937-38 and played in 15 league games. The player was freed by the club after a dispute on 8 February 1938.

Ab Grittar, hailed from Holland, and joined United's coaching staff in November 1990.

Fred Grubb, signed by manager Reggie Smith during the close season of 1955.

Barclay Gunn, signed by Jim McLean in April 1973 from Bankfoot Juniors. He had the distinction of being the first player with Bankfoot to turn senior. Later his colleague Paul Sturrock would break through to the rank of professional.

Billy Guthrie, played for St Johnstone, Y. M. Coupar Angus, and Auchterader Primrose. When with United he played in the position of inside-forward. In March 1952 he was working in the Naval Stores in Singapore.

Willie Guthrie, joined United for training on 24 November 1949 from Newburgh Juniors. The player made his United debut in a B-Division game against Albion Rovers on 26 November 1949 at Tannadice.

Jimmy Guy, signed by manager Willie MacFadyen in May 1952 on a free from Falkirk. Jimmy made his first team debut on 9 August 1952 against Dumbarton at Boghead. The player had previously played for Stirling Albion, joining them in 1948 after a spell with Third Lanark. The player was freed by United in May 1953.

Jim Gwynne, played in a first team trial match for United on 22 August 1957 in the 2-2 draw against Alloa.

Andy Haddow, was on loan to United from Clyde during season 1929-30. He had also played with Morton and Burnley. Andy played regularly for Morton until season 1926-27. Then he was transferred to Burnley, then went off to America for a short time. In January 1929 he signed for Clyde. The player made his United debut on 11 January 1930 against Dundee. Manager Jimmy Brownlie had signed Andy two days before his debut for the club. Andy was freed by Clyde on 10 March 1931, and returned to Tannadice two days later. He made his debut again for the club on 14 March 1931 against Arbroath at Gayfield. Then he made his Tannadice debut on 4 April 1931 against Albion Rovers. On 9 July 1931 Andy was signed to Irish club Ballymena.

Billy Hainey, joined Partick Thistle from Johnstone Burgh in October 1960. The player was signed by manager Jerry Kerr from Partick Thistle in March 1966. Billy made his first team debut on 19 March 1966 in the 5-1 victory over Motherwell. He was freed from the club in April 1968.

He signed for St Mirren in July 1968 and then signed for Portadown in June 1969. During his spell with United he featured in 46 league and cup games and scored eight goals for the club.

Henry Hall, was provisionally signed to Dundee from Kirkintilloch Rob Roy in November 1964. Dundee manager Bob Shankly allowed the player to leave in April 1965. Henry started his senior career with Stirling Albion, and then signed for St Johnstone on 7 November 1968 for £15,000. The player made his Muirton debut on 9 November 1968 in a 3-2 defeat from St Mirren. A leading goal scorer in the First Division, Henry had also trained as a Physical Education Instructor. By 1973, Henry was now an SFA Coach. In the close season of 1975 Henry came to Tannadice for a fee of 2,000. This also saw United's Duncan Macleod heading for St Johnstone in a swop deal. He made his club debut on 9 August 1975 in a game against his old club. United ran out winners 3-1. Henry was released by United in the close season of 1977. He signed for Forfar on 14 June 1977. Henry took over the manager's position in July 1986 after Doug Houston resigned on medical grounds. On 2 September 1989, he resigned as manager of Forfar. However, one month later he was back in football as a scout for Aberdeen. On 2 August 1991, he became a coach at Dens after Billy Kirkwood had moved onto Rangers. During his spell with United Henry played in 34 league and cup games and scored on eight occasions.

D. Halley, was a director with the club during the 1920s and 1930s. They re-elected him to the United board on 10 March 1930.

Vince Halpin, signed to United in June 1954 by manager Willie MacFadyen. The player had previously been with Hibs. Vince made his first team appearance for United on 16 October 1954 against Ayr United at Somerset Park. In September 1961, he was appointed player-manager with Pumpherston Juniors. In June 1966, he was given a free transfer from them.

Andy Hamilton, signed to United by manager Tommy Gray on 10 April 1957 from Dunfermline. Andy had previously spent two seasons at East End Park. The player made his first team debut for United on 13 April 1957 against Cowdenbeath at Tannadice. On 13 November 1957 United offered Andy a free transfer from the club.

Ian Hamilton, provisionally signed to the club by manager Reggie Smith in 1956. At that time the young player had been attending Harris Academy. In December 1956, Ian was showing up well with United's reserves.

Jim Hamilton, signed for United on 15 October 1953. Jim made his debut on 10 October 1953 in the second round of the Second XI Cup against Morton at Cappielow. The player made his first team debut on 17 October 1953 against Motherwell at Tannadice. While he was with the club, he played in 26 league and cup games.

Tom Hanick, became President of Dundee Hibs in March 1909.

David Hannah, born in Coatbridge on 4 August 1974, and signed from Hamilton Thistle in September 1991. David had the distinction of being the youngest player in the 1994 Scottish Cup winning side. On 27 December 1996 United transferred him to Celtic. David had been involved in a dispute over his contract. United reportedly sold him for £650,000. The player signed a four-and-a-half-year contract with Celtic. He made his Celtic debut on 28 December 1996, against Dunfermline at Celtic Park.

George Hannah, signed to Dundee Hibs by manager Jimmy Brownlie on 6 June 1923 from Hamilton Accies. George made his club debut on 15 August 1923 against St Johnstone. A few months after he signed the club changed its name to Dundee United. While he was with the club, he played in ten league games.

Jack Hannan, from St Johnstone, played in the first ever Dundee Hibs fixture. This match was played on 18 August 1909 and was a

1-1 draw against Edinburgh Hibernian. Joe also had the distinction of scoring the first league goal for Dundee Hibs on 21 August 1909. The side lost 2-1 against Dundee Wanderers. Jack was freed by the club in 1911, however, manager Pat Reilly re-signed him on 13 August 1913. The player also featured in the side that lost 3-0 to Albion Rovers in the Qualifying Cup Final game on 27 December 1913. While was with the club he played in eight competitive matches and scored one goal.

Bruce Harley, came to the club from Hearts in 1930. Bruce made his first team debut 11 January 1930 against Dundee at Dens Park. The player scored one of the goals in the record 14-0 win over Nithsdale Wanderers, played on 17 January 1931, in the Scottish Cup. During the summer football recess Bruce, who was also a professional golfer, went off to play in Norway. While he was at Tannadice he played in 24 games and scored one goal for the club.

Jimmy Hart, signed by manager Jimmy Brownlie during season 1934-35. While he was at the club, he made10 league appearances and scored six goals. In August 1935 he signed for Cowdenbeath.

Johnny Hart, signed for United during season 1927-28 by manager Jimmy Brownlie. Johnny had played for Albion Rovers, Motherwell, St Johnstone, and Ross County where he was their player-coach. Johnny spent 20 years at Tannadice as a player and then trainer. During his spell with United, Johnny played in 87 competitive matches and scored 22 goals for the club. Johnny died on 29 June 1963, aged 66.

Hart, played for Dunfermline Athletic and guested for United on 27 November 1943 against Hearts at Tynecastle.

J. Harvey, signed by manager Jimmy Brownlie in 1924 from St Johnstone. The player made his debut for the club on 16 August 1924 in the 2-2 draw with Bo'ness. While he was with the club, he played in 33 games and scored twice.

Robert Harvey, signed by manager Willie MacFadyen on 17 December 1948 on a free from Stenhousemuir, whom he joined in 1946. Robert made his United debut on 18 December 1948 in a C-Division game against Forfar.

Hugh Hay, signed by manager Tommy Gray during the close season of 1958 from Aberdeen. During his spell with United, Hugh played in 14 first team games and scored three times.

Ian Hay, signed for United in June 1944 from Aberdeen Mugiemoss.

J. Headrick, signed for Dundee Hibs from Stirling Emmet in October 1921. He made his debut for the club on 15 October 1921 against Forfar Athletic at Tannadice. In season 1921-22 he made 30 league appearances and scored twice for the club.

Paul Hegarty, born in 1954, and is now recognised as a Tannadice legend. He was signed by manager Jim McLean in November 1974 for £40,000, from Hamilton Accies. While playing for them, he had scored 12 goals since August 1974. Paul was originally a forward, until the manager moved him into a role in central defence – a role that would lead Paul to become capped for his country. He made his first team debut on 16 November 1974 in a game against Partick Thistle. Paul came on as sub in this match which United won 5-0. His first full game came on 14 December 1974 in a game against Morton. While at the club, manager Jim McLean teamed him up with fellow defender Dave Narey, and a partnership of the highest quality soon developed. As captain of United, Paul led the team to the League Championship, League Cup Finals, and many memorable nights with Europe's finest. In recognition of his service, they rewarded Hegarty with a testimonial game on 29 November 1989 against IFK Gothenburg before a crowd of 7,300. United announced that Paul was free to leave Tannadice on 6 December 1989. The board did want Paul to stay on in a coaching capacity. However, Paul still wanted to play, so the club agreed that they would not be difficult to deal with. On 22 January 1990, Paul left the club and joined St Johnstone. Paul made his debut for St Johnstone on 27 January 1990 in a game against Ayr United. While there, he won a First Division championship medal. After St Johnstone, he signed for Forfar Athletic where he became player-manager on 17 July 1990. He made his debut with Forfar on 2 August 1990 in a friendly game against Preston North End at Station Park. Paul parted company with Forfar on 7 April 1992. On 19 August 1992 he returned to Tannadice as coach, before joining the coaching staff at Hearts in 1995. Then, in 1997, he joined former Hibs manager Alex Miller as assistant manager of Aberdeen. Paul had a unique footballing record at Tannadice. He made 493 appearances in the Scottish League, appeared 58 times in Scottish Cup matches, and was capped for his country eight times. His first cap was in 1979 in a game against Wales. Paul was the Scottish PFA Player of the Year in 1979, and he played in the UEFA Cup Final against Gothenburg in 1987.

DUNDEE UTD WHO'S WHO

Ryan Hegarty, was 15 years old when he signed to the club on 1 September 1992 from Hutcheson Vale. His uncle Paul was a coach with the club when he signed. The club freed him on 8 November 1995.

Alex Henderson, signed by manager Jimmy Brownlie on 24 August 1926 from junior side North End. Alex played for United on seven occasions and scored one goal.

Andy Henderson, played in goal for Dundee Hibs in the early 1920s. Andy was in the Dundee Hibs side when they won the Forfarshire Cup against Dundee A on 1 May 1920. The keeper played in 29 league games with the club.

Atholl Henderson, became a coach with the club in September 1987. He left United and joined St Johnstone on 31 October 1994.

Bill Henderson, signed to Dundee Hibs by manager Pat Reilly in May 1913 from Grimsby Town, and had previously played for Dundee. The player made his debut on 16 August 1913 in the 0-0 draw with St Johnstone. Bill also played in the Qualifying Cup Final side that lost 3-0 to Albion Rovers on 27 December 1913. During that season he turned out 19 times for the club and scored one goal.

Bobby Henderson, signed to United in August 1956 by manager Reggie Smith. Bobby made his first team debut on 11 August 1956 in the opening game of the season against Ayr United at Tannadice. This was a League Cup clash, and United won that day 6-1. The goalkeeper had previously played for Dundee. Bobby was freed by United in April 1957.

George Henderson I, played for Dundee FC in the 1920s. George signed to United by manager Jimmy Brownlie on 24 July 1928. The former Rangers player went to play for Darlington before spending a season playing in America. He made his United debut on 7 August 1928 in a practise game at Tannadice. His first league appearance for the club was on 11 August 1928 in the 4-0 win over Bathgate. George scored the cup winning goal for United against Dundee in 1929. The ex-United player then made his way to Wales and joined Rhyll. He made his debut for them on 8 November 1930. His other clubs also included Forfar. In 1940 he was an SFA Referee. George then left Scotland and headed off to America. During his stay with United, George played in 69 first team games and scored 22 goals.

George Henderson II, signed for United on 16 March 1948 from Stirling Albion. He made his first team debut on 20 March 1948 against Raith Rovers at Tannadice. George appeared in five competitive first team games that season and scored three goals.

Jim Henry, born in Dundee and attended Lawside Academy. Jim signed for United in 1967 from Carnoustie Juniors. The young left half won his first major honour on 2 September 1970 when he was chosen to play for the Scottish League Team against the League of Ireland at Celtic Park. In 1972 Jim was due to sign for Fulham for a reported fee of £50,000. However, a few days later he was back at the club after Fulham pulled out of the deal. Dundee United transferred him to Aberdeen on 9 January 1974 for a reported fee of £20,000. He made his debut with Aberdeen three days later in a match against Rangers.

After leaving Aberdeen, Henry left for the United States on 19 March 1976 to play for San Antonio. When he returned from America a few months later, he signed for Forfar Athletic. Then after another spell in the States Jim returned to Forfar in February 1978. While he was with United he played in 94 league and cup games and scored seven goals.

Thomas Heraughty, joined the committee of Dundee Hibs in March 1909.

Johnnie Herbert, played for United on 22 December 1933 against his former club East Fife at Bayview. While he was at Tannadice, he made four league appearances and was later freed.

Gerry Hernon, signed by manager Jerry Kerr on 14 October 1966 from Ashfield Juniors. Gerry made his first team debut on 12 April 1967 against St Mirren at Love Street. The player was freed from the club in April 1968.

James Heron, signed to Dundee Hibs by manager Pat Reilly on 6 April 1916 from Arbroath. James made his club debut on 8 April 1916 against Leith Athletic at Tannadice. He was also in the Dundee Hibs side when they won the Forfarshire Cup against Dundee A on 1 May 1920.

Billy Higgins, signed by manager Jerry Kerr on 24 October 1969 on a three-month contract. At the time of signing, Billy had been playing in South Africa. His other clubs included Hearts.

Laurie Higgins, signed for the club on a free from Aberdeen on 7 September 1954. Laurie made his United debut on 11 September 1954 against Stenhousemuir at Tannadice.

Ernie Hiles, was captain of Fulham, and was fixed up to play for United as a War guest on 22 December 1943. He had played in 37 games for Fulham in season 1938-39. Ernie made his United debut on New Years Day 1944 against Aberdeen.

Peter Hinds, signed for United on 1 July 1989 for a fee of £65,000. At the time of signing he was playing for Japanese club Jujita. The 26-year-old had a superstar status in Japan. Peter made a scoring debut on 23 August 1989 in a Skol Cup match against Hamilton. United agreed to lend him to Portuguese side Martimo on 23 August 1990. Initially the player was to join them until the end of season 1991.

Davie Hogg, signed for United on 6 June 1968 on a free from Hibernian. The 21-year-old spent four seasons at Easter Road and made a few first team appearances. He signed to them from Tynecastle Boy's Club in Edinburgh. Davie played his first game for United on 19 June 1968 against Brann FC, during the clubs tour of Norway. He made his League Cup debut on 10 August 1968 against Dunfermline at East End Park.

Robert Hogg, signed for United on 28 September 1935. The player made his first team debut for the club the same day as signing against Dumbarton at Boghead. His former club's included Dundee, Partick Thistle, and Cork.

William Hogg, played for Dundee Hibs in the early 1920s signing to the club from Montrose. While he was with the club, he played in nine league matches and scored two goals.

William Hogg, affectionately known as 'Daddy' Hogg, he joined the the Board of Directors of Dundee Hibs in November 1922. In January 1927 he was club chairman. On 5 November 1927, William died, however his influence lived on in both First and Second Division circles in the 1920s.

David Hoggan, joined United on 25 July 1983 for a trial period. David had played for Bolton and had figured in the Scottish Under-21 squad.

Cornelius Holland, signed for United as a War guest on 18 June 1941. The 21-year-old was on Army service when he signed. Before the War he was playing for Grimsby Town.

John Holt, born in Dundee in 1956, and played for Invergowrie Boys Club when he signed an S-form with United. After leaving

Stobswell Secondary, Holt joined the club as an apprentice in February 1972 and made his debut two years later on the 19 January 1974. The game was against Motherwell and United lost 1-0. In September 1987 John was transferred to Dunfermline along with Billy Kirkwood. Then, on 16 December 1988, he signed for city rivals Dundee FC for a fee of £45,000. On 7 January 1989 John played in his first city derby, against his old club United..However, Dundee 1-0. On 30 April 1990, Dundee manager Gordon Wallace announced that John, along with several other players were open to offers. This was a direct response from the manager after Dundee were relegated from the Premier Division in season 1989-90. After this spell at Dens, John tried his hand at management by joining Forfar in January 1991 as player-manager. Then he went onto Highland League outfit Deveronvale, then became manager at Montrose on 24 March 1993. Ross Jack became his assistant at Montrose. John took over the managership from Jim Leishman. On 28 March 1995, Montrose sacked John. Shortly afterwards he returned to Tannadice as a coach. At present, United employ John as a Community Development Officer based at Tannadice.

Ben Honeyman, was fixed up by the club on 3 August 1992. His father Graham was also a player with United several years earlier. Ben made his first team debut on 27 September 1995 in the Challenge Cup Fourth Round tie against Clydebank. The player grabbed a goal in the game. The club freed Ben on 21 May 1996 and he joined Forfar soon after.

Graham Honeyman, played for East Fife and left them in December 1975 to play for Australian side West Adelaide. The player joined United on a short term contract in 1978. Graham played in a few reserve matches before his inclusion into the first team squad. His first team debut was on 18 November 1978 at Tannadice in a game against Motherwell. The final score was United 2 Motherwell 1.

Honeyman left United on 11 November 1978 after his Adelaide club could not reach an agreement with United. His son Ben was fixed up by United in 1992.

Bert Hood, played in goal for Brechin City, and joined United for a for a one-month trial in August 1949. The keeper made his first team debut on 13 August 1949 at Broomfield.

Bobby Hope, played in a first team trial match against Cowdenbeath on 23 April 1955. At the time he was playing for junior side Lochgelly Albert.

W. Hotson, signed by manager Willie Reid in August 1932. His former club was Falkirk and he had played for a spell with Armadale. He made his United first team debut on 13 August 1932 against Hibs at Easter Road. The player made only eight league appearances with the club, and was then freed a short time later.

Doug Houston, joined Queens Park from Giffnock North. In September 1962, he left Queen's Park, and signed for Dundee FC on 7 May 1962. He was then transferred to Rangers in 1973 for £35,000. Doug signed for United on 16 March 1974 from Rangers for a reported fee of more than £10,000. The player made his Tannadice debut for United on 30 March 1974 against Ayr United. United won that day 2-1. Then he signed for St Johnstone on 7 July 1977 for a fee of £4,000. He became reserve team coach at Muirton on 21 October 1978. Doug later became manager at Forfar, but had to resign on medical grounds in July 1986. On 7 August 1986 he took up a coaching position at Tannadice. During his playing days with United Doug played in 86 league and cup games and scored five goals.

T. Houston, played for junior side Roselea and played his first game for Dundee Hibs on 10 December 1921 against Alloa at Tannadice. During season 1921-22 he appeared in ten league games.

Bob Howe, signed for the club on 4 August 1938 and had played for St Johnstone the previous season. Bob made his United debut on 13 August 1938 in the 5-4 victory over Montrose at Links Park. While he was with United he played in 17 league games and scored twice.

Bert Howieson, signed for United on 27 October 1960 from Leeds United. Jimmy made his debut on 5 November 1960 against Third Lanark at Cathkin Park. United lost 6-1. The player made his first team debut at Tannadice Park on 19 November 1960 against Kilmarnock. United lost 4-2. The club freed the player in May 1965. However, he was not out of the game for long as Motherwell signed him on 5 June 1965. During his spell with United, Bert played in 67 league and cup games and scored on six occasions.

Jimmy Howieson, signed by manager Jimmy Brownlie in June 1925 from St Johnstone. Jimmy had the distinction of scoring United's first goal in the First Division. The game was between United and Raith Rovers at Stark's Park on 15 August 1925. United lost 4-2, with Jimmy scoring both goals in what, incidentally, was also his debut game for the club. Jimmy was transferred to St Mirren in September

1925 before joining Hull City. On 9 November 1927 he was placed on their transfer list. During his spell withUnited Jimmy featured in ten league games and scored five goals.

Joseph Hughes, signed by Dundee Hibs manager Pat Reilly on 18 March 1914 from Dundee Violet. Joseph made his club debut on 21 March 1914 in the Forfarshire Cup Final against Arbroath. This game ended 1-1. He played in three competitive games for Dundee Hibs during 1914. The following season he appeared in 24 games for the club. The player featured in the first city derby against Dundee on 13 March 1915.

Jimmy Hughes, was signed for a trial period by manager Jerry Kerr on 1 August 1961. His former club was East Stirling. However, Jimmy's stay at Tannadice was short as they freed him on 15 September 1961.

Tommy Hughes, signed on a month's contract with the club on 6 January 1978. The keeper was playing for Hereford United at the time of signing. He also had spells with Chelsea, Aston Villa, and was capped for Scotland at Under-23 level. His first game for United was in a reserve match on 14 January 1978 against Brechin City. United won 2-0. Hughes returned to Hereford on 2 February 1978 after his family decided to stay in England.

Lloyd Hull, signed for United by manager Willie MacFadyen on 21 March 1946 from Lesmahagow Juniors. Lloyd made his United debut on 23 March 1946 in the 2-1 win over Ayr United at Tannadice.

Willie Hume, signed by manager Willie MacFadyen during the close season of 1948-49. The player made his first team debut on 14 August 1948 against Dumbarton. In June 1954 he took up a coaching position with Penicuik Athletic. Willie featured in nine senior games with United.

Wilson Humphries, joined Motherwell in 1945. The player was in the Motherwell side that beat Dundee 4-0 in the 1952 Scottish Cup Fina, on 19 April 1952. Wilson was released by the Fir Park side in 1956. He played for St Mirren before joining United in May 1957. Wilson made his first team debut on 10 August 1957 against Clyde at Tannadice. The player scored within 45 seconds of the game kicking off. He was with United until April 1959 and then joined Hamilton. While he was with them, he played alongside Jim McLean. As a boy he attended Dalziel High School and in January

1960 he was back there again, this time as a teacher. While he was with United he featured in 54 league and cup games and scored 31 goals.

Hunter, signed for United in August 1945 and made his debut on 1 September 1945 in the 3-2 victory over Ayr United at Tannadice.

Ian Hunter, was playing for junior side North End when he was given a trial for United on 9 October 1954. The first team game was against Brechin City at Tannadice.

Jackie Hunter, signed to United by manager Tommy Gray in May 1958 on a free from Motherwell. Jackie made his first team debut on 9 August 1958 against St Johnstone at Muirton Park. During his spell with the club he played in 18 league and cup games and scored ten goals.

Husson, played for Dundee FC, however he guested for Dundee Hibs during the First World War. His first game was on 26 August 1916 against East Stirlingshire.

Daniel Hutchison, was the younger brother of Tannadice favourite Duncan Hutchison. The left-winger signed to the club from St Joseph's Juniors in 1937. Daniel played his first team game for the club on 10 April 1937 against St Bernard's at Tannadice. Dan played in 16 league and cup games and scored twice.

Dod Hutchison, signed for Dundee Hibs on 12 September 1922. He had previously played for Denbeath Star, and Lochgelly United. Dod made his club debut on 16 September 1922 against Aberdeen A in the Scottish Alliance League.

Duncan Hutchison, nickname 'Hurricane Hutch', and born in 1923. Played for the club between 1927-29. Then he was transferred to Newcastle United on 27 August 1929 for £4,000. His first appearance in a United shirt was on 9 August 1927 in a trial match at Tannadice. Duncan made his league debut for United on 13 August 1927 in a 4-2 win over Bathgate at Tannadice. The decision to sell Duncan Hutchison caused ugly scenes among supporters angry with the loss of their star player. Later Duncan went on to play for Derby and then for Hull. The player did return to United on 18 June 1935. Also included in the deal was the departure of Bobby Yorke heading for Hull. His first game back in United colours was on 3 August 1935. This was a trial match between Black & White against Red & White. More than 12,000 spectators turned up at

Tannadice that day to welcome the player. His first team game was on 10 August 1935 against St Bernard's at Tannadice. After retiring from the game Duncan became a publican at the United Bar in Castle Street Dundee. Once again he returned to Tannadice, this time in 1953 when he became a director. Eventually he became the club's chairman on 22 November 1963 taking over from Ernest Robertson. During his playing days at Tannadice, Duncan made 181 league and cup appearances and scored an incredible 119 goals. Duncan Hutchison died on 12 January 1973. Dundee United and Hibs players wore black armbands when they met on 13 January as a mark of respect.

William Hutchison, was one of the Directors who joined the club when they were known as Dundee Hibs in November 1922. He was also a Director when the club changed their name to Dundee United. On 14 May 1931 William announced that he was resigning as Club Chairman, due to health problems. However, he also announced that he was to continue as a director at the club. On 29 November 1939 William resigned from the United board because of business commitments. William died on 16 April 1943, aged 53.

Charlie Hutton, signed by manager Reggie Smith on 27 October 1956 from East Fife. The goalkeeper made his first team United debut the same day against Third Lanark at Tannadice. However, he was released by the club on 19 December 1956. Charlie had played in only three first team games. From February to May 1957 he played for Brechin City.

Johnny Hutton, took part in his first senior trial with United on 11 March 1939 in a 6-1 win over Leith Athletic at Tannadice. The player again appeared in United colours on 26 August 1939 in a 1-1 draw with East Stirling. Johnny then signed for United Juniors on 18 September 1940.

Iain Inglis, signed to United by manager Reggie Smith in 1956 from junior side Elmwood. Iain made his first team debut on 16 March 1957 against Forfar at Station Park.

Alan Irvine I, signed for the club in August 1987 for £100,000 from Liverpool. Before joining the Anfield side he played for Falkirk. Alan made his first team debut on 29 August 1987 in a game against Aberdeen at Pittodrie which ended in a 1-1 draw. On 11 February 1988 United sold him to Shrewsbury Town for a reported fee of £80,000. When he was at Tannadice Alan found it difficult to command a first team place each week.

Alan Irvine II, signed for the club in June 1987 from Crystal Palace. Alan had previously been with Everton and Queen's Park. He played in some friendly matches during the close season of 1987-88 with United in Norway. The player made his first appearance for the club on 8 August 1987 in a 1-1 draw with Rangers at Ibrox. In October 1989, Alan went on loan to Blackburn Rovers. On 22 November 1989, he signed for them for a fee of £30,000.

Andy Irvine, signed to United on 28 October 1958 on a free from Falkirk. Andy made his first team debut on 1 November 1958 against Alloa at Recreation Park. Andy was freed by United in April 1959. On 12 May 1959 he announced that he was to take on the responsibility of looking after Arbroath's reserve side. While he was with United, he featured in seven first team games.

Ian Irvine, signed to United in the close season of 1954 from junior side Violet. Ian made his first team debut on 14 August 1954 against Ayr United at Tannadice.

Jim Irvine I, born in Whitburn in 1940. Jim was signed to the club on 10 August 1959 from Whitburn Rovers and he had also played for Edinburgh Athletic. He played his first game in United colours in a reserve game against Queen's Park Strollers at Hampden on 15 August 1959. His first team debut was on 19 August 1959 against East Fife at Bayview. He was a member of the 1960 side that won promotion to the First Division. Jim was transferred to Middlesborough on 27 May 1964 for a reported fee of £25,000. On 18 May 1967 he was transferred from Middlesborough to Hearts for a fee of £15,000. After he retired from the playing side, he went on to coach Duntocher Hibs. Later, in June 1974, he was appointed coach with Armadale Thistle and later moved to Whitburn.

His son Alan signed an S-form with Hibernian in August 1976. While he was a United player Jim featured in 126 first team games and scored 63 goals.

Jimmy Irving II, signed by manager Willie MacFadyen on 27 March 1952. Jimmy made his United debut on 29 March 1952 in a reserve game against Hibs at Tannadice. His first game as club captain was on 23 August 1952 in a game against Dumbarton at Tannadice. This was a good omen for the player as he scored the only goal of the game. Jimmy scored within 25 seconds of the game kicking off. In May 1953 he was freed by United.

J. Izatt, signed for Dundee Hibs on 13 December 1910. The player made his club debut on 17 December 1910 against Arthurlie at Barrhead. Between seasons 1910-1913 he made 38 appearances for Dundee Hibs. As well as playing midfield for the club, he sometimes took on the task of playing in goal.

David Jack, signed for United in June 1944 from Dundee Arnot. David made his United debut on 3 June 1944 against Falkirk. This was in a 'Salute the Soldier' charity game at Brockville. The player signed for Forfar on 2 August 1946.

Andrew Jackson, signed to United by manager Willie Reid in August 1931 from junior side North End. Andrew made his first team debut on 15 August 1931 against Celtic at Parkhead. During season 1931-32 Andrew played in 26 first team games and scored five goals.

Darren Jackson, signed by manager Jim McLean on 15 December 1988, after the club paid a reported £200,000 to Newcastle United. Darren made his Tannadice debut on 17 December 1988 before a crowd of 18,745 spectators. The game was against Celtic, which United won 2-0. However, Darren's debut turned out to be a bit of a disaster for him. He lasted only four minutes when he was carried off suffering from an injured ankle. In July 1992, Darren signed for Hibs. On 12 July 1997, he signed for Celtic for £1.5 million. Darren was one of the first players to sign under new coach Wim Jansen. In August 1997 the medical profession diagnosed a neurological problem, but the player fought his way back to make a full recovery.

Jack 'Babe' Jackson, provisionally signed by Jerry Kerr on 29 October 1959 from Carnoustie Panmure. Before signing, Jack had played in two trial matches for United. The 17-year-old made his first team debut on 12 November 1960 in a game against Rangers at Ibrox. United lost 4-0.

Alec Jardine, the left-back was 19 years old when he signed for United on 4 March 1946 from Wishaw Juniors. The player made his United debut on 9 March 1946 in the 3-2 win over Dumbarton at Tannadice. On 16 August 1950 he signed for Millwall for a substantial fee. While he was with United he featured in 67 first team games and scored twice. Alec was forced to give up the game in December 1958 after recurring injury problems.

George Jeffrey, signed to the club by manager Willie MacFadyen in August 1946 from Hamilton Accies. The player made his United debut on 28 August 1946 against Dunfermline. George scored his first goal for the club on 7 September 1946 against Albion Rovers at Tannadice. During season 1946-47 George played in three league games and scored one goal for the club.

Iain Jenkins, born in Whiston on 24 December 1972, and signed by manager Tommy McLean on 26 March 1998 from Chester City. The reported fee for the player was £150,000. Iain had previously played for Everton, and had been capped for Northern Ireland. The player made his first team debut on 28 March 1998 against Motherwell at Fir Park. He made his home debut on 7 April 1998 in the 2-2 draw with Dunfermline.

Roy Jenkins, played in goal for junior side Stobswell. He played in goal for United on 10 October 1953 against Kilmarnock at Rugby Park. Roy stepped in to help the club out after normal United Keeper, Edmiston, was out injured.

Willie Jennet, signed for United on 24 August 1944 and had been playing for Glasgow Ashfield. On 26 August 1944 he made his United debut against Dundee. This was the first city derby match to be played between the clubs since 1939. Willie was placed on the United transfer list on 22 June 1945. The asking price was in the region of £50.

Joe Jermieson, of Aberdeen East End, played in a trial match for United on 28 September 1935 against Dumbarton at Boghead.

Grant Johnson, made his debut at Tannadice on 24 March 1992. Grant actually made his first team debut on 7 March 1992 against Dunfermline at East End Park. United ran out winners that day 1-0. On 17 October 1997 he returned from a loan spell at Burnley. Johnson left the club in 1997 after his contract had ended at the start of the season. He signed for Huddersfield for a fee of £100,000. The young player had been capped six times at under-21 level.

Johnston, played for Brechin City and played as a guest for Dundee Hibs during the First World War. His first match for the club was played on 3 April 1915, against Forfar Athletic, and ended 3-3.

Samuel Johnston, became the vice-president of Dundee Hibs in March 1909.

Alec Johnstone, played in goal for St Andrew's United and made his first appearance in a United shirt in a trial game played on 9 August 1927 at Tannadice. On 8 October 1927 he again played for the club in the 5-3 win over St Bernard's at Tannadice. Manager Jimmy Brownlie was suitably impressed by his performances and signed him on 19 October 1927. Alec appeared for the club on 18 occasions. In September 1928 Alec was playing for Queen of the South.

Davie Johnstone, made his first team debut on 30 September 1950 in the 5-3 win over Kilmarnock at Tannadice. His previous club was St Johnstone.

Derek Johnstone, joined United on loan from Chelsea on 24 October 1983. As a youngster he joined Rangers straight from Linlathen High School in 1970. After spending several years at Ibrox Derek signed for Chelsea in September 1983 for £30,000. Derek made his debut at Tannadice on 26 October 1983 in a League Cup tie against Morton. Later Derek would again return to Ibrox. On 26 June 1986 he became coach with Partick Thistle and worked in partnership with ex-Lisbon lion Bertie Auld who was manager then.

Douglas Johnstone, signed on S-form by manager Jerry Kerr on 17 July 1968 from United Crossroads.

Joe Johnstone, signed for United as a War guest on 1 October 1942. Joe had previously played for Motherwell. The player made his United debut on 3 October 1942 against Raith Rovers at Stark's Park.

Jimmy Jones, signed by manager Willie MacFadyen in September 1947 from Dundee FC. Jimmy made his United debut on 13 September 1947 against Cowdenbeath.

Siggi Jonsson, signed on 24 November 1997 from Orebro by manager Tommy McLean in a deal valued at £75,000. Siggi was born in Akranes, Iceland, on 27 September 1966. He was the first player from Iceland to appear for the club. His debut match was played on 25 November 1997 in a clash between United and Celtic reserves. The player made his home debut against Dunfermline on 6 December 1997. He had also played for Sheffield Wednesday, Barnsley, and Arsenal. Siggi played for seven years in England.

Henrick Jorgensen, was signed by manager Ivan Golac on 9 August 1994, from Vijborg. The goalkeeper was signed for a reported fee of £180,000. He had previously played for the club as a trialist when the club went on a tour of Malaysia during the 1994 close season.

He made his Premier League debut on 13 August 1994 against Hibs at Easter Road. However, this game was a disaster for him and the team as they lost 5-0. Ivan Golac fined the 12 players and himself £100 pounds for poor performance.

Albert Juliussen, played for North End juniors before joining United as a war guest in 1941. Juliussen was a prolific scorer of goals. The player notched up 83 goals in 70 games. He made his United debut on 13 August 1941 against a Scottish Command team at Tannadice. On 20 May 1944 he played for the Scottish Command that met Celtic at Somerset Park, in a benefit game for War Charities. The event was called 'Salute the Soldier.' Later the player returned to his first club, Huddersfield, and in 1945 was transferred to Dundee FC for £2,000. He left Dens in March 1948 and signed for Portsmouth for £10,000. After his spell with Portsmouth, he joined Everton during season 1948-49. Albert signed as player-manager of Consett, a Durham club on 17 August 1949. On 12 June 1953 he became a Dundee United player again after he signed to the club from Berwick Rangers. He made his first team debut on 8 August 1953 against Morton at Cappielow. It was a memorable debut for him as he scored a couple of goals. On 28 December 1953 he was freed by United and joined Brechin City.

Boye Karlsen, guested for United during the Second World War. He played inside-left and left-half for the club. Boye was stationed in Newport on Tay with the Norwegian Air Force. He played his first game for United on 25 September 1943 against Rangers. Boye made his last appearance for United on 2 June 1945. In a goodwill gesture by the club, they allowed him to captain the side that day. It was a memorable game for the player as United beat Falkirk 1-0 in a North-Eastern League game. The player had won several caps for Norway, including a cap that he won when he played against Scotland in 1954.

Kay, came to Dundee Hibs from Plymouth Argyle. In December 1920 he was transferred to Lochgelly United.

Dean Kay, signed for United on 27 March 1978 from Tartan Boys Club in Edinburgh. The player was called up as a full-timer in July 1978. However, the club freed Kay on 30th April 1979.

Jacky Kay, born in 1908, and signed by manager Jimmy Brownlie in 1928 from Motherwell Juniors. Jacky stayed with the club for nine years. In 1936 he was given a free transfer from the club and was then signed by Chester. Jacky stayed with them for three years. However, he did return to Dundee after the Second World War and in 1947 he became a trainer at Dens Park. In 1962 he was working as a commercial traveller with a Glasgow whisky company. While he was with United Jacky played in 222 league and cup fixtures, and scored 82 goals. Jacky died in August 1963, aged 55.

Jock Kay, born in 1899, and signed for Dundee Hibs on 6 June 1923 from Third Lanark by Jimmy Brownlie. Jock made his debut for the club on 15 August 1923 against St Johnstone. An extremely popular player with the crowd, United also awarded Jock a testimonial game played on 9 April 1928 against Hearts. Jock signed for Stenhousemuir on 15 November 1928 and retired from the game in 1931. While he was playing for United he featured in 177 league and cup matches and scored four goals. Jock Kay died in 1979.

Dick Keatt, played for Queen of the South and Morton, and played in a trial match for United on 5 August 1939.

Marino Keith, signed by the club on 10 October 1995 from Highland League club Fraserburgh for a nominal fee. Marino made his first team debut on 6 January 1996 in the 1-1 draw with Clydebank. Playing for the reserves against Berwich reserves on 8 January 1996, he scored six goals, Paddy Connolly scoring the other seven. The match ended in a 13-0 win for the United reserves. On 10 September 1997 he left United and signed for Falkirk for a reported fee of £35,000. While he was at Tannadice, he failed to command a regular first team place.

Keller, played for United as a War guest on 16 August 1941, in a 4-1 win over St Bernard's.

P. Kelly, played for Dundee Hibs, and during season 1921-22 he made 13 appearances in team. The player made his club debut on 14 January 1922 against Bo'ness.

Pat Kelly, signed for Aberdeen in June 1937 from Pirates FC Bloemfontein in South Africa. He made his Aberdeen debut on 5 April 1939 against Kilmarnock at Rugby Park. During the Second World War, Pat played in goal for Hamilton, and was released by them on 22 January 1943. The South African goalkeeper played for United on 1 January 1945 as a guest player against Arbroath. Pat also guested for Arsenal in April 1945, and he was picked to play for the Irish National side in September 1949.

Willie Kelly, played as a War guest for United, and featured in a game against Stenhousemuir. This match was played on 20 October 1945 at Tannadice, with United winning 7-0. The centre-half went onto play for Morton and was suspended *sine die* after being sent off in a game against Clyde in November 1946.

Kennedy, was a goalkeeper with junior side North End. He played his first game for Dundee Hibs on 19 August 1916. This game ended in a 5-1 victory over Lochgelly United at Tannadice.

John Kennedy, joined the committee of Dundee Hibs in March 1909.

Kermach, from Pitlochry, made his debut for Dundee Hibs on 17 August 1910 against St Johnstone.

A. Kerr, played in a trial match for United in a C-Division game against Raith Rovers at Tannadice on 8 November 1947.

Jim Kerr, signed for United on 20 December 1978 from Stonehouse Violet. The left-back was placed on standby for the 1979 tour of Japan. His first real taste of Premier Division football came on 29 September 1979 against Morton. However, it was to be a disappointing day as United lost 4-1. Jim was placed on the transfer list on 11 February 1981 after refusing to become a full-time player with the club. At the time he was working as a plater in Glasgow and did not want to change jobs. United eventually transferred him to Airdrie on 16 July 1981. Later he signed for Raith Rovers on 6 October 1982. In June 1986 Raith sold him to Falkirk for £9,000.

John Kerr, signed by manager Willie MacFadyen on 27 June 1947 from North End. After one season at Tannadice he was transferred to Irish side Glentoran on 9 May 1950.

Alan Kershaw, was 21 years old when he signed for the club on 18 December 1975. Born in Southport he had previously played for Brighton and Preston. He made his debut for the club in a reserve game against Dundee on 19 December 1975.

Lance Key, accompanied United as a trialist on their July 1996 tour of Denmark. The goalkeeper had been freed by Sheffield Wednesday. Lance signed for United on 25 July 1996. The keeper was released from the club on 12 February 1997 and returned to England.

David Kidd, signed by manager Jerry Kerr in September 1959 from Alloa. David played his first game in United colours on 19

September 1959 against St Johnstone reserves at Muirton. The player made his first team debut on 23 September 1959 against Dumbarton at Tannadice. During this season he played in 15 league and cup games for the club.

Kidd signed for United by manager Jimmy Brownlie on 12 May 1930 from North End.

Alec King, signed for United during season 1934-35 from Clyde. The player made his United debut on 11 August 1934 against Forfar. In season 1934-35 Alec played in 33 league games and scored 15 goals. On 16 July 1935 he signed for Alloa, and later moved to Brechin. United Director Greig re-signed Alec to United on 11 December 1936 from Brechin City. His comeback match was on 12 December 1936 in the 0-0 draw against East Fife at Tannadice. In season 1936-37 he made 14 league appearances and scored five goals.

Jimmy King, played for Dundonald Bluebells and joined Cowdenbeath from Army football in 1956. Jimmy was signed to United by manager Tommy Gray on 4 July 1957. The player made his United debut on 27 August 1957 against Dumbarton at Tannadice. He made three league appearances and one cup appearance. The player was freed by United in April 1958.

Tommy Kinloch, signed for United from Glasgow Secondary Juvenile Club. Tommy had also played for Anderston Benburb before beginning his senior career with Falkirk. The player was given a free transfer from United in May 1949. Tommy rejoined Falkirk on 5 May 1949, but on 5 July 1951 Carlisle United's manager Bill Shankly signed the player.

Paul Kinnaird, was an apprentice with Norwich City before coming to United in 1985. Paul had trouble settling at the English club so he came home to Scotland. On 4 March 1988 he joined Motherwell for a reported fee of £20,000. In 1992 Paul went on loan to Raith Rovers.

David Kinnell, signed by manager Willie MacFadyen in October 1950. David made his first team debut on 14 October 1950 in the 5-1 victory over Dunfermline at Tannadice. While he was at the club, he played in four first team games and scored one goal.

Alec Kinninmouth, played inside-left for St Andrew's Swifts. Alec was given a trial for United on 8 August 1960. At the time he was working as a painter and had just turned down the opportunity to sign for Luton Town. Later he signed for Dundee on 28 November 1960.

J. Kinsella, played for Dundee Hibs, and during season 1921-22 he appeared in eight league matches for the club.

Harry Kirk, played for Aberdeen Recreational Club. Harry played for United's reserve side in a game against Airdrie on 22 December 1962.

Jimmy Kirk, was United's scout in the West of Scotland in the early 1960s.

Jimmy Kirkham, guested with United during the Second World War. The player made his last appearance for the club in October 1942 when United beat Rangers 3-2. On 24 February 1944 the announcement had filtered through that Jimmy had escaped from a Prisoner of War Camp in Italy. He escaped via Switzerland.

Jimmy Knight, played for Dundee Violet, and signed for United during the 1951-52 close season. Jimmy made his first team debut on 15 September 1951 against Queen's Park at Hampden. United won 2-1. The player was freed by the club in April 1952.

Archie Knox, Archie Knox was 18 when he joined Forfar from Errol Rovers. He then signed for St Mirren in September 1970 before manager Jim McLean brought him to United on 6 January 1972 for a reported fee of just over £3,000. After spending four years with United he was released in April 1976.

He has visited many parts of the country in the intervening 20 years. First to Montrose as a player in August 1976 and made his debut against United in the Forfarshire Cup. On 22 November he became Forfar's new player manager. On 15 August 1980 Archie became assistant manager at Aberdeen under Alex Ferguson only to become manager of Dundee on 15 December 1983, taking over the position from ex-United keeper Donald Mackay.

He again became assistant manager at Aberdeen on 19 June 1986, only to incur the wrath of the home support when he left in November of the same year to join Alex Ferguson at Old Trafford. Ferguson had become manager of Manchester United in November 1986 and Archie was again to become his assistant.

On 24 April 1991 he teamed up with old Tannadice club-mate Walter Smith to become assistant manager with Rangers. When Walter joined Everton as manager he brought Archie Knox from

Rangers as his assistant. This took place on 1 July 1998. While he was with United, Archie featured in 56 league and cup games and scored 12 goals.

J. Knowles, made his debut for Dundee Hibs on 9 September 1914 in a friendly game against Dundee A at Tannadice. This match was in aid of the Prince of Wales National War Fund. The player was signed by manager Pat Reilly a short time later. He played in four competitive matches for Dundee Hibs during season 1914-15.

Bobby Knox, signed by manager Jimmy Brownlie for Dundee Hibs in 1923 from Third Lanark. Bobby made his club debut on 15 August 1923 against St Johnstone. A few months after he signed the club changed its name to Dundee United. In season 1923-24 Bobby made 13 league appearances.

Frank Kopel, born in Falkirk in 1949, Frank was signed for Manchester United by manager Matt Busby. At the time of signing Frank had just left Graeme High School in Falkirk. Manchester United transferred Frank to Blackburn Rovers for a fee of £25,000. He was then signed by Jim McLean on a free transfer from Blackburn Rovers in January 1972. He made his first team debut on 29 January 1972 in a game against Morton. United won 2-1. Frank was a member of both League Cup Winning sides, and appeared in the Scottish Cup Final teams in 1974 and 1981.

On 1 February 1982 Frank was given a free transfer. Within days of the announcement Frank was appointed player-coach with Arbroath, but the player returned to United on 2 December 1983 after leaving Arbroath. He retired from playing in 1984. However, he remained at Tannadice as a coach.

After leaving the club, Frank became a sales executive with Radio Tay, before starting his own business. In February 1989 Frank was back in football again when he joined the coaching staff at Forfar. Manager at the time was ex-United player Henry Hall, but on 15 January 1992 Forfar sacked Frank as assistant-manager. This was part of a cost cutting exercise. The manager at the time was Paul Hegarty, who had taken over from Henry Hall.

While he was at Tannadice, Frank played in 238 league and cup games and scored on seven occasions.

Scott Kopel, signed for United on S-form in August 1983 from Finlathen Boys Club. The young lad was following in his father's footsteps.

Scott was included in a Scotland Under-16 pool that played at Dens Park on 17 March 1986, against a pool of Dundee's S-signings. Other Tannadice youngsters included in the pool were Martin Feeney and John Bishop. Later Scott signed for junior side St Josephs.

Miodrag Krivokapic, born in 1959, and signed by manager Jim McLean on 3 August 1988 for £200,000 from Red Star Belgrade. The player played his first game for United in a reserve match against Rangers on 10 September 1988. Then on 24 September he made his first team debut in a 2-1 victory over Motherwell. There followed a lengthy spell when he could not play for United because of work permit problems.. In 1991 he played for United in the Scottish Cup final, incidentally against the club he would later sign for. He was released by United on 10 May 1993 and joined Motherwell. In April 1996 he signed for Raith Rovers as player-coach. In 1997 he signed for Hamilton Athletic, again as player-coach.

D. S. Laing, turned out for United on 18 December 1932 against Brechin at Tannadice and signed for them on 22 December 1932 During his spell with United he featured in 38 league and cup games and scored 16 goals.

Johnny Laird, signed by manager Willie MacFadyen in December 1952 from Rosyth Recreation. Johnny made his first team debut on 6 December 1952 against Dunfermline at East End Park. During his spell with the club he featured in 15 league games.

Bert Lamb, of junior side Dundee Violet, played in goal for United on 24 March 1934 against Dunfermline Athletic. This was after regular first-team keeper McIntosh was out through injury. Bert later signed for Dundee. However, he was freed by them in April 1936 and then signed for Irish side Portadown. On 16 March 1937 he was transferred to Chesterfield.

James Lamb, became a director with Dundee Hibs in April 1923. James replaced Hibs director William Burke.

M. Lamb, of St Bernard's, played at outside-right for Dundee Hibs on 9 November 1912. This match was played at Tannadice in the Qualifying Cup game against Inverness Caley. He featured in four competitive games for Dundee Hibs during season 1912-13.

V. Lawrence, played for Newcastle United, Manchester City, and guested for Dundee Hibs during the First World War. His first match for the club was on 18 September 1915 against Kirkcaldy United in the Eastern League. The match ended 3-3. He made his Tannadice debut on 2 October 1915 in the 2-1 victory over Dunfermline Athletic.

Henry Leadbitter, had been the club's doctor for many years. He was appointed to the Board of Directors at Tannadice on 18 February 1986.

F. Leckie, signed for Dundee Hibs by manager Pat Reilly in October 1913. The player made his club debut on 11 October 1913 against Albion Rovers. Leckie made seven appearances for Dundee Hibs during season 1913-14.

Gerry Lesslie, signed for United in July 1978 from Celtic Boys Club. Gerry played in the reserves for most of season 1978-79.

Ian Letford, signed by manager Jerry Kerr from Cambuslang Rangers. Ian made his first team debut on 16 August 1969 against St Mirren. The team won 1-0. He left the club in January 1971. The inside-forward signed for Stranraer after spending 18 months with United. Letford failed to make any real progress while at Tannadice.

Ted Leven, was 17 years old when he signed provisional forms with the club on 25 October 1948. Ted was transferred to Brechin City in December 1949.

Earnest Levett, played his first game for Dundee Hibs on 8 December 1917 in the 4-1 victory over Dunfermline at Tannadice.

Jimmy Lindsay, signed by manager Willie Reid from Bowhill Rovers in December 1932. Jimmy played in a trial game for United on 26 November 1932 against Leith Athletic. Dundee United freed Jimmy after season 1933-34. The following season he signed for Rhyll. He returned to Scotland before the end of that season and signed for Brechin. In January 1968 he was working at Rosyth Naval Dockyard.

Ally Link, was a former Middlesborough midfield player, and signed to United on 10 December 1977. Ally had previously played for the reserves on 6 December 1977 in a match against Falkirk and scored one of the goals. The match ended in a 4-0 victory for United.

Willie Linn, born in Dundee in 1890, and signed in November 1911 for Dundee Hibs by manager Pat Reilly from junior side North End. Willie made his club debut on 11 November 1911 in the 1-0 win over St Johnstone at Tannadice. He was a left-sided wing player and known for his speed and agility. The player was also a member of the Qualifying Cup Final team in December 1913. At the outbreak of World War One, he signed up for the forces, and returned to the club at the end of the war. For recognising his personal achievements at the club United awarded him a testimonial in 1922 for ten years loyal service. This game was played on 12 April 1922 against Dundee at Tannadice. Willie had made more than 100 league appearances at the club. Willie Linn died in 1959.

Alex Lister, signed by manager Willie MacFadyen on 17 October 1946 from Third Lanark. He made his debut as a signed player on 19 October 1946. This game was played against Dumbarton at Tannadice with United winning 2-1. Alex was United's top scorer in season 1948-49. The player was freed by United in May 1949. In March 1951 he was playing for Cowdenbeath. Later he moved to Alloa on 23 February 1950.

Dick Little, was a player with the club in the 1930s.

Bill Littlejohn, joined the United board of directors on 10 April 1992. His father was a board member with the club in the 1940s. Having been a fan of Dundee United since he was a child, Bill has a tremendous factual historical knowledge of the club.

Jimmy Lindsay, signed for United during season 1932-33. While he was with the club, he played in 37 league games scoring one goal. On 15 August 1934 he signed for Rhyll.

Livingstone, signed to United in 1949, and played his first game for the club on 16 September 1949 in a reserve game against Hibs at Tannadice.

Joe Locherty, signed for United on 22 January 1954. Joe made his United debut in a match against Motherwell at Fir Park. He also played for Lochee Harp before spending three years with Sheffield Wednesday. The player also had spells with Colchester United and Scarborough.

William Logie, played for Dundee Violet, and Portsmouth at the start of season 1930-31. The player was signed by United manager Willie Reid on 29 July 1931. During that season, he played in 20 first team games, and scored two goals.

Jimmy Lonie, played wing-half for Dundee Hibs, and featured in their first ever appearance in the Scottish League. This game was played on 20 August 1910 against Leith Athletic at Tannadice. Dundee Hibs lost 3-2 with two goals coming from Hibs striker John Collins. From season 1910-1913 Jimmy played in 39 competitive games for the club.

Albert Lorimer, was a groundsman with the club back in 1963.

Jim Lorimer, signed for the club provisionally in March 1977. The goalkeeper played for Broughty Athletic juniors.

Raymond Lorimer, signed to the club on S-form in 1977. The 16-year-old forward had played for Glasgow Celtic Boys Club.

Jimmy Lovie, joined United from Army football in March 1953, and was signed by manager Willie MacFadyen. Jimmy played in a trial game for the club on 28 February 1953 against Albion Rovers at Tannadice. The manager was suitably impressed by his performance and signed him a few days later. He played in his first team match on 7 March 1953, against Ayr United. Jimmy had previously played for Peterhead. United transferred Lovie back to Peterhead in August 1953.

Alec Low, signed for United as a War guest on 30 April 1942 from Raith Rovers. Alec had also played for Scotland in an International against Ireland in 1933. The player made his debut for United on 27 May 1942 against Rangers at Ibrox.

D. Low, signed for United as a War guest on 1 May 1942 from Matrix Rovers. They named him in a United pool that were to play Rangers on 2 May 1942.

George Low, signed for Dundee Hibs by manager Pat Reilly from Forfar Athletic. He played in 70 games and scored nine goals for the club. The player also featured in the first city derby against Dundee on 13 March 1915.

Walter Low, was a groundsman at Tannadice in the 1940s and 1950s.

Bill Lucas, signed by manager Tommy Gray in April 1957 from Broxburn Athletic. The keeper made his first team debut on 13 April against Cowdenbeath at Tannadice. The player was freed by United in April 1959. Bill was picked to play for the East of Scotland League who played an East of Scotland Junior XI in April 1961. While he was with United, he played in 51 matches.

Bruce Lyall, was called up by United on 10 January 1985. Bruce had attended Kirkton High School and was playing for Downfield Juniors. Later the player signed for Forfar. In 1987, he had teamed up with the ex-United men Craig Brewster, Ray Lorimer, manager Henry Hall and physiotherapist Andy Dickson.

Laurie MacBain, began his career with Queen's Park in the 1920s. His Father Alec had been chairman of Dundee FC for a time. Laurie was with St Johnstone from 1927-1933. However, they temporarily transferred him to Raith Rovers in January 1929 and his first game for the Muirton Park outfit was on 3 August 1927. Dundee United Manager Willie Reid signed him in September 1933 and the player made his United debut on 9 September against Morton at Tannadice. Laurie played in 15 league games and scored three goals for United. The player broke his leg while playing against Arbroath at Tannadice on 16 December 1933. This effectively ended his footballing career. Laurie died in September 1937, he was 29 years old.

Edward MacDonald, was a player for Dundee Hibs. The player also featured in the side that lost 3-0 to Albion Rovers in the Qualifying Cup Final game on 27 December 1913. On 11 May 1914 he re-signed for the club and featured in the first city derby against Dundee on 13 March 1915. During seasons 1912-1915 he played in 57 competitive games and scored six times for the club. During season 1921-22 he appeared three times for the club.

Ian MacFadyen, was the son of former United manager Willie MacFadyen. Ian made his debut for the club on 18 August 1950 in a reserve game against Falkirk at Tannadice. The player left United after Motherwell manager Bobby Ancell persuaded him to sign for them in 1954. However, on 9 May 1959, Ian again re-signed as a United player. Ian had the distinction of being a member of the 1960 promotion side that took the club into the First Division. In the 1960s Ian was a school teacher before opening two chemist's shops in Glasgow.

Alec MacFarlane, signed for United in September 1945, and made his debut on 8 September in the derby game against Dundee at Dens Park. He signed for Cowdenbeath on 12 August 1948.

James MacFarlane, signed by manager Jimmy Brownlie on 18 May 1936 from Fair City Athletic. James made his United debut on 23 September 1936 in a Quarter-Final Cup game against Dundee in the Forfarshire Cup. In his first season with the club he played in 26 league games and scored one goal. In season 1937-38 he made 13 league appearances before being freed.

Robert MacFarlane, joined United in January 1926 from Arbroath. The player made his United debut on 23 January in a 1-1 draw with Hearts. This was a Scottish Cup tie played at Tannadice Park. Robert made only two appearances in United colours.

Donald Mackay, signed for United from Forfar on 11 May 1962. The deal between manager Jerry Kerr, and Forfar chairman Will Callander, was conducted in his office at Station Park. Donald had signed for Forfar on 12 November 1958, from Jeanfield Swifts. He played his first League game for United on 11 August 1962 in a derby game against Dundee. United won 2-1. The goalkeeper was given a free transfer from United on 21 April 1972.

Mackay would later take up a coaching position with Bristol City in August 1974, and later still became the manager of Dundee FC in May 1980. In December 1983, Mackay resigned from his post after Dundee had accepted an offer from Aberdeen for a £90,000 transfer for Stuart McKimmie. His successor at Dens was former United player Archie Knox. After leaving Dens, Donald became an insurance salesman.

On 13 September 1984, he became the assistant manager at Coventry City and succeded to the manager's post on 28 December 1984 after Bobby Gould had left the club. On 12 May 1986, Rangers manager Graeme Souness offered him a post at Ibrox. He accepted, and was put in charge of the Reserve and Youth teams.

On 3 February 1987 Donald became manager of Blackburn Rovers. In November 1991 Donald left Blackburn, and Kenny Dalglish took his place.

Eric Mackay, signed for United by manager Jimmy Brownlie on 19 August 1930. Eric had signed for Dundee in season 1929-30, but could not get a regular first team spot, so he was freed.

Peter Mackay, the goalkeeper played for United on 4 September 1946 against East Fife at Tannadice. United lost 4-2.

Andrew Macleod, son of ex Scotland manager Ally. On 27 November 1991, he became the club's physiotherapist replacing Graeme Doig.

Ally MacLeod, signed for United from Hibs on a free transfer in July 1982. After being out through injury for a lengthy spell, he played his first game in a reserve match against Dundee on 1 December 1982.

Duncan MacLeod, signed by Jim McLean in April 1973 from Dundee FC. The player had spent 17 months at Dens, and had also played for Southampton for three years. Duncan made his first team debut against his old club on 23 April 1973. In 1975, United transferred him to St Johnstone in a swop deal that saw Henry Hall signing for United. Macleod signed for Brechin City in the close season of 1976.

Tom McAdam, signed by Jim McLean in October 1975 for a fee of £40,000 paid to Dumbarton. The player signed to Dumbarton in February 1971. Tom signed shortly after the departure of Andy Gray to Aston Villa. The media reported the fee as £37,000.

He scored twice in his first team debut on 1 November 1975 in a match against St Johnstone which United won 3-1 before a crowd of 4,850. In September 1977 United transferred him to Celtic for a reported fee of £60,000. On 27 February 1986 Celtic freed him.

Michael McAdams, signed for United on 12 March 1984. The goalkeeper was signed from Hamilton Thistle and played alongside Billy McKinlay when he was a player there.

Hamish McAlpine, born in Kilspindie in January 1948. Hamish 'the goalie' spent two decades at Tannadice. In 15 years Hamish made 586 first team appearances. He made his debut as first team keeper in March 1969 in a game against Hearts. For five seasons he fought among his fellow keepers Sandy Davie, and Donald Mackay for the first team shirt.

He became first team keeper in 1974. Hamish is the only postwar goalkeeper to captain a United side. On 19 January 1974, Hamish actually played outside left in a reserve game against Motherwell! During season 1978-79, United sent Hamish home prior to the Japan Cup Final after a dispute with the club. For a short spell Peter Bonetti took his place. The ex-Chelsea keeper had arrived in Mull and was offered a short term contract with the club. However, the matter between club and player was soon resolved, and Peter Bonetti was soon on his way out.

Hamish clocked up his 25th Scottish Cup appearance on 7 March 1981. It was a successful day for player and club as United beat Motherwell 6-1. As for international duty, Hamish played five times for the Under-21 side. On 13 February 1982, Hamish played his 500th game for the club. The match was against Hibs at

Tannadice and it ended 1-1. Then, on Saturday 5 March 1983, he made his 400th League appearance with the club. On Wednesday 17 August 1983, Tottenham Hotspur played at Tannadice in Hamish's testimonial game. More than 10,000 spectators showed up to honour the keeper. Spurs players included Glenn Hoddle and Steve Archibald.

In the season 1984-85, Hamish won the SFWA Player of the Year Award. At the end of season 1985-86, United released Hamish and on 11 April 1986, United chairman George Fox presented Hamish with a silver salver before the game at Tannadice. He was not quite finished with football and he went on to play for Raith Rovers and Arbroath.

In 1986, he opened his pub, 'Goalies', in Dudhope Street Dundee. Sadly the pub closed its doors several years ago after the area was redeveloped. Hamish helped out Celtic on 16 July 1988 when the Glasgow club took on Winterthur on their Swiss tour. Celtic's regular keeper was injured, so Hamish obligingly offered to help. Later that month Hamish signed for Arbroath. On 6 May 1991, Hamish joined the Dundee United Commercial Department.

Willie McAndrew, signed by Dundee Hibs manager Peter O'Rourke in 1922 from Third Lanark. After four months with the club, manager O'Rourke resigned, and Willie took over as player-manager. However, this arrangement lasted only a short period.

John McBain, signed for United on 4 January 1955 by manager Reggie Smith on a free from Arbroath. John had been with the Gayfield side for two seasons, joining them from junior side Elmwood. The player made his first team debut for United on 8 January 1955 against Airdrie at Tannadice. John was freed by United in May 1956, and headed off to Calcutta to work as a jute clerk in India.

Hugh McBride, signed by manager Jimmy Brownlie in August 1925 from Hamilton Accies. Hugh made his United debut on 15 August 1925 against Raith Rovers. While he was at Tannadice Hugh made 20 appearances for the club.

On 19 February 1927 Hugh played for East Fife in a cup tie against Dunfermline Athletic.

Bill McCallum, joined United from Y. M. Anchorage, and made his debut for United on 27 December 1930 against Alloa. Bill then signed for the club three days later. His debut as a signed player was on 1 January 1931 against St Johnstone at Tannadice. The player spent one season at Tannadice, and later played for Brechin City, signing for them in July 1933.

Denis McCallum, played for St Anthony's before turning senior with Celtic, whom he had been with since 1926. Denis was signed by manager Jimmy Brownlie on 23 October 1930. He made his first team debut on 25 October 1930 against Queen of the South at Tannadice. He returned to Celtic on 1 May 1931.

P. McCamon, signed for the club in August 1938 from St Mirren. McCamon made his United debut on the opening day of season 1938-39. The match was against Montrose at Links Park and United won 5-4. While he was with the club, he made only three league appearances.

Bert McCann, joined United from North End on 31 August 1953. Bert made his first team debut on 5 September 1953 against Dumbarton at Tannadice. He moved to Queen's Park in 1954 and subsequently spent season 1955-6 with Hamilton Accies. Then he joined Motherwell in 1956 staying with them until 1965. Bert won five Scottish Caps while he was at Fir Park.

McCann, was an ex-Celtic player who was signed by manager Willie MacFadyen during the close season of 1950-51. The player made his United debut on 12 August 1950 in the derby game against Dundee at Dens Park.

T. McCarthy, signed during season 1936-37, and made United debut on 22 August 1936 against Airdrie at Broomfield. The player only featured in four league games before being freed by the club.

Dave McClure, played in defence for United and St Johnstone. In March 1931, he was with Irish side Portadown.

McConnachie, turned out in goal for United on 21 April 1934 in a 5-2 victory over Raith Rovers. The club was experiencing injury difficulties at that time, so the player helped out.

Frank McCormack, signed by Jerry Kerr on 31 August 1964 after a spell with Charlton Athletic. The 17-year-old had also played for Edinburgh club Melbourne Thistle. Manager Kerr signed him after he played in a reserve game against Motherwell on 29 August 1964 at Fir Park. United freed Frank in May 1965.

J. McCormack, signed by manager Willie MacFadyen in February 1948 from Stenhousemuir. The player made his first team debut on

6 March 1948 against Leith Athletic. He was freed by United in May 1949.

A. McCulloch, played for Raith Rovers, Hearts, and Swindon Town before signing for Dundee Hibs in March 1922. The player made his debut for the club on 4 March 1922 against St Bernard's at Tannadice. During season 1920-21, he appeared in nine league games and scored one goal for Dundee Hibs.

Tom McCulloch, signed to Dundee Hibs by manager Pat Reilly in September 1917. Tom made his club debut on 8 September 1917 in the 3-1 win over Armadale at Tannadice.

Frank McCusker, took up the position of groundsman at Tannadice in August 1955.

William McCutcheon, was appointed chairman of Dundee United on 14 February 1940. William resigned as club chairman on 17 February 1943 due to his other business commitments. He had been at the helm for three years, and said that he 'deeply regretted having to sever his United connections'. His retirement meant that United had only five members on the board. They were A.S. Cram, John Carnegie, Ernest Robertson, J. Littlejohn, and William Robertson, who was on active service at that time.

McDermott, from Forfar Athletic, and played in the first ever Dundee Hibs fixture. This match was played on Wednesday 18 August 1909. The game ended in a 1-1 draw against Edinburgh Hibernian.

Charlie McDermott, signed for United on 7 August 1943 from Bradford City. Charlie made his United debut on 14 August 1943 against Hearts at Tannadice.

W. McDonagh, signed for Dundee Hibs in January 1922 from Croy Celtic. The player made his debut for the club on 28 January 1922 against Broxburn United at Tannadice. During season 1921-22 he appeared three times for the club.

Alexander McDonald, signed for Dundee Hibs by manager Pat Reilly. Alex made his club debut on 8 February 1913 against Queen's Park.

This game was in the second round of the Scottish Cup at Hampden. Dundee Hibs lost 4-2. While he was with the club, he made 17 appearances from 1913-14.

Donald McDonald, was called up by manager Jerry Kerr to begin training with the club on 20 July 1965. He had been playing with Drumchapel.

Iain McDonald, born in 1952. He played under Rangers manager Willie Waddell and made his debut at Ibrox in January 1960 when he was just 17 years old. Rangers released him in 1974, and he was snapped up by United manager Jim McLean. This was after his brother Tommy, who was then a Rangers player, phoned and told him about McDonald. The manager saw McDonald's potential as a winger for the club, and signed him in July 1974. He made his first team debut with United on 21 August 1974 in a game against Motherwell. However, injury problems affected the player, and he played in only three games during season 1975-76. Those injuries forced the young player to give up the game on 17 February 1976 at the age of 23. The club held a Testimonial game on Monday 11 October 1976 against Dundee. Guests included John Greig (Rangers) and Jocky Scott (Aberdeen). The score was seven each.

Jock McDonald, played for Blackburn Rovers, then he was transferred to Irish side Linfield in 1922. From there he signed for Dundee spending many seasons at Dens. Then he signed for United in July 1925 for £300, making his United debut on 15 August 1925 against Raith Rovers. Jock finished off his career at Tannadice. While he was with United he featured in 103 games and scored 12 goals. On 18 August 1943, Jock died after a long illness.

William McDonald I, from Law Scotia made his United debut on 5 September 1925 in a 1-1 draw with Motherwell. William made three appearances with the club.

William McDonald II, joined the club from St Joseph's on 11 February 1957. Willie played a first team trial for the club on 9 February 1957 against Stirling at Tannadice, scoring the two goals which secured United's victory. After his trial, manager Gray immediately signed the player. After spending five years at Tannadice he was transferred to Stirling Albion in March 1962. Then he joined Montrose. As a United player Willie played 91 times and scored 30 goals.

Bobby McEwan, signed for Dundee Hibs by manager Jimmy Brownlie in 1923 from Dumbarton. The player made his club debut on 15 August 1923 against St Johnstone. A few months after he signed the club changed its name to Dundee United. While he was with the club, Bobby made 10 league appearances. Bobby was freed by the club on 19 November 1923.

Ronnie McFall, signed for the club from Portadown in May 1966, and was called up for training by manager Jerry Kerr on 20 July 1966. Ronnie made his first team debut on 27 August 1966 in the derby game against Dundee. This match ended 1-1, and was played at Dens Park. The player was released by the club in May 1967.

Tom McGairy, signed to the club by manager Reggie Smith in December 1954. Tom made his first team debut on 4 December 1954 against Hamilton. During his spell at Tannadice, Tom featured in 28 matches and scored 11 goals.

Billy McGann, a goalkeeper with junior side Downfield who played a trial game for the club. Billy played in goal for United reserves on 31 October 1964, against Kilmarnock, because normal keeper Sandy Davie was suffering from flu.

George McGeachie, signed for St Johnstone in 1937, and turned out as a War guest for United on 23 December 1944 against Celtic reserves at Tannadice.

A. McGillivary, signed to United in September 1936, and made his club debut on 12 September 1936, against Dumbarton at Tannadice. The player made only two appearances in a United jersey before being freed.

Angus McGillivary, signed by manager Willie MacFadyen in December 1946 from Arbroath, and had also played for Raith Rovers. Angus made his United debut on 4 January 1947 in a C-Division Cup game against Forfar at Tannadice. The game ended in a 3-3 score-line.

Gary McGinnes, born in Dundee and educated at Lawside Academy. Gary signed for United on 10 August 1981. Celtic had released the 17-year-old in the close season of 1981. He got his first initial first team mention on Friday 19 February 1982 in the pool that met Rangers the following day. On 17 May 1982, he was called up for the Scotland Under-18 side by manager Andy Roxburgh. On 26 November 1983, he made his first team debut in a game against Aberdeen, United losing 2-0 at Tannadice. On 23 December 1987, Gary asked the United board to place him on the transfer list. He signed for St Johnstone on 8 February 1990 for £100,000 becaming St Johnstone's most expensive signing. He made his debut with that club on 10 February 1990 in a match against Falkirk. St Johnstone freed Gary in May 1995. After he was freed, he made his way to Hong Kong where he spent one season playing for Happy Valley.

J. McGinnis, played his first match for Dundee Hibs as a trialist on 17 August 1912 against East Stirling at Tannadice. He made seven club appearances with Dundee Hibs during season 1912-13.

George McGlynn, signed to the club by manager Willie Reid on 17 December 1931. George made his United debut two days later against Hearts at Tynecastle.

McGregor, signed by manager Pat Reilly on 24 March 1910. Prior to signing for the club McGregor had been playing for Dundee.

Bob McGregor, played for Aberdeen junior side Hall & Company. Bob played as a War guest for United on 7 April 1945 against Arbroath at Gayfield.

Harry McGregor, played in goal for East Stirlingshire and played in a practise match for United on 7 August 1928. Shortly after this game he was signed by manager Jimmy Brownlie. Harry made his United debut as a signed player on 1 September 1928 in the 1-0 victory over Dunfermline at Tannadice. While he was at Tannadice he turned out for United on 43 occasions. His brother Mickey also played for United.

Mickey McGregor, played for United and Arbroath. Mickey played in a trial match for Montrose on 4 August 1928. In 1929, he was playing for Arbroath. On 14 May 1931, Micky signed on for another season with Falkirk. In January 1937, Mickey was playing for Dartford.

Mitchell McGregor, signed by manager Jimmy Brownlie in March 1926 from Stobswell Juniors. The player made his United debut on 6 March 1926 in the 3-1 win over Raith Rovers at Tannadice. Between seasons 1926-1928 Mitchell appeared for the club on 55 occasions and scored five goals.

Frank McGrory, signed by manager Andy McCall on 9 May 1959. Frank had previously played for Arbroath, Dundee, and Forfar.

John McGuinness, played in a first team trial for the club on 26 January 1957 against Hamilton. At the time of his trial, John was a sergeant in the RAOC based in Gibralter. John signed amateur forms with the club on 30 January 1957.

James McGuire, played for St Johnstone, however, he turned out for Dundee Hibs during the First World War. His first game for the side was on 18 September 1915 in an Eastern League match played against Kirkcaldy United that ended 3-3. James first played at Tannadice for the club on 2 October 1915 in a match against Dunfermline Athletic which Dundee Hibs won 2-1.

Dennis McGurk, played for Dundee Violet and had just returned from Ireland when he signed for United in October 1937. Dennis made his first team debut on 30 October 1937 against East Fife at Tannadice. During that season he played in five matches and scored one goal for the club.

John McHugh, joined the club from Burnbank Athletic in February 1928. The keeper made his debut for United in a Scottish Cup tie against Dundee on 8 February 1928 at Dens Park. In October 1928 John went on loan to Montrose. John was transferred to Portsmouth on 19 November 1930.

Jim McInally, born in 1964, and signed to the club by manager Jim McLean from Coventry City in 1986. Also included in the deal was the signing of Dave Bowman. His career began with Celtic in 1982. However, the player was not getting a game each week so the club allowed him to go on loan to Dundee FC. After returning to Celtic, the player soon found himself transferred to Nottingham Forest on 19 May 1984. Then they transferred him to Coventry on 23 January 1986. Donald Mackay was manager of Coventry at that time and paid 80,000 for him. From there the player made his way to Tannadice. McInally played an integral part of the club's defence-midfield system. In October 1989, he walked out on the club after they had turned down his written transfer request. However, he returned to the club on 27 October, after the club and player had resolved their differences. Jim stayed with the club for seven seasons. The player left the club on 5 July 1995 and joined Raith Rovers for £150,000, where he later became a player-coach. On 23 February 1996, they formally announced that they had appointed Jim assistant-manager to Jimmy Thomson at Raith. This took place after the departure of manager Jimmy Nicholl to Millwall. When Tommy McLean arrived as manager of Dundee United, one of his first signings brought McInally back to the club on 2 October 1996. Within a year Jim was back on the move again, this time back to Dundee FC as player-coach on 13 June 1997. In April 1998, he won a First Division medal with Dundee after they were promoted to the

Premier Division. In his time at Tannadice, Jim made 302 Scottish League appearances and was capped ten times at full International level with Scotland. He was also a UEFA Cup Finalist in 1987.

Matthew McIlwain, signed by manager Willie MacFadyen on 30 September 1950. The player made his United debut that afternoon in a reserve game against Dundee at Dens. Matthew made his first team debut on 7 October 1950 against Stenhousemuir. He had spent three seasons with Ayr United. At the time of signing, he had just returned from a trial with Reading. During his spell with United he played in four league games and scored once.

Archie McIndiewar, signed by manager Willie MacFadyen in August 1950. He made his first team debut on 12 August 1950 in the 2-1 victory over Stenhousemuir at Tannadice. His former clubs included Rangers and Dumbarton.

Hector McInlay, was given a trial by United in December 1959. On 2 January 1960, United announced that they had invited the ex-Falkirk player back to the club for another trial. At that time Hector was playing for Armadale Thistle.

D. McInness, played for Dundee Hibs in the early 1920s. His previous clubs included St Johnstone and Raith Rovers. While he was with the club, he played in eight league games for Dundee Hibs during season 1921-22.

Chic McIntosh, goalkeeper, who was signed to United by manager Willie Reid on 29 July 1931 from Logie Juniors. On 11 December 1934 the keeper signed for Preston North End and on 7 May 1935 he signed for Luton Town. After the Second World War, Chic returned to Preston and opened a bakery business. He died in 1981.

Gordon McIntosh, was a goalkeeper with junior side North End. Gordon played in a trial match for United on 3 August 1946.

Jim McIntosh, was a former Montrose player who signed for Nottingham Forest for 15,000 in 1971. McIntosh had interested Jim McLean since 1975. In 1977, the player was signed from Hull City. The player was freed from United on 3 November 1977.

Robert McIntosh, signed for the club during the close season of 1936-37 from Blairgowrie. Robert made his United debut on 8 August 1936 against King's Park. He was freed by United in April 1937, then joined Alloa on 24 May 1937. While was with United he made 34 league appearances.

William McIntosh, born in 1881, was originally a director with Dundee FC for 21 years, from 1912 until he resigned from the board on 16 May 1933. McIntosh did his best to stop Dundee Hibs being reelected to the Scottish League in 1923. He claimed that the city could not support two sets of supporters. His opinion had little effect on those at the Scottish League, and they voted to reinstate Dundee Hibs' league status. On 26 February 1934, along with other prominent businesspeople, McIntosh helped save Dundee United from bankruptcy. In July 1934, he became club chairman, and retained this position for two years. After the Second World War, McIntosh again returned to the club on 8 September 1945 and he remained a board member until he died in 1955.

McIntyre, made his United debut on 10 February 1945 as a War guest. The player had been with Queen of the South, and he joined them from Glenafton Athletic.

Donald McIntyre, played for Drumochter Hibs, and featured in a trial game for United on 9 January 1954. This match was played against Arbroath at Gayfield.

John McIvor, was demobbed from his base in Singapore, and played for United on 14 April 1954 in a derby game against Dundee at Dens Park.

George 'Piper' McKay, was a firm favourite with the United faithful. George signed for United on 9 February 1943 from Elmwood Juniors and made his debut for United on 12 February 1943 against Aberdeen at Pittodrie. The player was swopped with Dundee's Jim Dickson on Christmas Day 1947. Two days later on 27 December 1947, he made his Dundee debut against Queen of the South. He was freed by East Fife on 28 April 1950 and signed for Morton on 7 August 1950. Then he went off to play in Vancouver in the 1950s.

Peter McKay, signed to the club on 9 September 1947, from Newburgh, by manager Willie MacFadyen. The player made his club debut on 13 September 1947 in a League Cup Tie against Cowdenbeath which United lost 1-0. Peter soon became a favourite among the fans. McKay had the distinction of being a high scoring centre-forward who scored 14 goals in 19 matches in his first season at the club. In 1951, Peter was working as a joiner with the Caledon Shipyard in Dundee. The player remained at the club for seven season's before being transferred for £3,000 to Burnley in May 1954. Peter made his debut for Burnley in September 1954. then he signed for St Mirren and later joined Corby Town. While at

Tannadice, Peter played in 238 competitive games and scored 202 goals for the club.

Frank McKee, signed to United by manager Willie MacFadyen from Lochgelly Albert. The player made his first team debut on 30 August 1947 in the 2-1 win over Alloa at Tannadice. Frank was later transferred from United to Birmingham in February 1948 and then he went to Gillingham during the close season of 1952-53 making his league debut on 10 September 1952.

James McKee, signed for the club on 8 September 1953 after a spell of two seasons with Doncaster Rovers. James made his first team debut with United on 19 September 1953 against St Johnstone at Tannadice.

Tommy McKeith, featured in several United reserve matches in 1968. However, the young player was freed by the club in April 1969.

Robert McKell, was signed by Jim McLean in the early 70s. The keeper went on loan to East Fife in November 1973. The club freed McKell, and in October 1974 he signed for Hamilton Accies. They transferred him to Clyde on 28 January 1977. In July 1977, he joined junior side Cumbernauld United.

Dave McKellar, signed from Ipswich Town in the close season of 1976. Dave played in goal for the club in July in a game against Brechin , and on 2 August 1976 in a game against St Mirren. United freed the keeper in April 1977. He had not played in any first team games. In July 1977, he joined junior side Ardrossan Winter Rovers.

McKendrick, was granted a free from Huddersfield. The player turned out for United in a C-Division game against Montrose on 24 April 1948.

Gibby McKenzie, signed for Airdrie in October 1947, then he was signed by United manager Willie MacFadyen on 24 January 1948. Gibby made his United debut on 30 January 1948 against Dumbarton and on 14 February 1948 he made his Tannadice debut against Cowdenbeath. The player had also played for Dundee FC. In August 1949, he was working as a coach with Kilmarnock. Later, in 1954, he was player-manager with Irish side Linfield.

On 13 July 1955, he took up the manager's position with Greenock Morton and in 1958, became manager for Irish side Portadown.

Ralph McKenzie, signed by Willie MacFadyen on 16 March 1948 on loan from Aberdeen. The player made his United first team debut on 20 March 1948 against Raith Rovers at Tannadice. Ralph signed for Dundee on a free from the Pittodrie club in 1956.

McKerragher, played in goal for Dundee Hibs. His first game for the club was on 30 October 1915 against East Stirlingshire in the Eastern League.

D. McKimmie, signed for Dundee Hibs in September 1921 from St Joseph's. Tottenham Hotspur was also after his signature. He appeared in ten games for the club in season 1921-22.

Stewart McKimmie, born in Aberdeen on 27 October 1962. Stewart was signed, on 19 March 1997, by manager Tommy McLean on a free transfer from Aberdeen, having spent 14 years there. While at Pittodrie, McKimmie won three Scottish League medals, winning his last in 1995. McKimmie had previously played for city rivals Dundee. He played his debut game at Tannadice against Raith Rovers on 22 March 1997, United winning 2-1. Capped for Scotland on 40 occasions, he gained his first cap in 1989 in a game against England.

Billy McKinlay, born in Glasgow in 1969. Billy was signed from Hamilton Thistle. The player made his first team debut with the club on 22 November 1986 against Hibs at Tannadice – a game United won 1-0. In 1989, he was voted the SPFA Young Player of the Year. On 3 January 1989, Billy signed a long-term contract with United that would keep him at the club until the 1990s. Towards the end of September 1995, he decided that it was time for a move and signed for Blackburn Rovers on 13 October 1995, for a reported fee of £1.7 million. Celtic were also trying to sign 'Badger.' To date McKinlay has played for Scotland on 20 occasions, winning his first cap in 1989.

Hector McKinlay, signed to Falkirk in 1958, then he joined Armadale. Hector made his first team debut with United on 23 March 1963, against Clyde at Tannadice. The final score that day was 4-1 for Dundee United, with Hector scoring in the 9th minute.

George McKinney, was 17 years old when he had a trial for the club. George played in several reserve games in October 1960.

Neil McKinnon, signed by manager Willie MacFadyen on 19 November 1945 from Rangers. Neil joined Rangers in January 1943. He made his United debut on 24 November 1945 against Albion Rovers at Tannadice. United later transferred him to Albion Rovers on 20 December 1946. On 2 May 1950, he was freed by Queen of the South.

Ray McKinnon, born in Dundee on 5 August 1970, Ray signed on S-form in August 1983 from Finlathen Boys Club. He made his first team debut for United on 8 April 1989 in a derby game played at Tannadice which United won 2-1. McKinnon had signed for the club in 1986, and later, on 26 June 1992, he was transferred to Brian Clough's Nottingham Forest for a reported fee of £750,000. Two years later he signed for Aberdeen. On 3 November 1995, he again signed for United for a fee of £200,000. He made his debut on 5 November in the League Challenge Cup Final against Stenhousemuir. During the close season of 1998 Ray left Tannadice.

David McLure, signed by United manager Jimmy Brownlie on 28 June 1928 from Nelson FC, and had previously played for St Johnstone. David made his league debut for United on 11 August 1928 in the 4-0 win over Bathgate. While he was with United, he had featured in 44 games for the club.

Neil McKinven, signed by manager Reggie Smith on 24 November 1955 from Arbroath. Neil made his United debut the same day he signed, against a United Service XI at Tannadice. He played again for United two days later, against Perth Celtic. He was freed by United in April 1956.

Andy McLaren, born in Glasgow on 5 June 1973, and signed on 20 June 1989 from Rangers Amateur Boys Club. Andy made his United debut on 17 August 1991 after he came off the sub's bench in the 1-1 draw with St Johnstone. He scored his first goal for the club on

21 August 1993 against Falkirk at Tannadice in a League Cup match which ended 3-3. However, United went through to the next round after they won 4-2 on penalties. Andy has also been capped for his country playing at Under-21 level. Andy's brother John, was signed on a short term contract with Dundee on 1 April 1997.

Paul McLaren, signed for United on 24 November 1987 from Whitehill Welfare. The 21-year-old right-back became a full-time player in December 1987.

Sandy McLaren, signed for United in November 1954 by manager Reggie Smith. The keeper first played for United in a first team game against Queen's Park at Tannadice on 20 November 1954 and during his spell with United he featured in ten league matches. His Father, Sandy, also played in goal for St Johnstone, Leicester City, and was capped for Scotland.

Desmond McLean, goalkeeper, signed for the club in January 1952 from Airdrie. His previous club was Arsenal. McLean made his debut in the League Cup in 1953-54. However, he played only three competitive games with the club.

James McLean II, signed for United on 29 February 1940 after spending four seasons with Hibs. The player was 17 years old when he was signed by Hibs manager Willie McCartney, and made his Hibs debut in 1936. James made his United debut on 31 March 1940 against Partick Thistle. At the time of signing, James was with the Army, and was stationed at an Army base close to Dundee.

Hugh McLeish, the 17-year-old centre-forward from Blackburn Athletic, joined the ground-staff at Motherwell. From there, Hugh then signed for United on 7 September 1965 having previously played in a trial match against St Johnstone, Then he played in another game against his old club on 3 September 1965. After that match, manager Jerry Kerr was impressed enough to sign him. The player was freed by United in May 1967.

Joe McLeod, United allowed him to go on loan to Dumbarton on 16 February 1987. The player was still training full-time with United during this period. It was announced on 12 April 1990 that he had walked out on the club having failed to report for training the previous Friday. He settled his differences with the club and returned to Tannadice in July 1990. On 7 September 1990, he signed for Motherwell for a reported fee of £80,000. Joe made his Motherwell debut on 17 November 1990, against Rangers.

Gordon McLeod, the 16-year-old became the youngest player to be included in the Scotland Under-18 squad in May 1984. He was also on the subs bench at Tannadice when United met Hamrun Spartans in season 1983-84. Gordon joined Airdrie on 16 November 1988 for a reported fee of £100,000. In March 1989, he signed for Dundee for £70,000. Also included in the deal was Alan Lawrence .

Tommy McLeod I, signed by Jerry Kerr in August 1960. Tommy made his first team debut on 20 August 1960, against Stenhousemuir at Tannadice. The score was 3-3, and Tommy scored all United's goals. The club freed the player during the close season of 1961. He signed for Morton, and was released by them in November 1961. He then turned out for Inverness Caley on 2 December 1961.

Tom McLeod II, signed for United on 10 August 1954. The player had been with Liverpool from 1946-51, then from 1951-51 he played with Chester City, before being placed on the transfer list again. Tom made his United debut on 14 August 1954 in a game against Stenhousemuir at Tannadice.

Dave McLure, signed by manager Jimmy Brownlie during season 1928-29. While he was with United, he played in 44 games.

McMahon, played for Dundee Hibs during season 1920-21. On 28 June 1921 he signed for Lochgelly United.

Jimmy McManus, signed by manager Jerry Kerr on 23 November 1962 from Edinburgh Norton Club. Jimmy played his debut game for United on 30 November 1962, in a reserve match against Falkirk at Tannadice. The player made his first team debut on 24 October 1963 in a Scottish League game against Aberdeen at Pittodrie; final score Aberdeen 2 United 0. In October 1965, he was playing for Falkirk, and in the team were ex-United men Doug Moran and Johnny Graham. He was freed by Falkirk on 20 December 1968.

Mick McManus, played for junior side Lochee Harp. On 15 March 1989, the 32-year-old was a trialist for United reserves. This match was played against St Mirren.

James McMichael, signed by manager Jerry Kerr on 17 November 1960, from Bathgate Thistle. James made his United debut on 26 November 1960, in a reserve match against Aberdeen at Tannadice. He made his first team debut on 31 December 1960, against Hibs at Easter Road. United lost the match 2-0.

Jimmy McMillan, manager Willie MacFadyen provisionally signed Jimmy on 26 January 1951, the player was called up in August 1951. Jimmy made his debut on 28 August 1951 against Stenhousemuir at Tannadice and on 9 August 1952, he made his first team debut against Dumbarton at Boghead. Before he signed for United, he was playing for Whitburn Juniors, and was employed as a miner. The player was freed by United in May 1953.

Peter McMillan, made his United debut on 12 September 1925 in the 1-0 win over St Johnstone. Peter made his Tannadice debut on 19 September 1925 in the 1-0 win over Celtic. The player appeared on three occasions and scored one goal for the club.

Tom McMillan, played in Scotland's World Cup Under-16 squad in 1990. To give the young player some early experience with the full Scottish squad, he was allowed to travel with the squad to Italia 1990. Unfortunately, he had to give up the game in October 1992 due to recurring knee problems.

Charlie McMullen, signed by United on 11 August 1952 and had a spell with Arbroath and Hamilton before signing for the club. Charlie made his first team debut on 13 August 1952 against Stirling Albion.

John McNeil, came to United on 30 December 1982 on loan from Morton. Part of the deal included Ian Gibson and Graeme Payne heading for Greenock. John made his debut at Tannadice that night in a reserve game with Dundee. He made his first team debut on 8 January 1983 when he came on as a sub. The match was at Ibrox and United lost 2-1. John returned to Morton on 22 February 1983 after he failed to make the grade.

M. McNeil, played for Kilsyth Emmett, and played in a trial match for United on 6 October 1928 in the 3-0 win over Morton at Tannadice.

J. McNally, signed by manager Jimmy Brownlie 6 August 1929 from Motherwell Juniors. While he was with the club, he played in ten competitive matches.

Mark McNally, joined United on 11 March 1998 for a trial. Mark was placed on the transfer list by Stoke City, and manager Tommy McLean offered the player a try out. The player had also played for Celtic, and was a former Scotland Under-21 internationalist. Mark later returned to Stoke after his loan expired. He was later signed by manager Tommy McLean on 8 July 1998 from Stoke. United bought out the remainder of his contract with the club. He made his Premier League debut on 1 August 1998 against Kilmarnock at Rugby Park.

Ian McPhee, born in Perth in 1961. Ian had attended Letham Primary and Perth Academy. He was signed by Jim McLean for a fee of £45,000 from Forfar Athletic, and signed for the club in August 1987. On 19 August 1987, he made his first team debut in a Skol Cup tie against Partick Thistle at Tannadice. In 1986, he joined Celtic, and made 18 appearances with the club. In November 1988, Celtic transferred him to Airdrie for a fee of £50,000. He spent three years with the club. On 24 September 1991, he joined Forfar for a fee of £50,000 and in December 1996 he became their player-manager.

Archie McPherson, signed by manager Bobby McKay on 29 August 1939. Archie had previously played for East Fife during season 1938-39. His other clubs included Rangers, Sheffield United, and Falkirk. He made his United debut on 2 September 1939 against Leith Athletic at Tannadice.

Charles McPhillips, signed for Dundee Hibs by manager Pat Reilly on 23 July 1913. He previously played in goal for Hearts. Charles made his debut for Dundee Hibs on 16 August 1913 in the 0-0 draw with St Johnstone. He featured in the Dundee Hibs side that lost 3-0 to Albion Rovers in the Qualifying Cup Final game on 27 December 1913. He made 11 appearances for Dundee Hibs during season 1913-14.

Jamie McQuilken, signed for United on 4 November 1995 from Celtic, for £150,000. He signed for Celtic at the age of 16, where he was on a Youth Opportunities Scheme. Jamie was at Celtic Park for five years before he signed for United. Later the player would sign for Hibs.

Willie McRitchie, signed by manager Jimmy Brownlie during season 1934-35. Willie spent two seasons at Tannadice leaving in 1936. During his time with United he made 55 league appearances.

John McRoberts, signed by manager Jimmy Brownlie in 1924 from St Johnstone. John made his debut for the club on 16 August 1924 in the 2-2 draw with Bo'ness. While he was with the club he played in 40 league games and scored one goal.

Alec McSpayden, turned out as a guest for the club during the Second World War.

Gary McSweegan, was born in Glasgow on 24 September 1970. He signed for the club on 6 October 1995 from Notts County, for a fee of £350,000. Gary is a proven goal scorer who is fast and durable.

He made his first team debut on 7 October 1995 against Dumbarton. Gary had spent seven years at Ibrox and played several times for Rangers. However, Gary was unable to command a regular first team place with them, so he took the decision to move. It was during his time with Rangers that United manager Billy Kirkwood noticed him, and then brought him to Tannadice. In his first season at Tannadice Gary scored 17 league goals and ultimately helped United back into the Premier Division after a season of First Division football. Gary feels that one of the biggest highlights of his career was when he came off the subs' bench and scored against his former club Rangers at Ibrox. His main personal ambition is to be successful and to help the club win as many trophies as they can. He would also love to represent Scotland at international level, and hopes that he has not missed the boat yet. In his spare time he enjoys the odd game of snooker, however, his young son, Kieran, is keeping him occupied at the moment. He is married to Pauline.

Raymond McWalter, played for Celtic Boys Club in Dundee. The 16-year-old was showing promise in the reserve team in January 1980.

Ronnie McWalter, signed for United in October 1943. Ronnie played his first match since signing for the club on 9 October 1943. This match was against Falkirk at Tannadice.

Edison Machin, signed for United in April 1992 for a reported fee of £200,000. They had voted the Uruguayan their Player of the Year for 1992.

James Mackie, signed by manager Jimmy Brownlie for Dundee Hibs in August 1923 from Bo'ness. The player made his club debut on 12 September 1923 in the 2-0 win over St Johnstone at Tannadice in the Wallace Cup. James was released by the club on 19 December 1923. Within days he was off to Kings Park.

W. Mackie, signed by manager Jimmy Brownlie in November 1924 from Albion Rovers. He made his club debut on 8 November 1924 in a 2-1 win over Forfar Athletic at Tannadice. While he was with United he played in 16 games and scored on seven occasions.

Alexis Magallanes, from South America, and played for United in a friendly game against St Mirren at Love Street on 18 July 1998.

Alan Main, goalkeeper, born in Elgin in 1967. Alan was signed by manager Jim McLean from Highland league club Elgin City on 26 November 1986 for a reported fee of £8,000. When he was 15-years-old, he was playing in the Highland League with Lossiemouth before signing for Elgin. Before turning full time with United, the young 21-year-old was working as a plumber's mate. He played his first city derby match against Dundee on 28 March 1987 at Tannadice and it ended in a 1-1 draw. United originally signed Alan as cover for Billy Thomson, but shortly after his arrival he replaced Thomson as the first team choice, despite being only 21-years-old. Alan signed a four-year contract with the club on 7 February 1990. He also played in the 1991 cup final, seeing off a challenge from Guido van de Kamp. On 5 January 1995, the club sold him to St Johnstone for a fee in excess of £100,000. Scotland's coach, Craig Brown, has now recognised his fine goal keeping skills.

Malcolm, signed by manager Willie MacFadyen in August 1947. The player made his first team debut on 30 August 1947 in the 2-1 win over Alloa at Tannadice.

J. Malloy, signed for the club in August 1938, and had previously played with Cowdenbeath. The player made his United debut on 13 August 1938 in the 5-4 victory over Montrose at Links Park.

Thomas Malone, joined the committee of Dundee Hibs in March 1909.

Maurice Malpas, was born in Dunfermline, on 3 August 1962. Malpas signed S-form with the club on 21 August 1978 from Leven Royals. In 1979 he signed as a full-time player. Later, in recognition of his experience he became part of the coaching set up at Tannadice. During his career he was capped for Scotland at Under-21 level, and then went on to gain 55 caps at full international level.

His first cap was in 1984 in a game against France. This was the biggest day in Maurice's life, and he clearly remembers feeling a lump in his throat as the National Anthem was played. Maurice has won a League Championship badge from season 1982-3 and captained the squad when they won their first Scottish Cup Final against Rangers in 1994. He also holds a runners-up medal from the 1987 UEFA Cup Final against Gothenburg. On 23 April 1991, it was announced that he had won the Scottish Football Writers Player of the Year Award.

He became player-coach at Tannadice on 17 July 1991. His testimonial game was played on 31 July 1991, against Rangers, United won 3-1 in front of a crowd of 12,438. On 14 September 1991, he made his 500th United appearance in a game against Rangers at Ibrox. The final score was Rangers 1 United 1. Maurice also has the distinguished honour of being the first United captain to hold aloft the Scottish Cup when the team won it in 1994. He is married to Maria and has two children, Darren and Zoe, and when he gets the opportunity, he enjoys playing golf. Maurice also has an Honours degree in Electrical and Electronic engineering. His father pushed him into further education and Maurice appreciated his advice.

Jim Mann, played in a first team trial match for United on 11 January 1958 against Dumbarton at Tannadice. At that time Jim had been playing for junior side Rutherglen Glencairn.

Fabrice Mannucci, arrived at Tannadice in July 1998 for a trial.

John Markie, was showing up well in United's reserve side in December 1956.

Peter Markie, played centre-forward for Lochee Harp. On 13 September 1947 he turned out for United's reserves against Arbroath at Tannadice. The player scored a couple of goals in the 5-3 victory.

Stewart Markland, signed on a month's contract with the club on 9 August 1968. At the time of signing, Stewart had recently been freed from Berwick Rangers.

Goran Marklund, born in Stockholm, Sweden, on 2 October 1975. Goran s was signed from Vasalund on 15 August 1997 for a reported fee of £100,000. When the player signed for United he was just completing his National Service with the Swedish Army, so technically he could not play for United until the end of August. Marklund did turn out for United in a trial match against Orebro during the club's tour of Scandinavia in 1997. Several clubs were chasing his signature including Gothenburg, Leicester City and Derby County. He made his first appearance in a United shirt on 2 September 1997 in a reserve match against Aberdeen at Tannadice. Goran made his first team debut on 13 September 1997 against Kilmarnock, after he came off the sub's bench. The player played his first game from the start on 27 September 1997 against Celtic at Tannadice. On 29 April 1998, it was announced by manager Tommy McLean that Goran was to return to Sweden. His short-term contract had ended.

A. Marshall, in season 1910-11 he played in seven competitive games for Dundee Hibs and scored three goals.

Graham Marshall, signed for United in April 1978. The big centre-half made his first appearance in a tangerine shirt on 27 April 1978 in a charity match against Dundee University.

David 'Collie' Martin, born in 1890, he signed for Dundee Hibs by manager Pat Reilly on 21 July 1913 from Brechin City. He had previously played for Dundee. David made his debut for Dundee Hibs on 16 August 1913 in the 0-0 draw with St Johnstone. While in the Second Division, Collie was the leading goal scorer of the division for two seasons. The player also featured in the side that lost 3-0 to Albion Rovers in the Qualifying Cup Final game on 27 December 1913. His name was also linked to Sheffield United. However, Martin refused to sign for them. At the end of season 1913-14, Collie was the Division Two's leading scorer with 28 goals. David also featured in the first city derby against Dundee on 13 March 1915. His last game for Dundee Hibs was on 6 November 1915 against St Bernard's. Three days earlier he had signed up for the Black Watch. David left Dundee to fight in the First World War and in 1917 he was killed in action.

Tommy Martin, signed by manager Tommy Gray in September 1958. Tommy made his first team debut on 6 September 1958 against St Johnstone at Muirton. It was a memorable debut for the player as United won that day 4-3.

Willie Martin, played as a War guest for the club on 17 November 1945 against Dunfermline at Tannadice. Before the War started, Willie was a player with Bradford City.

Alan Massie, signed by manager Reggie Smith on 18 November 1954 from Dundee. The player had played for Aberdeen for two years before signing to the Dens Park club in May 1945. Alan made his first team United debut on 20 November 1954 in a match against Queen's Park at Tannadice.

Willie Masson, made his United debut on 4 November 1933 against Albion Rovers. The big 19-year-old was signed by manager Willie Reid in October 1933. At the time of signing he was a student of Physical Education at Jordanhill College.

Ally Maxwell, signed by manager Billy Kirkwood on 16 June 1995 from Glasgow Rangers. He was Kirkwood's first real signing and cost the club a reported £250,000. Born in Hamilton, on 16 February 1965, Motherwell snapped him up from Fir Park Boys Club when he was 16 years old. He joined Rangers in 1992, and manager Walter Smith paid the 'Steel-men' £300,000. Maxwell has found it difficult to displace first team keeper Sieb Dijkstra. Other former clubs include Clydebank, Liverpool, and Bolton Wanderers. During the close season of 1998 he left Tannadice.

G. Maxwell, signed for United on 28 August 1943 after he had played in a trial game for the club on the same day against Raith Rovers at Tannadice.

P. Maxwell, played for Edinburgh Hibs but turned out for Dundee Hibs on 4 March 1922 against St Bernard's at Tannadice. While he was with the club, he appeared for them on five occasions.

Eddie May, was 14 years old when he signed an S-form with United on 13 March 1982. At the time had been attending Holyrood High School in Edinburgh. Eddie left Tannadice on 10 January 1985 after suffering from homesickness. In 1986 he was playing for Hibs.

George May, turned out for United as a War guest on 8 August 1942 against Rangers at Ibrox.

Rafael Meade, first came to United for a trial on 30 July 1988. His former clubs included Arsenal and Sporting Lisbon. Eventually the player did sign for United on 3 August 1988. He made his first team debut on 24 August 1988 in a Skol Cup tie against St Mirren at Love Street. The player scored when he came off the subs bench. Rafael made his Tannadice debut on 27 August 1988 in a 2-2 draw with Aberdeen.

Jimmy Meagher, signed by manager Jimmy Brownlie on 1 March 1927 on loan from Dundee. His first game in a United shirt was on 5 March 1927 against Partick Thistle at Firhill. Jimmy made his first Tannadice appearance on 19 March 1927 against St Johnstone. While he was with United, he turned out on nine occasions and scored three goals.

Eddie Meaney, came from Dublin and signed for United on 4 December 1987. Also signed that day was Vincent Arkins who was also from Dublin. The 17-year-old made his first appearance in United colours on 7 December 1987 in a Youth Cup tie against Hearts.

Gary Mearns, signed for the club on 28 September 1987. The 16-year-old had attended Menzieshill High School and played for the Dee Club. Gary became a full-time player in December 1987.

Terry Meigham, joined the club on 4 March 1977 as a Public Relations Officer.

Andrew Meikleham, signed for the club on 9 August 1938, and had previously played for St Johnstone, Alloa, Leith Athletic and Raith Rovers. Andrew made his United debut on 13 August 1938 in the 5-4 victory over Montrose. In his first season with the club he played in 33 league games and scored one goal.

Steve Mellon, signed for the club in 1974, from North End. Mellon made his debut in a reserve match against Hibernian on 12 January 1974.

James Menzies, played in a trial match for United on 27 October 1946 against Brechin City in a C-Division game played at Glebe Park. United ran out 6-3 winners.

Jim Melville, signed for Rangers in 1939 from Blantyre Vics. Jim first turned out for United reserves on 24 August 1941 as a War guest. The keeper took over from Alec Edmiston who had been called up for his Army service.

Chris Meyers, was born in Yeovil on 1 April 1969 and was Ivan Golac's first signing when he took over the manager's job at Tannadice. The manager knew of Meyers capabilities having watched him while he was at Plainmoor. He signed for the club on 2 August 1993 and cost a reported fee of £90,000. Chris made his Premier League debut on 14 August 1993 in a 2-1 victory over Partick Thistle. Plagued by injury, Meyers struggled to gain a first team place each week and eventually he went back to England. He spent a month with his former club Torquay United, but returned to United. During 1995, he suffered serious injuries and did not appear for the club. Meyers was freed at the start of season 1995-96, and had trials with Dunfermline and Wrexham. Chris eventually signed for Exeter City in March 1996 and played eight competitive games for the club. He was released from Exeter during the summer of 1997. Now he is playing for non-league clubs in the area.

Harry Michie, signed by manager Jimmy Brownlie in December 1927 from Alva Albion. Harry made his club debut on 17 December 1927 against Armadale. While he was with the club, he appeared in 32 games and scored 13 times.

Johnny Millar I, was transferred from Dunfermline to Rangers on 12 January 1955, for a fee of between £6,000 and £7,000. Johnny made his debut with Rangers on 29 January 1955, against Dundee at Dens Park. The player signed for United on 18 July 1967, after being freed by Rangers. He made his first team debut for United on 5 August 1967, in a friendly game at Tannadice against Sheffield United. Then on 12 August 1967, he played in the first League Cup game of the season against Celtic at Parkhead. He played for United from 1967 until 1969, and played in 22 league and cup games and scored three goals. While he was at Rangers, he played 285 games and scored 148 times for the Ibrox outfit. His brother Tommy also played for United. On 10 February 1969, he became manager of Raith Rovers.

Tommy Millar, was born in Edinburgh in 1938 and signed to United in March 1962, by manager Jerry Kerr from Colchester. He made his first team debut on 17 March 1962, in a match against Motherwell at Tannadice. The score was 1-1. Tommy played 256 league and cup games with United and scored ten goals. He was freed by United in April 1969.

Miller, became the new goalkeeper for Dundee Hibs in January 1920. He made his Tannadice debut on 17 January 1920. This match was played in the Northern League against Aberdeen A. Dundee Hibs ran out winners 2-1 that day.

Andrew Miller, joined United in September 1926 from Larkhall Thistle. The player made his club debut on 4 September 1926 against Kilmarnock at Tannadice. Then he was transferred to Hearts for 1,000 in April 1927, and then he later joined Dundee. Andy signed for Raith Rovers on a free from Dundee on 12 June 1934. In 1958 he was a director with Hamilton Accies.

Alec Miller, joined United as a war guest, and made his debut on 18 May 1940 against Dunfermline. Alec was signed by manager Willie MacFadyen on 27 May 1946 from Motherwell for 400. He had also played for Celtic, and Preston North End during the War. The player made his United debut in a B-Division game on 10 August 1946 in a 3-1 win over Dunfermline. Alec was transferred to Morton on 22 October 1947.

Joe Miller, signed by manager Tommy McLean on 8 July 1998 from Aberdeen. The player was signed under the Bosman ruling. Joe made his United debut on 18 July 1998 in a friendly game against St Mirren at Love Street. His Premier League debut for United was on 1 August 1998 against Kilmarnock at Rugby Park.

Tom Miller, played in the first ever Scottish League match that Dundee Hibs featured in. The game was played on 20 August 1910 against Leith Athletic. Dundee Hibs lost 3-2.

During season 1910-11 he played in 15 competitive games for Dundee Hibs and scored one goal. Tom went to Vancouver in March 1911.

A. Milliken, played for Rutherglen Glencairn and Kilmarnock. The goalkeeper played in 33 league games for the Rugby Park side in season 1932-33. On 14 July 1933 he was signed to United by manager Willie Reid. He made his first team debut for United on 12 August 1933 against East Fife at Tannadice.

Arthur Milne, born in 1915, the player signed for the club on 13 October 1934, from Brechin Victoria. On his club debut, the 19-year-old scored on four occasions. This match was played on 28 November 1934, against Edinburgh City. United won 9-6 that day. His teammates nicknamed him Li'l Arthur because he was only 5ft 6in. The nifty little player scored 85 times in 81 outings in a period of three years. However, problems began to develop between Milne and manager-director George Greig. This involved an argument between the men involving Milne's pay. The player asked for a transfer, and went on loan to Liverpool on 11 March 1937. This led to a confusion over the player's registration, which left the player to act on his own behalf. In other words, he was one of football's first free agents. Milne signed for Hibs on 13 May 1937, and United did not receive any transfer money. United received only £750 as compensation. They had previously refused a £3,000 bid from Chelsea for him. The player did return to the club in August 1939. His first game as a War guest was on 11 August 1939 in a 2-2 draw with St Johnstone at Tannadice. Little Arthur also played for United in the 1940 Emergency War Cup Final against Rangers. Eventually he signed for St Mirren. On 31 May 1950, he left Scotland for a spell as player-coach with Irish club Coleraine. Shortly after this he retired from football.

Douglas Milne, signed for United on 5 July 1937 from junior side Broughty Ex-Service.

Jimmy Milne, joined United when he was 18-years-old, and at that time he had been working as a porter at Lochee West Station in Elmwood Road Dundee. He was transferred from United to Preston North End on 5 October 1932 for £750. He broke off with Preston during the Second World War to become a police officer in November 1939. In 1934, he was in Preston's promotion winning side. On 11 May 1961, Jimmy became manager of Preston North End. Back in 1961, his son Gordon was a wing-half with Liverpool.

John Milne, signed by manager Jimmy Brownlie during season 1935-36. John made his first team debut on 16 November 1935 against Leith Athletic at Marine Gardens. While he was at Tannadice, John made 49 league appearances and scored seven goals.

Maurice Milne, signed by manager Reggie Smith in April 1955 from junior side St Joseph's. Maurice had played in a first team trial on 16 April 1955 against Arbroath at Tannadice. The club signed him shortly after this game. The player signed for Brechin City on 25 September 1959. In January 1960 he was given a trial for Forfar.

Ralph Milne, born in Dundee in 1961, and signed an S-form with United on 16 January 1976 while he was attending Craigie High School. Ralph signed for United in 1977 from local team Celtic Boys. His first team debut was in August 1979 against Dunfermline and he scored the third goal in the game. As a player Milne was one of the most exciting wingers ever to put on a United jersey. Unfortunately, off the field activities were to dominate his personal and professional life and this led to many arguments with manager Jim McLean. These conflicts resulted in Milne leaving the club in January 1987 for Charlton Athletic. In April 1988 he signed to English Third Division side Bristol City for £50,000 and in November 1988, he signed for Manchester United for £170,000. In season 1988-89, he played 19 league games and seven cup games, and scored three times for Manchester United. He made only one appearance as a sub in 1989-90, and did not feature in any first team games in season 1991-92. Manager of Manchester United was Alex Ferguson.

Jimmy Milton, signed by manager Jimmy Brownlie on 28 May 1936, the goalkeeper had previously played for King's Park. Jimmy made his United debut on 8 August 1936 in the 4-2 victory against his old club. While was with the club he made 34 league appearances. After leaving United, Milton joined East Fife on 5 July 1937, on a free transfer and was part of the East Fife team that won the 1938 Scottish Cup Final, beating Kilmarnock 4-2 after extra time in the replay.

Jean Jacques Misse Misse, born in 1969, and signed by Tommy McLean in January 1998 on a short term contract. The big striker was known to the Tangerine supporters as he had played for Turkish club Trabzonspor in the UEFA Cup against United on 26 August 1997. The player left Trabzonspor for Sporting Lisbon in 1997, for a fee of £350,000. Misse left the Turkish club after they stopped his wages reported to be in the region of $600,000 per annum. The player did not cost United a fee, however, his wage demands were high. He has 55 International caps for Cameroon. Manager Tommy McLean announced on 10 March 1998, that the player could leave the club, should he wish to do so as his short-term contract had run out, and he had failed to hold down a regular first team spot. The player had also said that he felt his long-term future lay in England. The player was offered a week's trial with Chesterfield United on 11 March 1998 but turned down their offer. A few days later, the player reconsidered and decided to take up their offer of a trial.

A. Mitchell, played in 16 competitive matches for Dundee Hibs during season 1911-12.

George Mitchell, signed for the club from Aberdeen Sunnybank by manager Willie MacFadyen. George played in his first team debut for United on 1 January 1949 against St Johnstone. The player had previously turned out for the reserve side on Christmas Day 1948 against Montrose. George made his Tannadice debut on 8 January 1949 against Dumbarton.

He was freed by United in April 1952. On 13 December 1952, he made his Forfar debut against his old club at Tannadice. Unfortunately, his new club lost 4-1 to United that day. The player signed to the Station Park outfit from Dundee.

Ian Mitchell, born in Falkirk in 1946. He was signed for United by Jerry Kerr when he was 16 years old on 18 July 1962. He made his debut against Hibs on 29 September 1962. United won 5-0. Mitchell played 261 League Cup, Scottish Cup and European games for United, finding the net on 125 occasions. Mitchell signed for Newcastle United in 1970, for a fee of more than £50,000. The fee made the club's record books, beating the previous best of £30,000 when Liverpool signed Ron Yeats in 1961. On 21 October 1971, he was transferred back to the club in a straight swap deal that saw Alec Reid moving to Newcastle. Eventually he ended up playing for Falkirk and was freed by them on 1 May 1974. In March 1976, he was playing for Brechin City. After retiring from the game he opened a shop in Strathmartine Road, Dundee, selling business supplies. Ian died after a long illness in April 1996, he was only 50 years old. On 6 April 1996, there was a minute's silence for Ian before the game against Dumbarton at Tannadice.

Neil Mochan, signed to United on 17 November 1960 by manager Jerry Kerr. Neil made his first team debut on 19 November 1960 in a game against Kilmarnock at Tannadice. Kilmarnock lost that gane 4-2 with Neil scoring two of United's goals. Neil was with the club for three years. One of his last appearances for United was on 7 March 1963 in a game against Aberdeen at Pittodrie which United won 2-1. His last match for the club was on 23 May 1963, in a reserve match at Tannadice. The same evening the club freed him but his contract with United did not run out until 30 June 1963, and that was his official date for starting with Raith Rovers. He joined them formally on 4 July 1963. Neilly was with Celtic from 1953-60. He had played for Morton and Middlesborough before signing for United. In February 1964 he joined Celtic again, this time as a trainer. Neil was also part of the set-up when Celtic won the European Cup on 25 May 1967. Neil was capped for his country on three occasions. He played in a World Cup qualifying game against Norway in Oslo in 1954, in the same year he played against Austria and Switzerland.

Harry Mollison, signed by Jerry Kerr in the close season of 1971, from St Francis Boys Club Dundee. The 17-year-old made his first team debut on 27 October 1971, in a game against Motherwell. United won that day by 2-1.

Tonny Mols, signed by manager Tommy McLean on 30 July 1998 for a nominal fee paid from Lokeren. Tonny made his United debut on 30 July 1998 in a friendly game against a United White team played at Tannadice. He made his Premier League debut on 1

August 1998 against Kilmarnock at Rugby Park. The player had also had spells with FC Bruge and RWD Molenbeek.

Mariano Montefiori, arrived at Tannadice in July 1998 for a trial. He was playing for Argentinian side Athletico Rafaela, and was one of three South American players who manager Tommy McLean was showing interest in. The other two were Alexis Mallaganes and Jose Valeriani. Mariano played his first game in United colours on 18 July 1998 in a friendly game against St Mirren at Love Street. United won 2-1 that day.

Bill Montieth, played in goal for Dundee Hibs, and played in 17 competitive games for the club. In season 1911-12, he signed for Albion Rovers.

Bobby Moodie, played for United during the Second World War. Bobby went to Falkirk. However, he returned to United on 11 November 1944.

Graham Mooney, signed for United on 18 February 1974 from Salvesen Boys Club. Mooney made his first appearance for the club on 16 February 1974, in a reserve game. His performance so impressed Manager Jim McLean that he signed the player two days later.

J. Moore, played for Aberdeen and Crystal Palace and joined United in August 1926. The player made his United debut on 4 September 1926 against Kilmarnock at Tannadice.

James Moore I, played in a trial game for the club on 4 February 1950, in a reserve match. At that time he was playing for Crieff Earngrove.

James Moore II, signed to United by Jerry Kerr on 26 April 1963. The player was called up by the club during the close season of 1963-64. He played his first game for the club in a reserve match on 2 May 1963 and then was formally called him up for training on 29 July 1963. As a professional player he made his debut for United reserves on 10 August 1963 against Aberdeen reserves at Pittodrie. Jim made his first team debut on 28 August 1963, against Hibs at Tannadice. He was freed by the club in April 1968.

Doug Moran, signed by manager Jerry Kerr on 26 June 1964, from Ipswich Town. Doug had previously played for Hibs and Falkirk. He made his first team debut on 8 August 1964, in the 3-2 victory over Dundee at Dens Park. In October 1965, he was playing for Falkirk.

Also playing for them at that time was Jim McManus and Johnny Graham. Both men were ex-players with United. Doug was freed by Falkirk in April 1968.

Stephen Moran, was 16 years old when he signed for the club in January 1978. Moran, who was from Greenock had just left school when he joined the ground staff at Tannadice.

Jimmy Morgan, born in Freuchie, Fife, and joined Dundee from Bowhill Rangers. During the Second World War he guested with Third Lanark and United. He guested in a game played on 6 December 1941 against East Fife in the North-Eastern League Cup Semi-Final. He was fixed up by United manager Jimmy Allan to play for the club in season 1942-43. This took place on 8 August 1942. Jimmy was called up for Naval service on 20 December 1943.

Dave Morris, signed by United manager Willie Reid on 17 December 1931. Dave made his United debut two days later against Hearts at Tynecastle. In March 1934 Dave was playing for Leith Athletic.

Henry Morris, signed for United in May 1953 from East Fife. The club freed Henry on 27 November 1953. Henry played in only two first team games in the opening League Cup ties.

George Morrison, signed for United on 26 January 1950 from Thornton Hibs by Manager Willie MacFadyen. The player made his debut on 18 February 1950 in a reserve game against Arbroath at Tannadice. At the time of signing he was living in Windygates, and working in the local paper mill. George was freed by United in May 1953.

Robert Morrison, played for Airdrie before signing for Southport in the early 1930s. Robert was signed by United manager Jimmy Brownlie on 9 August 1935 and he made his first team debut on 10 August 1935 against St Bernard's at Tannadice. While he was at Tannadice he made 33 league appearances before signing for Alloa Athletic.

Stewart Morrison, signed by manager Jerry Kerr on 2 October 1959, from Whitburn Rovers. The goalkeeper made his first team debut on 2 April 1960, in the 4-0 win over Forfar at Tannadice.

Andy Moule, was 17 years old when he was given his first taste of Premier League football. Andy came off the sub's bench and made his first team debut on 22 October 1994. This game was against Hibs at Tannadice.

Marc Moulin, arrived from France for a trial with the club in July 1998.

George Mudie, played as a War guest for the club on 24 November 1945 against Albion Rovers at Tannadice.

J. Mudie, during season 1912-13 the player made one appearance for Dundee Hibs.

Tommy Muir, from Bridgeton Waverley, made his Tannadice debut for United on 12 April 1947 in a 2-2 draw with Stenhousemuir. While he was with United, he featured in only three league games. The keeper also played for Irish side Derry City.

Willie Muir, played in goal for Hearts during season 1909-10, and had also played for Dundee for many years. Willie was signed to Dundee Hibs by manager Pat Reilly on 23 May 1910.

Mullaney, played in a trial match for United on 11 February 1939 against Edinburgh City at Tannadice.

Jochen Muller, signed for the club on 9 August 1991 for a reported fee of £75,000, paid to his former club Mannheim. He played his first game for United on 10 August 1991, in a Premier League game against Celtic at Tannadice which United lost 4-3. It was announced on 23 January 1992 that the player had to quit football due to a back injury and had returned to Germany in December 1991.

John Mulholland, was the team captain of Dundee Hibs when they won the Forfarshire Cup on 1 May 1920 against Dundee A.

Alan Munro, signed from Partick Thistle in 1974. The outside-right made his first team debut on 14 September 1974 in a game against Dundee. Munro scored that day and United ran out winners by 3-0.

Francis Munro, born Dundee in 1947, and attended St Michael's Secondary. Spent one year with Chelsea then came back home to Dundee because he was homesick. Francis was then signed by manager Jerry Kerr on 29 July 1963. The 16-year-old was desperate to make a name from himself at the club. In his first game he scored the winner against Dundee on 8 August 1964. This match ended 3-2 for United, and it was played at Dens Park. While Frank was at Tannadice, he played in 70 competitive matches and scored 22 goals. Munro was later transferred to Aberdeen on 13 October 1966 and made his debut for them on 15 October 1966, in the 2-0 victory over Ayr United at Pittodrie. Frank Munro spent two years with Aberdeen before he signed for Wolves in 1968. Frank made his debut for Wolves on 6 January 1968 in a 2-1 defeat by Everton. In 1971, while he was playing for Wolves, he won his first cap for Scotland. In October 1977, Munro was placed on the transfer list and on 14 October, his 30th Birthday, he signed for Celtic on a month's loan. Eventually he signed for them for £20,000. Munro made his debut on 15 October 1977. Celtic released him in April 1978. He was capped for his country on nine occasions.

Iain Munro, signed to Rangers in November 1976. Iain was signed from Sunderland in March 1984 and played his first game for United on 31 March 1984 against Hearts at Tynecastle. The result was Hearts 0 United 0. He left United in March 1985 and signed for Hibs. In 1989, he was assistant manager at Raith Rovers under Jimmy Nicholl. Later he became the manager of Dundee. On 27 July 1990, he became manager of Dunfermline. After his appointment as manager, a bitter disagreement erupted between the fans and board at East End Park, the fans being angry at the departure of Pars manager Jim Leishman. His stay at East End Park was short lived however as the club sacked him on 17 September 1991. One month later, on 7 October 1991, he was appointed manager of Dundee but a few months later he resigned his post at Dens on 21 February 1992. On 11 June 1992, he made another comeback, with another club, this time as manager of First Division Hamilton Accies. Iain was appointed manager of Raith on 16 September 1996, after Tommy McLean left to take up the manager's post at Tannadice. He had his contract terminated by the Raith board on 14 April 1997.

Jimmy Munro, signed by manager Willie MacFadyen in August 1952 from St Johnstone. Jimmy made his first team debut on 13 August 1952 against Stirling Albion at Tannadice. In May 1953 the club freed the player.

J. 'Monty' Munro, signed up for the club during season 1932-33. Monty made his first team appearance on 16 December 1933 in the 4-4 draw with Arbroath at Tannadice. While he was with the club, he made nine league appearances, and scored two goals.

James Murphy, was an ex-Celtic player who signed for United in June 1954. He played in a game against Ayr United on 14 August 1954, at Tannadice.

Kenny Murphy, was signed in 1974, from St Columba's Boys Club. The player made it to the subs bench in December 1974. He was released by the club in April 1976. The winger then signed for Forfar Athletic. However, he emigrated to Australia in August 1976 to play for Essondon of Melbourne.

Murray, played for East Craigie and played his first senior game for Dundee Hibs on 13 November 1915. This match was played at Tannadice against East Fife. He was also in the Dundee Hibs side when they won the Forfarshire Cup against Dundee A on 1 May 1920.

Derek Murray, was born on 3 August 1962, and was 16-years-old when he signed for the club on 30 March 1977, from Oakley United. The youngster had just started work and was called up by the club in January 1978. In September 1986, he was playing for Motherwell.

Fred Murray, formerly played for Cowdenbeath before United manager Willie Reid signed him on 5 July 1933. Fred made his United debut on 12 August 1933 against East Fife at Tannadice. He was freed by the club on 22 November 1933 at his own request.

R.A.C. Murray, came on loan to United from Clyde during season 1935-36. The player made his United debut on 2 November 1935 in a 4-1 win over Forfar at Tannadice. While he was with the club he made 21 league appearances and scored one goal.

Steve Murray, born in 1944, signed by Jim McLean in 1979. Steve made his United debut when he came on as a sub on 24 November 1979. In his early career he had played for Dundee, making his debut for them on 8 August 1964, against United. Dundee lost that game 3-2 at Dens. He also played for Aberdeen and Celtic, playing his last game for them on 10 January 1976. Murray also had a managerial stint with Forfar Athletic that lasted only 72 hours. He was appointed manager on Monday 18 August 1980. Then he was gone. However, he took up the managership of Montrose in April 1982. On 18 January 1983, he resigned his post at Montrose following a defeat in the Scottish Cup at the hands of Brora Rangers. When Jim McLean signed Murray, it was purely as a coach. The player had been forced to retire from Celtic four years earlier through injury. Murray ended up having treatment to the injury and found that he could play again. He was a member of United's League Cup winning side in 1979, having received a medal after coming on as a substitute in the first game at Hampden. On 20 July

1989, it was announced that Murray would again return to the club. This time it was as Jim McLean's assistant-manager. After four months in the job, Murray walked out on the club on 15 November 1989.

Jackie Myles, signed from Edina Hibs in January 1976. The club freed the mid-fielder in April 1978.

Andy Napier, signed for United by manager Andy McCall on 17 January 1959 from Newburgh Juniors. Andy played in a first team trial game against Morton in December 1958. He made his home debut for United on 24 January 1959 in a 1-1 draw against East Fife. The player scored his first goal for the club on 21 March 1959 in the 3-0 victory over Montrose.

Dave Narey MBE, was born in Dundee in 1956, and attended St John's Secondary School. Dave has the distinction of being one of United's top players and signings. He was originally signed on S-form by the club on 6 January 1972. At the time of signing the young Narey was playing for St Columba's Boys Club. He made his debut for United on Wednesday 21 November 1973 in a game against Falkirk which United won 2-1. Since then he has played over 600 league games for United. Narey went on to achieve what most professionals dream about. He became the first United player to be capped at International level for Scotland, gaining 35 caps. Dave's first International cap came in 1978, when he played his first game against Portugal. He was also part of the finest historical days at Tannadice. He was part of the Championship winning side and shared in the two League Cup victories. As part of his testimonial year United managed to secure Tottenham Hotspur as their guests. The match was played on 7 August 1988 and 10,000 fans turned up. Spurs' lineup included Paul Gascoigne and Paul Stewart. Both these men were recent signings at a cost of £2 million each. On 27 November 1990, Dave made his 800th appearance for the club. To mark the occasion, Dave was presented with crystal glasses and a decanter before the game against St Johnstone at Tannadice. Dave was presented with his MBE on 18 November 1992 at Buckingham Palace. Dave made his 600th League appearance on 27 March 1993 and vice-chairman of the club, Doug Smith, made a presentation to Dave at Tannadice before the United v. Celtic game. By the time the Scottish Cup final took place in 1994, Dave had slipped out of the first team and on 20 May 1994, the club freed him. After leaving Tannadice, he joined Raith Rovers and helped manager Jimmy

Nicholl win the Coca-Cola cup and get promotion. Dave Narey has now retired from playing side of the professional game, although he did turn out for United reserves in 1997. On the team lines they reported him as a trialist! From 1973 to 1994, Dave played in 603 games for the club, scoring 22 League goals. He played in 70 Scottish Cup games. Dave appeared in 108 League Cup games, scoring six times. He also made 75 European appearances scoring on six occasions. Dave represented Scotland on 35 occasions, gaining his first cap against Sweden in 1977. We will always remember Dave Narey for his professional style and play, and he is a legend at Tannadice Park. On Tuesday 10 February 1998, Dave returned to Tannadice Park as a coach. This followed shortly after Jocky Scott's departure to Dens Park to take up the manager's job after the Dundee directors had sacked their previous manager John McCormack. Dave still turns out for the odd game and can be regularly seen with the All-Star XI. This team is made up of ex-United and ex-Dundee players. They play other local teams for a small fee and all the monies raised go to local charities. Included in the All-Star side from United are Hamish McAlpine, Ian Gibson, John Holt and George Fleming. And from Dundee Les Barr, Jocky Scott, and Bobby Glennie.

John Naulty, joined the committee of Dundee Hibs in March 1909.

Bert Neal, made his first appearance in a Dundee Hibs shirt on 27 August 1915. This match was against Lochgelly United at Tannadice.

James Nelson, played for Dundee in season 1929-30, and signed for United by manager Jimmy Brownlie on 8 August 1930. The player made his United debut on 9 August 1930 against Armadale.

John Nelson, played in two reserve games for United in 1950. On 3 March 1951, he went on trial with St Johnstone.

Martin Neil, signed for United on 27 March 1992, from Berwick Rangers for a reported fee of 25,000. He made his club debut on 30 March 1992, in a reserve game against Montrose at Gussie Park. United sold Martin to Berwick Rangers on 31 March 1993.

Derek Neilson, was 18 years old when he signed a provisional form with the club from Tartan Boys Club Edinburgh. The young lad was included in a 17-strong United pool in September 1977.

Tommy Neilson, signed to Hearts from Armiston Rangers in 1953. He was transferred from Hearts to East Fife in 1957 and from there he signed for United in 1959. Tommy was part of the United side that won promotion to the First Division. The player played in 295 competitive games at the club, and scored ten goals, remaining with the club until 1968, when he emigrated to South Africa.

Alf Nevens, guested for United during the Second World War. In June 1943, he was playing for the Navy team.

Laurie Nevins, was a War guest at the club, and had previously played for Newcastle United. He received permission from them on 15 April 1942 that he could turn out for United. Laurie made his United debut on 18 April 1942 in the 8-1 win over Rangers at Tannadice.

Peter Newbury, was given his first taste for first team football on 12 March 1960. This was in a friendly game played at Tannadice Park against Derby County. The score that day was United 3 Derby 2.

Watt Newton, left United on 6 January 1960, and headed for Alloa. At the time Watt was training with Forfar at Station Park. His brother Pat was also training there. In May 1963, he was playing for junior side Kirrie Thistle. In July 1964, he was transferred from Kirrie to Alyth United.

Joe Nibloe, signed to United in 1949.

George Nicol, signed for the club on 3 August 1981 from Stirling Albion. George was on the subs bench for a first team match played on 8 August 1981 against Ayr United. He joined Dunfermline on 12 November 1981 for £5,000.

Dave Nicoll, joined United in January 1926 from Forfar Athletic. His previous clubs included Dundee. Dave made his United debut on 23 January 1926 in the 1-1 draw in the Scottish Cup game at Tannadice. While he was with United, he appeared twice for the club.

Nicholson, played for Arbroath, and turned out for Dundee Hibs as a guest during the First World War. His first game was played on 9 October 1915 against Bathgate in the Eastern League.

George Nicholson, played in a trial match for the club on 25 September 1937 in a 2-2 draw with Alloa at Tannadice. He was signed by the club on 29 September 1937 from junior side Kirrie Thistle.

Harry Nicholson, signed to United on 25 October 1933 by manager Willie Reid. He had departed from his old club St Johnstone at the end of season 1932-33. Harry made his United debut on 28 October 1933 against Dunfermline at Tannadice.

Jack Nicholson, signed for United on 1 December 1951 from Brentford City. Before he joined them, he was playing for Dennistoun Juniors. Jack made his United debut on 1 December 1951 in a reserve game against Montrose at Tannadice.

Syd Nicholson, played for Scunthorpe United and Bournemouth before joining Barnsley. He was transferred from there to Aberdeen in 1937. Syd played as a War guest with United on 17 February 1945 against Dunfermline at Tannadice.

Jimmy Nielson, signed by manager Jerry Kerr on 22 October 1959 from East Fife. The player made his first team debut for the club on 24 October 1959 in the 0-0 draw with Albion Rovers at Tannadice.

Jerren Nixon, born in Trinidad on 25 June 1973, and signed by manager Ivan Golac on 29 November 1993, from EMC Motown for a reported fee of £220,000. The deal was not finalised until 21 December 1993 due to work permit problems. He made his first team debut on 8 January 1994, when he came off the subs bench in the game against Hearts. This game was played at Tannadice, and United won 3-0. Golac once said that the young player was worth millions! However, when manager Kirkwood took over, he did not share his predecessor's view. On 3 July 1995, Kirkwood announced that Jerren Nixon was unlikely to return to Tannadice. They sold him to FC Zurich for a reported fee of 200,000 on 18 July 1995. Nixon was an exciting prospect, but never fulfilled his full potential at the club. The player did return to the UK in January 1997, when he went on a month's loan with Watford. Jerren had appeared for his national side Trinidad and Tobago on five occasions.

Bobby Norris, signed for United by manager Andy McCall on 4 April 1959 from Rutherglen Glencairn. Bobby played in a first team trial match for the club on the same day as he signed. This match was against Stranraer at Tannadice. He played his first game as a signed United player on 18 April 1959 against Morton at Tannadice. United ran out 4-1 winners that night. Bobby was a member of United's promotion side to the First Division in 1960. The club freed him on 6th February 1961. In August 1961, he joined English non league side South Shields. In the 1980s, Bobby was working for Rolls Royce and running a newsagent's business.

Paul O'Brien, was a striker with United's reserve team. They transferred him to Hearts on 11 February 1980. Then he signed for St Johnstone on 11 November 1981.

James O'Gara, played in the first ever Scottish League match that Dundee Hibs featured in. The game was played on 20 August 1910 against Leith Athletic. Dundee Hibs lost 3-2 that day. From seasons 1910-1912, James featured in 23 competitive games for Dundee Hibs and scored five goals.

Duncan Ogilvie, signed to the club on 5 August 1948 at the age of 37. Manager Willie MacFadyen knew all about Ogilvie's playing capabilities as both had played together at Motherwell. Both men also appeared in the Scottish International Team that drew with Austria in the 1930s. In March 1936, Ogilvie signed for Huddersfield. The player did not settle there and returned to Fir Park a short time later. Duncan was signed to United on 5 August 1948, and played his first game for the club on 7 August 1948 in a friendly game at Tannadice.

Kelham O'Hanlon, signed for United on 9 September 1994, from Preston North End. The reported fee was 40,000. The goalkeeper made his first team debut on 8 October 1994, against Kilmarnock at Rugby Park. United won 2-0 that Saturday. In July 1996, Kelham returned to Preston North End to continue as a coach. However, United signed him on a month's contract in August 1996 so that they could thrash out a suitable fee for the keeper.

Joe O'Kane, signed by manager Jimmy Brownlie for Dundee Hibs in 1923 from Celtic. Joe made his club debut on 15 August 1923 against St Johnstone. A few months after he signed the club changed their name to United. While he was with the club, he played in 42 league games and scored 15 goals. Joe was granted a free transfer at his request in February 1925.

Andy Oliphant, played for junior side Dundee Violet, and appeared in a United reserve side in April 1948.

Kjell Olofsson, was born in Gothenburg, Sweden, on 23 July 1965. Kjell originally came to United on 23 October 1996, for a trial period. He made his first team debut on 26 October 1996, against

Hearts. The player scored his first goal for United on 2 November 1996, in a match against Motherwell. United ran out 3-1 winners that day. The big striker impressed Manager Tommy McLean and was signed by him officially on 15 November 1996. The reported fee was in the region of £400,000 from Norwegian club Moss F. K. The big striker has scored several match winners for the club. In his first season, Olofsson scored 13 goals for the United. Olofsson is a plumber by trade, and before joining United on a full-time basis he was assembling wheelchairs in Norway. Dundee United is Kjell's first professional club and he appreciates that United gave him the opportunity to play in Scotland's Premier League. Kjell is married and has three children, Charlotte, Tobias and Patrick. His personal ambition is to win more trophies with the club, but feels that he is now too old to win any caps at international level for his country. His hobbies include golf and his family.

Emanuelle Omoyinmi, arrived at Tannadice on 20 February 1998, on loan from West Ham United. The player had lived in London for eight years before arriving from Nigeria. He made his United debut on 21 February 1998, in a 2-2 draw with Dunfermline at East End Park. Emanuelle left United on 30 March 1998 after his loan period expired.

John O'Neill, was just 18 years old when he was in the starting line-up in the friendly match against Brondby played on 3 March 1989. John scored a goal for United in that match. He was transferred to St Johnstone on 2 August 1994, for a reported fee of £100,000.

Michael O'Neill, born in Portadown, Ireland, on 5 July 1969. On 14 October 1987, United failed in a bid to bring him to Tannadice for £80,000. The player decided to sign for Newcastle. United had to wait until 14 August 1989 before they signed him from Newcastle United for a reported fee of £350,000. Michael made his debut at Tannadice on 16 August 1989 in a Skol Cup Tie against Partick Thistle. He scored his first goal for the club in that match. The player spent four seasons with the club, but his potential failed to materialise. On 20 August 1993, Hibs manager Alex Miller signed him for £245,000. Then he moved onto Coventry City three years later. On 31 December 1997, soon after Alex Miller was appointed to manage Aberdeen, he attempted to sign him again. However, they agreed that O'Neill would be on loan to the club for a period of three months. Michael left Aberdeen on 2 March 1998, and went on loan to Reading.

Sean O'Neill, was a former player with Leeds United and Chesterfield. Ivan Golac appointed him team coach on 16 July 1993.

Orchison, played for Brechin and Forfar and turned out for United on 14 April 1934 against Dundee at Dens in the Penman Cup.

Gibby Ormond, signed from Airdrie on 25 February 1960 by manager Jerry Kerr. The player made his first team debut on 27 February 1960, against Albion Rovers; the score that day: 4-1 for United. He made his home debut at Tannadice on 5 March 1960 against Hamilton. Gibby was a member of the promotion-winning side of 1960 when United beat Berwick Rangers 1-0 on 30 April 1960, and secured a place in the First Division. The club freed the player in May 1962. His late brother, Willie, became manager of St Johnstone on 24 March 1967. Willie was Scotland's manager for the 1974 World Cup campaign. In the 1980s, Gibby was working as a scout for Rangers.

Hugh Ormond, signed by manager Willie MacFadyen on a free from St Mirren. Hugh made his Tannadice debut on 11 November 1950 against Dundee reserves. The player then made his first team debut on 9 December 1950 in the 3-2 win over Queen's Park at Tannadice.

Peter And Michael O'Rourke, were the sons of Dundee Hibs manager Peter. Their father signed them to the club in the 1920s.

Osborne, played for Leicester City and guested for United on 1 January 1944 against Aberdeen.

Jacky Osborne, played for Lochee Central, and played for the club as a trialist in a game against East Fife on 20 September 1924. The game ended with a 1-0 win for United, and Jacky was signed after the game. His first game as a signed player was on 27 September 1924 in a 2-2 draw with Bathgate. While he was with United, he appeared in 29 games. In October 1930, Jacky was playing for Brechin City.

Willie Oswald, played for Dundee Celtic and played his first trial game for Dundee Hibs on 29 April 1922 against Armadale at Tannadice. Willie scored two of the goals in the 4-1 victory that day. The player was with the club when they became Dundee United. After finishing with United, he went off to America to play football there in 1928, and settled in Massachusetts. When he returned to Scotland, he went to work in the engineering industry.

Kinnaird Ouchterlonie, signed by manager Willie MacFadyen on 3 September 1948 for a trial period of two months. He made his United debut on 4 September 1948 against St Johnstone reserves. Prior to signing for United, Kinnaird had played for Dundee and Ayr United. Kinnaird was freed by United a short time later.

Willie Ouchterlonie, played for junior side Osborne, and featured in several United first team games from 1932-34. He signed for Raith Rovers on 26 June 1934, and released by them in April 1935. On 16 May 1935 he signed for Irish club Portadown.

Mixu Paatelainen, was born in Helsinki on 3 February 1967, and signed for the club on 30 October 1987 from Valkeakosken Haka for a reported fee of £100,000. He made his Tannadice debut on 31 October 1987 against St Mirren at Tannadice. The score that day was United 2 St Mirren 3, with the player scoring on his debut, before a crowd of 7,607. Mixu soon became a favourite at Tannadice and was in the 1988 Scottish Cup squad beaten by Celtic 2-1.

On 28 March 1992, United transferred him to Aberdeen for a fee of £400,000. By 1994, the player was off to Bolton Wanderers. Then he joined Wolves in 1997 for £200,000. He joined Hibs in September 1998.

Emilio Pacione, signed by manager Willie MacFadyen on 3 November 1945 from Lochee Harp. His first senior game for United was on 20 October 1945 when he guested for the club against Stenhousemuir at Tannadice. It was a memorable day for the player as he scored one of the goals in the 7-0 win. Emilio played for the club from 1946 until 1950. When United freed him, Emilio was signed for Coleraine by former Hibs and United centre-forward Arthur Milne. Emilio stayed in Ireland for two months and then came back to Scotland. He then signed for Brechin City. His brother, Sid, played for Hibs and Aberdeen. Sid signed for Hibs on 14 July 1945. He later went on to become a PE Instructor at St Michael's Secondary.

Jimmy Page, joined United from Celtic Boys. Along with club mate John Clark, they were included in Scotland's Under-18 pool that met Wales on 15 February 1983. Jimmy made his first team debut on 28 April 1984 in a game against Motherwell. However, his debut turned out to be a bit of a disaster for him because he broke his leg in the second minute of the game.

Michel Pageau, played in goal for the club's reserve side in January 1994. On 26 February 1994, he was signed by Dundee for a reported fee of £80,000. The keeper left Dundee during the close season of 1996-97, and joined his old French club Valenciennes.

Alec Palmer, signed by manager Willie MacFadyen on 11 August 1948 on a free from Third Lanark. At the start of season 1949-50, he was playing for Clyde's C. Division side. In May 1951, he finished the season with Airdrie.

G. Parker, made two appearances for Dundee Hibs during season 1912-13.

T. Parker, was on Celtic's playing list before joining United on 16 March 1928, he had also played for Bathgate. The player made his United debut on 17 March 1928 in the 4-3 win over Third Lanark at Tannadice. While he was with the club, he featured in three league games and scored once.

Bill Paterson, signed by manager Jimmy Brownlie in June 1925 from Dunfermline Athletic. The goalkeeper had been playing in the United States before he signed for United. Bill made his United debut on 15 August 1925 against Raith Rovers. Between seasons 1925-1928 Bill made 77 appearances for the club. On 17 January 1928 United transferred Bill to Arsenal. Bill was transferred from Arsenal to Airdrie in July 1929. He returned to Tannadice in 1932 to

THE PLAYERS

help out in goal for the club. Bill featured in only a limited amount of games.

Jim Paterson, born in Belshill on 25 September 1979. Jim was handed a starting line place in the United lineup in a friendly game against Wolves at Tannadice on 19 July 1997. Manager Tommy McLean decided to reward the young man for all his work in the reserves.

Neil Paterson, was an author and signed as an amateur player on 1 July 1936 from Leith Athletic. He made his United debut on 8 August 1936 in the 4-2 win over King's Park. While he was with the club, he appeared in 26 league games and scored nine goals. In January 1960, Hollywood awarded him a scroll that recognised him as being one of the famous five of Filmdom's Screenwriters for the Past Year. This was in recognition for his work on John Braine's movie *A Room at the Top.*

Darren Patterson, signed by manager Tommy McLean on 10 July 1998 from Luton Town under the freedom of contract ruling. The Northen Ireland internationalist was signed on a three-year contract by the club. At the time of signing he had gained 17 caps for his country.

George Pattie, provisionally signed by manager Jerry Kerr on 3 April 1962, from Blairgowrie Juniors. George played in a trial match against Rangers at Ibrox on 4 April 1962. He made his first team debut for the club on 23 April 1962, against Partick Thistle at Firhill. George was given a free from the club in May 1963. The player signed for Brechin, and was playing for them in 1964.

Graeme Payne, born in Dundee in 1956, and made his first team debut on 11 August 1973, at the age of 17. This was in a League Cup tie against East Fife which United won 2-1 at Methil. A year later he was to feature in the Scottish Cup Final team. Sadly, the team was beaten 3-0 by Celtic. On 30 December 1982, Graeme left Tannadice on loan to Morton. Also included in the deal was Ian Gibson on loan. In return, United got John McNeil on loan. He returned to United in June 1983 along with Ian Gibson. However, Arbroath eventually signed the player in May 1984 for a fee of £5,000. On 28th March 1985, Graeme moved from Arbroath and joined Brechin City.

Jacky Peat, played centre-forward for Leith Athletic, and played for Cowdenbeath. Jacky signed for United in February 1954, and made his debut for United on 13 February 1954. This game was against Falkirk in the third round of the Second XI Cup, played at Tannadice.

Erik Pedersen, was born in Porsgrunn, Norway, on 11 October 1967. Erik arrived at Tannadice for a trial period on 23 October 1996 and made his debut on 26 October 1996 against Hearts. They listed

him in the first team lines as a trialist. The midfield-defender signed for United on 1 November 1996, from Viking F.K. International Honours include: Full Caps – 10, B-Caps – 1, Under-21 Caps – 10. Eric is married and has two children, and his wife thoroughly enjoys living in Dundee. His favourite games have been against Rangers, and he loves to turn out for United each week. He also enjoy his rapport with the fans. His hobbies include golf and fishing and he enjoys his family life in Scotland. Before he joined United he was working as an electronics engineer. He also enjoys coaching the younger kids and had his own football coaching school in Norway.

Bob Penman, signed by manager Reggie Smith on 23 March 1955 from Jeanfield Swifts. Bob made his first team debut on 17 August 1955 against Motherwell at Fir Park.

Willie Penman, joined United on 14 December 1955 on a free from Montrose. Willie had played with Raith Rovers for 11 seasons and then transferred to Montrose in 1953. The player made his first team debut for United on 17 December 1955 against Berwick Rangers. Willie was freed by United in April 1956.

Frank Penson, signed by manager Jimmy Brownlie on 8 August 1930 from Fairfield. Frank made his United debut on 9 August 1930 against Armadale. He was freed by United in April 1933.

Perriam, played as a War guest for United on 4 September 1943 against Dunfermline at East End Park. At the time the player had been playing for Huddersfield.

Orjan Persson, born in 1942, and signed by manager Jerry Kerr on 2 December 1964 from Orgryte Sweden. There was no fee involved in bringing the player to Scotland. Persson was the first internationalist and foreign player to join the club. He made his club debut on 5 December 1964, against Hearts at Tynecastle. United lost 3-1 that day. He played his last game for the club on 3 May 1967 in a game against Celtic. On 3 August 1967, United transferred the left winger to Rangers. Included in the deal were Wilson Wood and Davie Wilson who made their way to Tannadice. His first game for the Ibrox outfit was on 9 August 1967, against Eintracht Frankfurt. Persson had appeared nine times for the Swedish national side.

Mark Perry, was born in Aberdeen on 5 February 1971, and signed from Cove Rangers on 3 August 1988. Mark made his club debut on 12 December 1992 against Aberdeen. On 18 October 1997, Perry made his 100th appearance for the club in a game against Motherwell. On 2 July 1998, Mark was signed to Aberdeen by manager Alec Miller.

Gordan Petric, born in Belgrade on 30 July 1969. The player was signed by Ivan Golac on 17 November 1993 for a reported fee of 750,000 paid to Partizan Belgrade. Golac had previously worked with Petric when he was manager of Partizan. He made his debut on 20 November 1993, in a game against Motherwell at Fir Park. In 1994, he played in the winning Scottish Cup Final team. After some poor performances, United sold Petric to Rangers on 26 July 1995, for a reputed fee of £1.5 million.

Peters, signed by manager Willie MacFadyen during close season of 1947-48 from Stobswell.

Willie Pettigrew, born in 1953. In September 1972, Willie was playing for East Kilbride Thistle and was beginning to come to the attention of the senior clubs in Scotland. The high scoring forward was signed by Jim McLean in August 1979, from Motherwell. The fee was £100,000. He made his debut on 11 August 1979 against Dundee.

Within three months of joining the club, Pettigrew found himself in the League Cup Final, and scored twice. On 12 December 1979, with the help of Pettigrew, United had their first major trophy. In 1980, he again won a League Cup medal after the team beat Dundee 3-0 in the final. He was also a member of the 1981 Scottish Cup Final side. On 18 September 1981, Billy, along with Derek Addison, were transferred to Hearts. They reported the transfer fee for both players was £180,000.

Ian Phillip, born on 14 February 1951, and joined the club on 29 November 1978 for a fee of £25,000 paid to Dundee. The player also has the distinction of playing for both city clubs. Playing first at Dens Park, he made his first team debut on 25 November 1969 against Falkirk in the Dewar Shield Semi-Final replay at Brockville. He was eventually sold to Crystal Palace in 1972 for a fee of £72,500. Within a year he was back at Dens. The player made his debut against Celtic on 16 December 1978. He came on as a sub and the game ended in a 1-1 draw. Phillip stayed with United for five years before signing for Raith Rovers. He was part of the League Cup winning teams of 1979 and 1980. A Scottish Cup finalist in 1981, and a League Cup finalist in 1981.On 8 May 1986, Raith freed him. Ian is now employed as a civil servant working for the DSS in Dundee.

Jose Luis Pochettino, signed for the club on 27 March 1992. Jose had played for the Mexican First Division side Cobras. The player made his debut in a reserve game against Montrose at Gussie Park on 30 March 1992. On the 3 April 1992, he made his first team debut at Tannadice in a game against St Johnstone.

Jim Porter, signed by Dundee Hibs manager Jimmy Brownlie in 1923 from Hearts. Jim made his debut for the club on 15 August 1923 against St Johnstone. A few months after he signed, the club changed its name to United. Jim played in 39 league games and scored twice. On 1 December 1924 he was given a free transfer by the club.

Philip Prain, was 15 years old when manager Jerry Kerr took him onto the ground staff on 25 August 1966. The schoolboy had previously spent two weeks guesting with Peterborough United before signing. The club cancelled Philip's registration papers on 27 November 1967. This allowed him to return to Peterborough.

Steven Pressley, born 11 October 1973, in Elgin. Manager Billy Kirkwood signed him for United on 25 July 1995 from Coventry City, and he soon became a very polished player. Steven made his first team debut on 29 July 1995, in a friendly game against Brechin at Glebe Park. He made his First Division debut on 12 August 1995, in a game against Morton at Tannadice. The player was a former Under-21 internationalist winning 26 caps. The former Rangers player had spent four seasons with them after signing from Inverkeithing Boys Club. On 1 July 1998, after he was offered a lucrative contract by United, Steven, who was by then out of contract, chose to sign for Hearts

Alan Preston, from Edinburgh, was called up as a full time player in 1985. He made his first team debut on 7 May 1988 in a match at Tannadice against Hearts. The player came on as a sub that day. Final score was United 0 Hearts 0. The crowd that day was 9,820. On 1 October 1992, he was transferred to Hearts in a deal that saw Hearts player Scott Crabbe joining United. Crabbe had signed to United for a reported fee of £215,000. Later the player signed for Dunfermline, and then transferred to St Johnstone.

Terry Preston, signed by manager Jerry Kerr in December 1964, from Tranent Juniors. Terry made his debut with the club in a reserve game on 23 December 1964, against Partick Thistle at Tannadice. In May 1966 he was freed by the club.

Peter Prior, was given a month's trial by the club on 11 December 1959. Peter joined Raith in December 1958. The player made his first team United debut on 12 December 1959 in the 1-0 victory over Falkirk at Tannadice. Later he joined Hamilton, and was freed by them on 2 May 1961. In August 1961, he joined his old club Fauldhouse United.

Pat Purcell, signed for the club in season 1967-68. Pat made one league appearance on 9 September 1967 against St Johnstone. The result was 2-2. The player was freed by the club in April 1968.

Frank Quinn, born in 1926, and joined United on 18 August 1948 from Celtic on a free transfer. Frank made his United debut on 18 August 1948 in a reserve game at East End Park against Dunfermline. United won 5-4 with Frank scoring a hat-trick. He made his first team home debut for the club on 23 October 1948 against Arbroath. The former Celtic player scored 90 goals for the club and made 157 Scottish League appearances. Frank featured in 196 League and Cup games with United and scored 107 goals. In 1954, he left the club and signed for Hamilton Accies. He left Hamilton after a season and then finished off his career with Cowdenbeath.

Henry Quinn, joined United on a two-month trial period on 24 July 1967. Clyde had recently released Henry. His previous clubs included Celtic and St Mirren.

Jack Qusklay, joined United in August 1927, and was club trainer. Jack left United, and became Celtic's trainer on 1 May 1932. He resigned from this position in December 1934. Then he officially joined Dundee on 1 July 1935, and retired in 1936. For several years after the war, he was chief sports officer at Dundee University.

George Radcliffe, signed by manager Willie Reid from Albion Rovers in July 1931. The player signed for Falkirk in January 1932. While he was at Tannadice, George played in 15 league games and scored one goal.

Ally Rae, signed by manager Tommy Gray on 21 March 1958 on a free from St Johnstone. He made his first team United debut on 22 March 1958 in the 3-0 victory over Hamilton at Tannadice. Ally was freed by United in April 1959.

David Rae, freed by the club in the close season of 1977. Benny Rooney, the Morton manager signed him on 11 June 1977.

Jock Rae, signed for Dundee Hibs on 26 January 1922 from Albion Rovers. Jock made his debut on 28 January 1922 against Broxburn United at Tannadice. During season 1921-22 Jock turned out for the club on 13 occasions and scored one goal.

Len Rae, signed by manager Willie MacFadyen on 22 March 1946 from Inverurie Locos. The player had provisionally signed for Aberdeen in 1937.

Johnny Raeburn, went on trial with United in February 1953. At that time he had been playing for Lochgelly Albert. Johnny played in United's first team on 14 February 1953 against Hamilton, and he scored the only goal in the game.

Archibald Ralston, signed to United by manager Jimmy Brownlie on 11 August 1927 from Law Scotia (Lanarkshire.) He made his United debut on 13 August 1927 in the 4-2 victory over Bathgate at Tannadice. While he was with United, he featured in seven games and scored four goals for the club.

Ramsay, from Brechin City, played in the first ever Dundee Hibs fixture. They played this match on Wednesday 18 August 1909 at Tannadice. It ended in a 1-1 draw against Edinburgh Hibernian.

Billy Ramsay, was the club's physiotherapist in the 1980s taking over the position after Andy Dickson retired. He had previously worked with Airdrie FC.

Brian Rankin, was signed by Jim McLean in November 1971, from Vale of Clyde. He was the nephew of Tannadice favourite Dennis Gillespie. Rankin made a number of first team appearances after signing. The player was just beginning to breakthrough to the first team by December 1973. However, they transferred him to Hamilton on 20 November 1974.

John Reddington, signed by Jerry Kerr on 26 April 1963 from Lochore Welfare. He was called up by the club on 29 July 1963, the day the players returned from their break.

Ian Redford, signed to Dundee from Errol Rovers in 1973. Redford signed for Rangers in 1980 for £210,000. Ian made his first appearance for the Ibrox outfit on 5 April 1980 in a game against his former club. He signed for United on 15 August 1985 for a reported fee of £75,000. The player made his United debut on 17 August 1985 in a 1-1 draw with Aberdeen at Tannadice. Ian signed for Ipswich Town on for a reported £200,000 on 14 November 1988. Their manager was ex Dundee player John Duncan. He signed for St Johnstone on 6 August 1991 for a fee of £60,000 paid to Ipswich. Ian, who was appointed player-manager with Brechin on 19 June 1993, quit as manager on 15 August 1994. Within days of his resignation he signed for Raith Rovers. He made his debut with them on 27 August 1994, against Dunfermline.

Alec Reid, born on 2 March 1947, joined the club on 3 July 1968. The player signed by Jerry Kerr previously played for Rangers. He joined Rangers from Glasgow Perthshire in 1964. Alec made his United debut in a League Cup tie against Dunfermline on 10 August 1968 at East End Park. In October 1971, Reid was involved in a swap deal that saw him move to Newcastle, and Ian Mitchell returning to Tannadice. Reid had played 113 games for United, and scored 15 goals. Reid left Newcastle in November 1972, and then signed to Greenock Morton. He signed for Ayr in 1976 for £7,000. Reid had played only two games with them when he injured his knee and was forced to quit the game.

Bobby Reid, joined United from Arbroath on 23 January 1963. The goalkeeper signed to Arbroath from Swansea in September 1960. In June 1964, United transferred him to Raith Rovers. The goalkeeper did not feature in any first team games while he was at Tannadice.

Dave Reid, signed for United by manager Jerry Kerr in October 1960. Dave made his first team debut on 15 October 1960, in the 2-0 victory over Raith Rovers at Stark's Park.

Donovan Reid, signed provisionally for the club on 2 September 1935 by manager Jimmy Brownlie. At the time of signing, the young man was playing for Aberdeen East End. Don made his United debut on 7 September 1935 against Falkirk at Tannadice. While he was with the club, he featured in 23 league games and scored four goals. Don re-signed for United on 15 July 1938. In his second spell with United he played in nine league games and scored one goal.

Ian Reid, played for Drumchapel Amateurs and Queen of the South. Signed by manager Jerry Kerr in 1970, arrived from Nottingham Forest.

James Reid I, played in a first team trial on 26 March 1955 against Hamilton at Tannadice. Jimmy was just 18 years old when he had this trial, and he had been playing for junior side St Joseph's. He also played for East Fife, and was transferred to Bury on 24 January 1957. Jimmy was re-signed to United in June 1959 from Stockport. In December 1959 he signed for East Fife. The player signed for Arbroath on 12 September 1960.

James Reid II, played in goal for junior side Brechin Vics. James turned out as a guest for United on 2 January 1946 in the 4-1 win over Dumbarton at Tannadice.

Lomond Reid, signed as a War guest for United on 16 September 1941 from Leith Athletic. The player made his United debut on 19 September 1941 against Dunfermline at Tannadice.

Walter Reid, played for St Mirren and Stirling Albion, before signing for United. He made his home debut on 1 December 1951 in a reserve game against Montrose.

Willie Reid II, signed by manager Jimmy Brownlie on 25 May 1936 from Aberdeen. He had joined the Don's from junior club Hall Russell during the close season of 1934-35. The player made his United debut on 8 August 1936 in the 4-2 victory over King's Park.

Willie was freed by United on 29 October 1936 at his own personal request. He signed for Forfar on 27 January 1937 and made his debut for them on 6 February 1937 against Leith Athletic at Station Park. He later signed for Hibs, however, he was freed by them in April 1938.

Jed Reilly, goalkeeper, was signed by Jerry Kerr in September 1969 from Montrose. Reilly was playing for North End juniors when signed for Meadowbank Thistle on 6 September 1978.

John Reilly, born in Dundee in 1962, and signed an S-form for the club on 28 January 1977. At the time he was attending Linlathen High School and playing for Tayside Boys Club. The player was given his first reserve outing on 3 April 1979 in a game against Hearts. As a player he never really broke through into ranks of first team football. In August 1985, United transferred him to Motherwell for a reported fee of £50,000. However, a serious injury ruled him out of football for some time. The player then received some revolutionary surgery that enabled him to resume his career at Motherwell. In 1991 he was transferred to Dunfermline. East Fife later signed the player, and he was appointed manager on 12 October 1993. He would later manage Cowdenbeath.

Alec Rennie, began his senior career with Rangers having signed for them from United Crossroads in June 1964. Rennie was freed by then and then signed for Stirling Albion in June 1967. On 28 October 1967, he joined St Johnstone in exchange for Bruce Munro. The player was with the club for eight years. He joined United in the close season of 1975 on a free transfer from St Johnstone. Rennie made his first appearance in a tangerine jersey on 28 July 1975 in a friendly game against Fraserburgh. They advised Alec to quit the game on 19 January 1979 after sustaining an eye injury in an accident during a match against Ayr United in 1978. Alec later became a coach with Hearts. On 24 April 1980, he became manager of St Johnstone after turning down an offer to become assistant manager with Hearts. In 1988 he was manager with Stenhousemuir.

J. B. Revell, played as a War guest for United. The goalkeeper played for Brighton.

John Reynolds, signed for United on 22 March 1979 on an s-form. The 16-year-old became a full-timer in season 1979-80.

Dave Richards, signed by Dundee Hibs manager Jimmy Brownlie in 1923 from Port Vale. Dave made his club debut on 15 August 1923 against St Johnstone. Shortly after he signed for the club they changed their name to United. While he was with the club, he played in 48 league games and scored three goals. On 1 June 1925 Dave was signed by Luton Town.

Andrew Richardson, signed for Dundee Hibs in November 1912 from junior side Blairgowrie. Andrew made his club debut on 7 December 1912 in the 1-1 draw with St Johnstone at Tannadice Park. During his spell with the club he played in two competitive matches and scored one goal.

William Richmond, signed by manager Jimmy Brownlie on 14 August 1928. The previous season he had been playing for Raith Rovers. William made his club debut on 15 August 1928 in the Dewar Shield Cup tie against East Stirlingshire at Tannadice.

Alistair Riddle, signed from Montrose in the early 1960s. United later transferred him back to them on 10 January 1963. On 26 January 1967, Montrose gave the player a free transfer.

R. Rintoul, played his first game for United on 17 January 1925 against Arthurlie. The player made his Tannadice debut on 24 January 1925 in the 5-1 win over Aberdeen University in the Scottish Cup. While he was with the club he played in three matches and scored one goal.

Dragutin Ristic, signed for United in July 1994. He played his first game for United on 20 July, in a friendly against Bayern Munich. This game was played in Malaysia when United were on tour in the close season of 1994. It ended in a 1-1 draw. Ristic made his Tannadice debut on 30 July in a game against the Australia Olympic XI. He made his Premier League debut on 13 August against Hibs at Easter Road. Hibernian won 5-0. Ivan Golac fined himself and his players £100 each for the trouncing.

Billy Ritchie, was playing for junior side Osborne when he played in a trial match for United on the opening day of the 1954 season. This was on 11 September 1954 against Stenhousemuir at Tannadice.

J. M. Ritchie, signed for Dundee Hibs on 28 April 1921 from Aberdeen. While he was with the club he played in 23 league games and scored twice.

John Ritchie, signed for the club on 22 April 1974 on a free transfer from Bradford City. The keeper had been with Bradford for three seasons.

Chick Robbie, was signed by manager Willie MacFadyen on 1 October 1952. Chick made his United debut on 4 October in a reserve game against Clyde at Tannadice. A crowd of 1,500 watched the United beat Clyde 3-0. Chick had previously played with St Johnstone and Brechin City.

A. Robertson, played for Y. M. Anchorage, and appeared for United in a first team game on 19 March 1938 against Stenhousemuir at Tannadice.

Albert Robertson, signed for United on 5 July 1937 from junior side East Craigie. During season 1937-38, he played in 21 league games and scored nine goals.

Bert Robertson, affectionately known as 'Doodles.' Bert stepped up from junior side Stobswell. He married an Australian girl during his service in the Second World War. Then after the war, he emigrated.

Charlie Robertson, signed by manager Tommy Gray on 27 September 1958. He joined the club after the manager was suitably impressed by his style of play in a trial match played at Tannadice against Stenhousemuir. His first game after he officially signed for the club was on 18 October against the Scottish Command at Tannadice. Charlie was freed by United during season 1959-60.

Ernest Robertson, was a director with the club and later became United's Chairman. He was also one of the oldest serving club directors in Scottish football. Ernest first joined the club in 1923 when they were known as Dundee Hibs. Chairman Jim McLean spoke about one of his most personal moments when the club won the League Cup for the first time in 1979.

Jim recalled the moment when he saw tears trickle dowm Mr Robertson's face as the team lifted the trophy. That personal memory will always be treasured by Jim. Ernest's association with Dundee United extended to over 50 years. It should also be noted that Ernest, on numerous occasions, wrote personal cheques to pay the United staff. These were paid out of his own pocket, and on most occasions he never told anyone about it. His contribution to Dundee United Football Club, and to Jim McLean, can never be fully documented. Until he retired, Ernest was the head of the family firm Robertson's Fruit Products Ltd. On 11 January 1982, Ernest died, he was 90 years old.

Hugh Robertson, turned out for United as a War guest on 2 December 1939 against Dunfermline at Tannadice. United won by 5-2.

Jimmy Robertson I, signed to United on 19 June 1939 from Wellesley Juniors. Jimmy had previously played in a couple of games in season 1938-39 before signing. The player made his debut on 12 August 1939 in a 3-2 win over Edinburgh City. He also played left-half for United in the War Cup Final against Rangers in 1940. In 1951, Jimmy became a scout for the club in the Fife area.

Jimmy Robertson II, made his debut for United on 18 August 1954 against Dunfermline at East End Park. The player had previously played for Plymouth Argyle.

John Robertson I, bought 50 shares in Dundee United Football Club in 1926. He later transferred the shares to his son Ernest, who then became a director and later chairman.

John Robertson II, played centre-half for Dundee Hibs, and played in the first ever Scottish League match that Dundee Hibs featured in. The game was played on 20 August 1910 against Leith Athletic. Dundee Hibs lost 3-2. While he was with the club, he played in 31 competitive matches. In November 1911, he was transferred to Ayr United and made his debut for them on 25 November 1911 against Leith Athletic.

Malcolm Robertson, signed for the club in season 1981-82.

Norman Robertson, signed by manager Jerry Kerr from Clackmanan Juniors. He was called up by United on 17 July 1968. However, the player did not last long at Tannadice and was freed in April 1969.

Peter Robertson, played in goal and signed by manager Jimmy Brownlie during the close season on 1934-35.

Sandy Robertson I, was a trainer with the club in the 1920s. After retiring from the game Sandy became a newsagent.

Sandy Robertson II, signed by Billy Kirkwood on 25 July 1995 from Coventry City. Sandy was signed at the same time as Steven Pressley. He made his debut for United in a friendly game at Brechin on 29 July, at Glebe Park. The player made his First Division debut on 12 August, against Morton at Tannadice. He was freed by the club on 13 May 1997.

Tommy Robertson, signed for United on 12 November 1954 by manager Reggie Smith. Tommy made his first team debut the following day against Dunfermline at East End Park.

Bobby Robinson, signed by Jim McLean in 1977 from Dundee for a reported fee of £14,000. Later the player signed for Hearts. He was released by them in the close season of 1980-81and he signed for Raith Rovers on 22 July 1981. Bobby was released by Raith on 12 May 1983. In April 1989, he came back to Tannadice to help play for the club's reserve team. Manager Jim McLean felt his experience would help his up and coming young stars. By the late 1980s, Bobby had been turning out for junior side Forfar Albion, and Coupar Angus. In December 1996, Bobby died after a long illness; he was just 46 years old.

Paddy & Peter Rock, along with Paddy Reilly, were founder members of Dundee Hibs.

John Roe, was released from Colchester United, and played in a trial game for United on 6 August 1960. Manager Kerr was suitably impressed, and signed John after that game. The player was given a free transfer from the club in May 1963.

Walter Rojas, signed for the club on 28 August 1991 from San Lorenzo. Rojas returned to Argentina in November 1991, failing to make the grade for Premier League football. He never featured in any first team games with the club.

Andy Rolland, born in 1943, and signed by manager Jerry Kerr in September 1967 from Cowdenbeath for a fee of £8,000. Andy made his first team debut on 30 September 1967 in the 2-0 defeat by Airdrie. On 28 November 1975 the player was suspended for breach of contract. The dispute was over Rolland's housing arrangements. Manager Jim McLean had insisted that all his players resided locally but Andy had moved his family out of the area and back to Glenrothes. The club lifted the suspension on 17 December when Andy agreed to stay in digs in the area. On 17 March 1976, Rolland was in the Scottish League pool that played England. Andy left Tannadice for the last time on 11 April 1978, and headed off to America. On 24 June 1978, he joined the Los Angeles Aztecs in a swop deal that saw George Best going to Fort Lauderdale. Andy returned to Scotland and was signed by

Dunfermline in season 1978-79 but rejoined Cowdenbeath on 2 November 1979. Andy became manager of Cowdenbeath in December 1980. In February 1982, Andy resigned as their manager after 14 months in charge. In September 1984, Andy became manager of Glenrothes juniors. In the 1990s, Andy was working for a telecommunications company in Fife.

George Rollo, signed by manager Jerry Kerr in September 1965, from Carnoustie Panmure. Before being signed he had played in two trial matches, one against Dundee and the other against St Johnstone. George played his first game after signing on 24 September against St Mirren at Tannadice. However, in May 1966 he was freed from the club. In 1975 he was a minister in Arbroath.

Gerry Ronald, signed to the club on a month's contract in the close season of 1987-88 from Clydebank. Gerry went on the Norwegian tour in the summer of that year, and played in a couple of friendly games. However, he did not feature in any of Jim McLean's plans and was released on 2 September 1987.

Rooney, signed for Falkirk from Strathclyde in season 1941-42. He temporarily signed for United as a War guest on 7 May 1942. He made his United debut on 9 May in the North-Eastern League Cup Semi-Final against Rangers. The player had the privilege of scoring United's first goal in the game in the 20th minute. The game ended in a 2-2 draw at Ibrox.

Benny Rooney, signed for the club on 6 June 1963 after he was freed by Celtic. He joined them from junior side Petershill in 1960. At the time of signing for United, his father, Bob, was a trainer at Celtic Park. He made his Scottish League Cup debut with United on 10 August 1963. This match was played against Aberdeen at Tannadice and ended 1-1. The player played his last game for United on 12 March 1966, in the 3-2 victory for Falkirk at Tannadice. Incidentally, that was the first time that Falkirk had beaten United at Tannadice in six and a half years. Benny left United on 14 March 1966, and joined St Johnstone. He made his debut for them on 19 March, in the 1-0 victory over Dundee at Muirton Park. He played his last game for the Saints on 15 September 1977 against Aberdeen at Muirton. He would later manage the club.

Bobby Ross, signed for United in 1945 from Crosshill. His United first team debut was on 10 August 1946 in a B-Division match against Dunfermline. Dundee United ran out 3-0 winners at

Tannadice. The player remained at Tannadice until he signed for Millwall on 14 August 1952. The last United player to be transferred to Millwall was Alec Jardine. After leaving them, Bobby returned to his native Fife. He ended his career with Cowdenbeath. Bobby died in April 1984, he was 58 years old.

George Ross I, signed by manager Jimmy Brownlie on 10 January 1929 from Dalkeith Thistle. The player made his United debut on 6 February 1929 in a Scottish Cup replay match against Stenhousemuir. It was a memorable debut for George as the side won 2-0. George was later transferred to Portsmouth in 1930. On 21 July 1933 he was re-signed to United by manager Willie Reid from Portsmouth. In May 1937 he signed to Leith Athletic.

George Ross II, of Forthill Athletic, played for United in a trial game against Cowdenbeath on 31 December 1938. He signed for United on 13 January 1939, and made his debut as a signed player on 14 January against Dunfermline at Tannadice. United paid £20 to Forthill for his services. After spending only a couple of months at Tannadice, he was then transferred to Hibs on 9 March 1939.

George Ross III, signed for United on 13 June 1939. He hailed from Glasgow and had played for Bradford City and Gillingham.

Jock Ross, signed by manager Jimmy Brownlie in July 1929 from Dundee. Jock made his United debut on 10 August 1929 in the 3-3 draw with Clyde at Tannadice. While he was with the club, he featured in 35 competitive games. He signed for Welsh club Connah's Quay on 18 August 1930.

John Ross, joined United at the beginning of season 1939-40, and played in only one game for the club before the Second World War began. John signed for Arbroath in March 1940, and made his Gayfield debut on 23 March against Dunfermline. On 5 July 1947 he signed for Montrose.

Robert Ross, played for Crosshill Hearts and signed for United on 6 January 1945. Robert made his first team debut for the club on the same day that he signed in a match against Rangers at Ibrox. The 19-year-old player made his Tannadice debut on 13 January 1945 in the 5-2 victory over Raith Rovers.

Sammy Ross, signed by manager Willie MacFadyen from Motherwell on 3 July 1946, for a fee of £340. MacFadyen had also appointed Ross as club captain. Sammy made his first team debut in a B-Division game against Dunfermline at Tannadice. It was a memorable debut for him as United ran out 3-0 winners. Sammy left United in October 1947.

Thomas Sharp Ross, signed to United by manager Jimmy Brownlie on 10 December 1934 from junior side Osborne. It was nearly three months before he made his first team debut for United on 30 March 1935 in the 4-0 win over East Stirling at Tannadice. Incidentally, United scored their 100th goal in this game for season 1934-35.

Joe Roy, joined Dundee FC from Clydebank juniors in July 1954. He was freed from Dundee in July 1956 and signed to Third Lanark, and released by them in April 1957. On 18 May 1957, he signed for United and played for a season. The doctors advised to retire from the game due to a knee injury and he did so on 16 October 1958.

Willie Rumbles, signed for United on 10 January 1938 on a free transfer from Brechin. The player made his United debut on 15 January against Forfar at Station Park. Willie played his last game for the club on 26 February 1938 in a 4-2 win over Alloa. He then emigrated to Australia. During his brief stay with United he featured in five league games and scored six goals.

Jimmy Russell, played for Rosslyn juniors and was signed to the club in 1924 by manager Jimmy Brownlie. While he was with United, he played in 17 league games and scored six goals. Later Jimmy played for Raith Rovers.

Vic Ruse, signed for Dundee on 27 September 1944. The player made his debut for the Dens park side on 30 September against Hearts. Vic played for United as a War guest and had a spell with Raith Rovers. He signed for Arbroath, joining them in February 1948. He was the cousin of Hollywood actresses Olivia de Havilland and her sister Joan Fontaine.

Jimmy Salmond, played for United as a War guest. In October 1946 he was playing for Brechin City.

Johnny Samuel, signed for United in May 1953 by manager Willie MacFadyen from Third Lanark. Previously he had played for Morton and Meadowbank. He made his first team debut for United on 8 August 1953 against one of his old clubs, Morton.

Willie Savage, was recruited as a War guest for the club in October 1943 from Queen of the South. His first game in United colours was on 30 October 1943 against an RAF Select side.

Ernest Schofield, was fixed up by United as a War guest on 10 December 1942, from Sheffield Wednesday. The player made his debut on 12 December 1942 against ITC at Muirton Park.

Dick Scott, played for Lochee Harp, and signed to United in January 1945. The player made his United debut on 13 January 1945 in the 5-2 win over Raith Rovers at Tannadice.

Ian Scott I, born in 1946. The club freed Ian on 10th April 1971, having joined in 1966 from Mussleburgh Athletic. Ian made his first team debut on 22 April 1967 against Partick Thistle, the game ending 2-2 at Tannadice. He played 57 league and cup games, and scored 18 goals. One week after he was freed, he joined Dundee FC.

Ian Scott II, signed by manager Tommy Gray in September 1958 from Brechin. The player made his first team debut for United on 27 September in a 5-2 victory over Stenhousemuir at Tannadice. The player was freed by the club in April 1959.

Jocky Scott, signed for Dundee on 5 August 1964 and made his debut on 26 August. Scott was with Dundee for 11 years, joining them as a 16 year old from Chelsea. He was transferred to his hometown of Aberdeen in August 1975. On 23 November 1977 he again joined Dundee, signed by Manager Tommy Gemmell.

On 19 June 1986 he started his managerial career by succeeding Archie Knox at Dundee, who had left to become assistant manager at Aberdeen. On 1 June 1988 he resigned as manager and was succeeded by Dave Smith, appointed by Chairman, Angus Cook. The merry-go-round continued and soon afterwards Jocky became manager of Aberdeen, taking over from Ian Porterfield. Later, on 20 September 1991; he became manager of Dunfermline Athletic, only to lose his job when he was dismissed on 19 May 1993.

It was on to Arbroath as manager in January 1994, but he resigned the position on 13 April 1994. In 1996, he became manager of Hibs, and one of his first signings was Rab Shannon from United for a fee of £90,000

On 29 September 1997, Jocky joined the coaching staff at Dundee United. However, Jocky Scott again became manager of Dundee when he was appointed to the position on 9 February 1998.

John Scott I, signed for United on 28 March 1952 from Cowdenbeath, joining them from Third Lanark. John made his first team debut on 29 March 1952 against Dumbarton at Boghead.

John Scott II, signed by manager Jerry Kerr in October 1959. The 17-year-old had been playing for junior side St Joseph's. His senior career with United began in a reserve game against Queen of the South on 17 October. John made his first team debut on 25 November against Arbroath at Tannadice. This was in the First round of the Forfarshire Cup.

Richard Scott, signed for United in December 1944 from Lochee Harp. Richard had previously played for Glasgow Parkhead in season 1938-39.

Alf Scrimgeour, played for Stobswell juniors. The centre-forward was on United's books in 1954-55. In November 1977, he was a coach with Dundee Violet.

Dave Scrimgeour, played for Dundee Hibs and was later transferred to Portsmouth on 21 April 1913. While he was with the club, he played in 28 games and scored eight goals.

Finn Seeman, signed by Jerry Kerr on 24 October 1965. He made his first team debut on 27 October against Rangers at Ibrox. His home debut match was played on 30 October, in the 4-2 win over Morton. Finn played his last game for the club on 20 April 1967 against Dunfermline. He was transferred to DWS Amsterdam for £25,000 in July 1967.

Frank Sergeant, played for Tottenham Hotspur, and joined United as a War guest. Frank made his United debut on 21 February 1942 against Dunfermline at East End Park.

Joe Shandley, played in a trial game for the club on 11 August 1925 at Rockwell Park. His previous club was Queen of the South. Joe made his United debut on 26 August 1925 in a match against Dundee in the Penman Cup at Dens Park. While he was with United he featured in two games and scored one goal. On 13 February 1926 he turned out for Dundee in a Second XI Cup tie against Aberdeen at Pittodrie.

Rab Shannon, signed by Billy Kirkwood on 3 July 1995 from Motherwell. Rab made his First Division debut on 12 August, in a game against Morton at Tannadice. He was transferred to Hibs for £90,000 on 15 November 1996.

James Sharp, received permission from his club Chelsea to turn out as a guest player for Dundee Hibs. He played on 11 September 1915 against Bathgate at Tannadice. James made his last appearance for the club on 1 April 1916, in the Forfarshire Cup Final against Montrose at Dens Park. Shortly afterwards he joined the Black Watch.

Alec Shaw, signed by manager Willie Macfadyen in February 1950, from junior side Strathclyde. He made his first team debut on 18 February 1950 in the 3-0 victory over Forfar at Station Park. Alec made his home debut for United on 25 February 1950 in the 2-2 draw with Morton.

Robert Shaw, signed for United on 9 December 1950, on a free transfer from Alloa. Robert made his first team debut on 16 December 1950 in a C. Division game against his old club.

John Shearer, was signed from Airdrie on 12 December 1953, and played in United's first team the same day against Albion Rovers. John made his Tannadice debut on 23 December against Stenhousemuir.

James Sheridan, played for Dundee Hibs in 1910. The club was fined £1 because he was still a registered player with his former club Alloa when he turned out for United. He had played as an amateur and the club had paid him a fee, which they should not have done. On 30 April 1910 the Emergency Committee suspended the player for his involvement until 1 January 1911.

Bob Sherry, joined United as an amateur player by manager Willie MacFadyen on 23 June 1949. The previous season Bob had been playing for Kilmarnock, and before that he had a spell with Queen's Park. Bob made his United debut in a C-Division game against Montrose reserves at Tannadice on 13 August 1949. He made his first team debut on 20 August against Arbroath at Gayfield.

Alec Shirley, signed by manager Charlie McGillivary on 17 May 1945 from Arbroath. Alec made his United debut on 19 May in the first round tie of the Mitchell Cup against Falkirk at Tannadice. United ran out winners by 3-2.

Frank Shufflebottom, played for Nottingham Forest, Raith Rovers, and Kilmarnock. Frank turned out for United as a War guest, and he played in several first team games for the club. The player made his first appearance in a United shirt on 8 September 1945 against Dundee at Dens Park.

Eric Sibley, received permission from his club, Blackpool, to turn out as a War guest for United on 17 July 1941. At the time, Eric was stationed close to Dundee with the RAF.

George Sievwright, signed from Broughty Athletic, and gave up his job as a baker to become a full-time player at Tannadice. George made his first team debut on 14 October 1961, against St Mirren at Tannadice, United winning 3-1. The player was freed by the club in May 1963. On 11 June 1963, he signed for Luton Town. On 30 April 1964, Luton placed him on the transfer list.

Albert Simmons, played for Arnot, and turned out as a War guest for United on 6 March 1943 against Hibs at Tannadice. On 8 March 1943, he was signed by United as a fully-fledged player. Albert was 17 years old at the time of signing.

David Simpson, was club secretary of Dundee Hibs, and remained on the board after several prominent business people invested in the club in 1922. New board members were James Dickson, William Hutchison who became club chairman, William Hogg and William Burke Junior.

Jimmy Simpson, born in 1908, in Ladybank, Fife. Manager Jimmy Brownlie signed the player from Newburgh West End, on 13 August 1925. He was also a schoolboy Internationalist when he played for Morgan Academy. Jimmy had also previously played for Auchtermuchty Bellvue in 1923. On 15 August 1925 he made his debut for United against Raith Rovers. He remained with United for two years before he signed for Rangers on 12 May 1927, for a fee of £1,000. This took place after the club was relegated. During a fine career with Rangers, Simpson went on to play for Scotland. He played at international level on 14 occasions, playing his first game against England at Hampden in 1935. Scotland won 2-0. Jimmy returned to play for United as a War guest on 9 August 1941. This was in the opening match of the newly-formed North Eastern-League, against East Fife, and ended 1-1. In 1946, he became manager of Buckie Thistle. Later he became manager of Alloa in December 1947 and remained there for two years. After retiring from the game, Jimmy went into the licenced trade in the west coast. His son, Ronnie, played for Celtic and also gained five caps for his country. Ronnie played in Celtic's European Cup winning side in 1967. Jimmy Simpson died in 1972.

John Simpson, signed by manager McKay on 9 August 1939 from St Monance Swifts. John made his United debut on 12 August 1939 in the 3-2 win over Edinburgh City. This game was played one month before the outbreak of the Second World War.

Robert Simpson, played in a trial match for the club on 3 August 1946. After the game, manager Willie MacFadyen signed the player who had previously played for Hull City. Robert made his United debut as a signed player on 10 August 1946. This match was against Dunfermline with United winning 3-0. Robert was freed by the club in May 1949.

Ronnie Simpson, signed for United in June 1962 from Armadale. The 5ft 4in tall player had also played for Greengairs United. The player gave up an engineering apprenticeship to go full-time with the club.

He made his first team debut on 5 October 1963, in a game against Airdrie at Tannadice. United won 9-1. Ronnie was freed by the club in May 1964. (Not to be confused with the Celtic goal-keeper of the same name.)

Tommy Simpson I, played for junior side Osborne, and made his club debut for United on 2 January 1924 against Alloa at Tannadice. Between seasons 1924-1927 he featured in 101 games and scored 14 goals. In season 1927-28, Tommy played for New Brighton.

Tommy Simpson II, signed to the club in December 1954 by manager Reggie Smith. Tommy made his debut for United on 18 December 1954 against Forfar at Tannadice.

Davie Sinclair, born in Dunfermline on 6 October 1969. The player also spent six years with Raith Rovers and gained a League Cup Winners medal after the shock win against Celtic. Former clubs included Kelty Under-21's, and a loan spell with Portadown. Signed by manager Tommy McLean on 31 January 1997 for £90,000, the 27-year-old made his first team debut on 8 February 1997, when he came off the subs bench in a 0-0 game against Hibs at Tannadice.

Malcolm Sinclair, signed by manager Willie MacFadyen on 14 October 1947 on a free transfer from Falkirk. He had turned senior in 1938 with Third Lanark, then transferred to Falkirk for a fee of £1,500. Malcolm made his first team debut for United on 18 October against Dumbarton at Tannadice.

Singleton, turned out for United as a War guest. The player made his debut on 14 August 1942 against Hearts.

Dave Skelligan, was a hard-hitting defender who was signed for the club on 13 June 1935 by manager Jimmy Brownlie from Brechin City. He made his first team debut on 10 August against St Bernard's at Tannadice. Dave was also a team member when the club lost 5-0 to East Fife in the Scottish Cup game played on 12 February 1938. Previous clubs included Dundee and Montrose. In 1967, after retiring from the game, Dave went to work in Dundee Royal Infirmary. He retired from the hospital in February 1974.

Billy Skinner, became a full time player in September 1983. However, he became homesick and returned to the Highlands. Dundee United then farmed out the 16-year-old to Inverness Thistle.

Magnus Skoldmark, born 22 September 1968, in Langsele. Magnus was signed from a Chinese club Dailen Wanda, by Tommy McLean on 18 September 1997. The Swedish internationalist made his first

team debut on 20 September against Hearts. Magnus had spent seven seasons with Orebro. He had previously played with another Tannadice favourite Lars Zetterland. While he was playing with the Chinese side, he picked up a Championship medal.

Ian Smart, turned out for United as a War guest on 16 August 1941 against St Bernard's, the game ending in a 4-1 victory for United. Ian played for the club from 1946-52.

When he first signed for United, they farmed him out to junior side Dundee Violet and first team debut was on 20 August 1946, in a League Cup tie against Stenhousemuir at Ochilview. His last appearance with United was on 14 April 1952, when the side lost

3-2 to Falkirk at Tannadice. The player was freed shortly after that game. Ian played in various positions with United. He played nine times at right-back, 62 times at left-back, eight times as a centre-forward, once at outside-right and 35 times at outside-left. As well as playing for United, Ian was also a schoolteacher in the city. While he was at Tannadice, Ian played in 97 games, and scored ten goals.

Harry Smillie, signed by manager Jimmy Brownlie for Dundee Hibs on 22 January 1923 from St Johnstone. Harry had previously played for Hearts and Yoker Athletic. The player made his club debut on 24 January against Nithsdale Wanderers, in the second round of the Scottish Cup at Tannadice.

A. Arrick Smith, retired from the United Board of Directors 14 November 1940. United Chairman Will McCutcheon presented him with a clock to mark his retirement.

Alec Smith, signed by United in the close season on 1959-60, from Frances Colliery. The 22-year-old was freed by United on 29 April 1961.

Archie Smith, signed by manager Willie MacFadyen in May 1953, and made his first team debut on 22 August against Morton. His previous club was East Fife.

Barney Smith, played for Edinburgh Hibs and turned out for Dundee Hibs on 3 September 1921 against East Stirling at Tannadice. Barney made his first appearance after signing for the club on 10 September against St Johnstone at Tannadice. During season 1921-22 he played in two games for the club.

Bobby Smith I, played in goal for United and was given permission by the club to play for any club that required his services. On 2 March 1940, he guested for Celtic in a game against Raith Rovers.

Bobby Smith II, was signed for United by manager Jerry Kerr, on 23 January 1962. His previous club had been Burnley who had kindly cancelled his registration so he could join United. Bobby made his debut in a reserve game against St Mirren at Tannadice on 10 February, United winning 3-2. On 4 August 1966, he was transferred to St Johnstone. Bobby later acted as a scout for the Club but resigned from this job on 24 October 1974.

Dave Smith, played for Leeds United, and signed as a War guest for United in August 1941. Dave made his United debut on 6 September against Leith Athletic in the North-Eastern League.

Doug Smith, born in Aberdeen, and has been one of the club's best loved and loyal servants since 1958. Doug played his first senior game with United in a League Cup match against Falkirk at Tannadice on 2 September 1959, losing 3-0. His first league game was against Dumbarton at Boghead on 9 September, United losing 3-2. His big chance came after Ron Yeats signed for Liverpool in 1961. Smith was a big strong centre-half and controlled the club's defence. Doug's family was all active in the football scene. His brother Hugh, was given a trial at United on 8 September 1961, in a reserve match against Dundee. At that time Doug's younger brother was a Junior International player, and had been playing for Aberdeen East End. Doug's other brother David signed for Aberdeen when he was 18 years old. David made his debut for them at Pittodrie on 10 October 1962 against St Johnstone. On 20 June 1966, the board signed Doug for another three years and this proved the high esteem that the board felt for the player. Doug captained the side when they reached their first-ever Scottish Cup Final in 1974. During his playing career that spanned 18 years, Doug turned out in an incredible 587 times in Scottish league and cup games. Doug played his last game for United on 5 May 1976 in a reserve game against Ayr United.

On Tuesday 9 August 1977, United held a testimonial game for Doug in recognition of his achievements. Guests included Ally Donaldson (Dundee), Joe Harper and Willie Miller (Aberdeen), Tommy McLean (Rangers), Bobby Lennox (Celtic), Dennis Gillespie, Jimmy Briggs and Ron Yeats. After retiring he became a publican who always welcomed the club's supporters into his hostelry. In 1983, he was invited to join the Tannadice board. Presently he is the Vice-Chairman of the club and he became President of the Scottish League in 1997.

Edward Clark Smith, signed by manager Jimmy Brownlie on 1 October 1929 from Carluke Rovers. Edward made his United debut on 6 October against St Mirren. While he was with United he played in eight matches and scored twice.

George Smith I, of Dundee Arnot, turned out for United as a trialist on 24 November 1938 in a game against Brechin City at Tannadice with United winning 1-0.

George Smith II, became a United player on 1 February 1964, from Partick Thistle. A deal was struck between both clubs, George coming to Tannadice, with Norrie Davidson heading to Firhill. He made his debut later that day against Airdrie. United lost 3-1 at Broomfield. George asked the club to free him in 1965 so that he could become player-manager with Irish side Ballymena.

Harry Smith I, signed for United from St Joseph's. Harry was freed by the club on 10 October 1960.

Harry Smith II, played for junior side Stobswell, and played senior football with Dundee. Harry guested for United on 22 December 1945 against Airdrie at Broomfield.

J. Smith, played one competitive game for Dundee Hibs during season 1910-11.

James 'Snider' Smith, signed by manager Jimmy Brownlie on 22 June 1924. His previous clubs were Third Lanark, Clyde, Port Vale, and Fulham. James made his United debut on 16 August 1924 against Bo'ness, and scored the two goals in the 2-2 draw. The player made only three appearances and scored three goals for the club.

Jack Smith, signed by manager Willie MacFadyen in December 1948, from Loanhead Mayflower. Jack made his United debut on 11 December 1948 against Queen's Park Strollers at Hampden. The player was freed by United in May 1949.

Jimmy Smith, signed by manager Jimmy Brownlie during season 1934-35 from Hearts. While he was with United, Jimmy played in 51 league games and scored 19 goals.

Mick Smith, got his first chance at first team football with United on 12 March 1960. This was a friendly game between United and Derby County at Tannadice. The score was 3-2 for United.

Paul Smith, signed to Dundee from Tynecastle Boys in 1980. He was freed by Dundee on 2 June 1982. The lad from Edinburgh joined United at the beginning of season 1982-83, for a trial period. He scored his first goal on 31 July 1982 in a United XI game against Queen's Park. Paul signed for Raith Rovers on 14 January 1983, with no fee being involved.

Peter Smith, signed by manager Jerry Kerr on 21 July 1959 from Hearts. However, on 29 June 1960 he left United and signed for Alloa. In his first season with Alloa he scored 27 goals in 26 appearances.

R. Smith, played for Stoke City and turned out for United as a War guest on 21 February 1942. This game was played at East End Park against Dunfermline.

Robert Smith, made his debut on 13 August 1938 in the 5-4 victory over Montrose. Robert had previously played for Beith Caledonia's, and Ayr United. In his first season with United he made 30 league appearances.

Sid Smith, played for Norwich City and guested for United on 27 September 1941 against East Fife. On 31 January 1942, Sid won the Midlands Lightweight Boxing Championship held in Brechin.

Walter Smith, born on 24 February 1948. Signed by manager Jerry Kerr from Ashfield Juniors in November 1966. While at Tannadice he played in 127 matches and scored three goals. Walter played in the 1975 Scottish Cup Final team that lost to Celtic. He was transferred to Dumbarton on 18 September 1975. By 1976 Walter was back with United coaching young defenders and on 27 February 1977 Dumbarton and United agreed terms for him to resume playing. His comeback game was on 27 February against Rangers, United winning by 3 goals to 2.

In 1979, Walter was Andy Roxburgh's assistant in charge of the Scottish Youth team. On 18 February 1986, he was appointed by United to the Board of Directors.

But two months later, on 15 April 1986, he was on his way to Ibrox as assistant manager of Rangers under Graeme Souness. He became manager on 16 April 1991 when Souness left to become manager of Liverpool. Walter enjoyed great success at Rangers until on 28 October 1997. he confirmed that he was to step down as Rangers manager at the end of that season. Rangers held a testimonial match for him on 3 March 1998 against Liverpool when over 50,000 turned up at Ibrox to see the light blues win 1-0.

On 1 July 1998 Walter Smith became manager of Everton, with Archie Knox as his assistant.

'Zander' Smith, played in a trial match for United on 23 January 1937 in the 2-1 win over Stenhousemuir at Tannadice. The young player had been with junior side Forfar East End.

Dickie Sneddon, played in a trial game for the club on 10 March 1951 against Brechin reserves. At the time he was playing for Lochore Welfare. Manager Willie MacFadyen was suitably impressed by the player as he signed the 20-year-old on 17 March 1951.

Douglas Sneddon, played for United as a War guest on 24 February 1945 against Raith Rovers at Stark's Park.

Dave Soutar, played in a United first team trial game on 17 January 1959 against Stenhousemuir at Ochilview. At the time of the trial he had been playing for Carnoustie Panmure.

Doug Soutar, played for Butterburn Youth Club, and told manager Jerry Kerr on 22 January 1963, that he would sign for United at the end of the season. The 17-year-old signed up for the club on 11 April 1963. Doug made his first team debut for the club on 27 April, against Airdrie, United losing 4-2. Doug made his Tannadice first team debut on 10 January 1964, in a 4-1 win over Third Lanark.

In January 1965, he went on loan to Forfar, however he did return to Tannadice later that year. In May 1966, Doug was freed by the club.

William Spence, signed by manager Pat Reilly for Dundee Hibs from junior side Stobswell. He made three appearances for Dundee Hibs during season 1913-14. William also featured in the first city derby against Dundee on 13 March 1915. The following season he turned out for the club on 21 occasions.

Stalker, signed by Dundee Hibs manager Pat Reilly in December 1917. His debut for the club was on 29 December 1917 in a 5-1 win over East Fife at Tannadice. He was also in the Dundee Hibs side when they won the Forfarshire Cup against Dundee A on 1 May 1920.

Jim Stalker, played for Dalry Thistle and played in a United first team trial match on 6 March 1959, against Ayr United at Tannadice. The player was signed by manager Andy McCall on 21 March 1959 after his third trial match for the club. Jim played his first official game as a signed player on 28 March against Arbroath at Gayfield. He was freed by United during the close season of 1960. The inside-left signed for Stranraer on 13 May 1960. Jim later joined Stenhousemuir, and he was freed by them on 1 May 1962.

Derek Stark, born in 1958. Formerly with Glenrothes Juniors, the 16 year old's first game for United was on 22 January 1975 in a reserve game against Partick Thistle. Manager McLean gave him his first team debut on 2 March 1978 in a game against Clydebank, United losing 2 0. He very soon established himself as a first team regular. The player was forced to retire in August 1985 because of recurring knee problems.

In his nine years at Tannadice, Stark played in 164 league games, and was a League Cup medal winner in 1979 and 1980. He was in the losing Scottish Cup Final teams of 1981 and 1985 and of the League Cup final team of 1981.

H. Steel, signed to Dundee Hibs by manager Pat Reilly in January 1915. The goalkeeper made his debut on 16 January at Tannadice in the 2-1 win over Abercorn. He had previously played for Dundee Wanderers. While he was with Dundee Hibs he made only two appearances.

Billy Steele, signed on a free transfer from Rangers in April 1975. The 18-year-old striker had gone to Ibrox from Oakley in 1971. Steele made his debut with United on 9 August 1975 in a game against St Johnstone, caming off the sub's bench and scoring the winner. The match ended United 2 St Johnstone 1. The player signed for Dumbarton on 24 September 1976 for a fee of £5,000. On 27 August 1977, Steele signed for Cowdenbeath.

Ian Steen, was 18 -years-old at the time of signing for the club in 1973. The player made his first team debut in the Forfarshire Cup game against Dundee on 23 April 1973. He was released by United and joined Raith Rovers. He was released again in January 1983 and signed for East Stirling. His father had played for Forfar.

Jock Stein, joined Albion Rovers from Blantyre Vics in 1942 and twice played for Dundee United as a War guest.

He went to Llanelly in 1950 before joining Celtic as a player in 1951. Later he enjoyed a spell with Celtic as a player coach, 1956 and coach, 1958, before leaving to become manager of Dunfermline on 15 March 1960. He resigned his post to take over as manager at Hibs, on 30 March 1964. He left Hibs, where he was replaced by Bob Shankly, to become manager of Celtic in February 1965, where he was to enjoy outstanding success, as Celtic became the first British team to win the European Cup in May 1967.

He was to leave Celtic in May 1978 and became manager at Leeds United for a surprising 44 days.

He became the manager of the Scottish national side in 1978, and died in September 1985.

Gijs Steinmann, signed by the club on 4 October 1990, from FC Utrecht for a reported fee of £100,000. The 28-year-old was a former Dutch Under-21 Internationalist and made his debut on 6 October 1990, in a game against Dunfermline at Tannadice. This match was abandoned after 63 minutes when torrential rain made the pitch unplayable.

Alec Stenhouse, made his first team debut for United on 16 January 1954 against Kilmarnock at Tannadice. The player had previously played for Auchterader Primrose. While he was with United, he made 27 appearances. Alec signed for Portsmouth on 20 February 1957 for a reported fee of £1,000.

Sandy Stephen, signed by manager Reggie Smith on 11 November 1954 from junior side Elmwood. Sandy made his first team debut on 13 November at East End Park against Dunfermline. After he was released from his National Service, Sandy returned to Tannadice and resumed his playing career in a first team game on 11 January 1958 against Dumbarton at Tannadice.

Morris Stevenson, played for Musselburgh, then signed to Motherwell in 1958 spending four years with them. The inside forward signed for United from Luton Town on a free transfer in 1970. He spent one year with Hibs in 1962, before joining Morton in 1963, spending five seasons there. He was transferred to Luton Town for £5,000 in November 1968. The player made his Tannadice debut on 25 February 1970, against Motherwell. His last game for United was on 4 December 1971 against Hearts, United losing 3-2 at Tynecastle.

Stewart, joined United in 1943, and made his debut for the club on 6 February 1943 against Rangers at Tannadice.

Alec Stewart, was freed by the club on 15 September 1961. The player had signed for United when he was freed by Airdrie. On 2 February 1965, he signed to Brechin City.

Andy Stewart, born in Dumfries on 2 January 1978, and turned out for United. Andy signed a contract in May 1998 that would keep him at Tannadice until the year 2000. Manager Tommy McLean had been impressed by the young player's performances in the reserve side.

Eddie Stewart, signed to the club from Dundee Junior side Osborne on 24 September 1954. Eddie was United manager Reggie Smith's first signing. The player played in a trial match for United in the opening game of season 1954 against Stenhousemuir at Tannadice. Eddie made his debut as a signed player on 25 September against Third Lanark at Tannadice. Stewart left the club in March 1959 after United transferred him to Arbroath.

Ian Stewart I, went on loan to Forfar on 26 July 1980 from United. The defender staying with them for 18 months. Then he spent five years with Brechin City before moving to Meadowbank Thistle. Later Ian signed for Forfar on 7 October 1987.

Ian Stewart II, signed by manager Jerry Kerr on 23 September 1965, from Arbroath. The reported fee paid to Bert Henderson's Arbroath was £5,000. He made his first team debut on 6 November 1965, against Hearts, the match ending in a 2-2 draw. Ian went to Morton after the clubs struck up an exchange of players deal. This saw Cappielow star Jackie Graham heading for Tannadice, on 15 August 1966.

J. P. Stewart, made his home debut for United on 16 November 1946 against Dumbarton. United winning 2-1, with the player scoring his first goal for the club.

Jimmy Stewart, played for Lawside Academy, and then signed for Chelsea in 1962. Stewart returned to the city and signed for United in January 1965. However, he was released at the end of the season and he signed for Dundee where he spent season 1965-66.

Mr And Mrs John Stewart, were appointed to run the United player's hostel at Seafield Road, Broughty Ferry. Club President George Fox made the announcement on 22 March 1966.

Raymond Stewart, signed by manager Jim McLean while he was playing for Sunday boys' team Errol Rovers. Stewart made his debut in a reserve match against Dundee on 19 December 1975. On 2 September 1976, he made his first team appearance against Celtic in a League Cup game. The score was United 1 Celtic 1. On 30 August 1979, at the age of 19, Stewart signed for West Ham United for £400,000. He had made only 44 League appearances with United. The player had been capped at under-21 level, and has ten full caps at International level. Stewart gained his first cap in 1981 in a game against Wales. Manager McLean put the player's transfer fee to good use by financing a new-covered enclosure for the fans. He was freed by West Ham, and signed to St Johnstone on 27 June 1991. While he was there, he acted as a player-coach. Ray was released by St Johnstone on 17 May 1994. This was part of a cost cutting exercise after they had been relegated from the Premier League. After his free transfer, he signed for Stirling Albion during the close season of 1994-95 and is presently assistant manager.

Tom Stewart, signed by manager Jimmy Brownlie on 19 May 1930 from Dundee Violet.

Willie Stewart, played for Dundee Wanderers, then Carlisle United, and then played for Dundee Hibs in their first season. Willie was killed in December 1915, in the Dardanelles, while fighting for his country in the First World War.

Ed Stirling, was in the Dundee Hibs side when they won the Forfarshire Cup against Dundee A on 1 May 1920. He also played for Dundee Hibs on 15 August 1923 against St Johnstone. Ed played in 31 league games for the club during season 1923-24. Manager Jimmy Brownlie freed him at the end of that season.

Fred Stoessel, signed for Dundee Hibs by manager Pat Reilly on 6 August 1913 from Dundee. He made his club debut on 16 August 1913 in the 0-0 draw with St Johnstone. Fred also featured in the side that lost 3-0 to Albion Rovers in the Qualifying Cup Final game on 27 December 1913. During his first season with the club he played in 17 competitive matches and scored six times. The following season he made just three appearances for the club. In 1914 Fred left the club to serve in the forces during the First World War.

Strachan, from junior side St Joseph's, played in the first ever Dundee Hibs fixture, on Wednesday 18 August 1909. It ended in a 1-1 draw against Edinburgh Hibernian.

Alec Strang, signed for United on 7 September 1961, from Shotts Bon Accord in Lanarkshire. The 16-year-old defender was signed by Jerry Kerr. The player was released by United on 28 February 1962.

David Stratton, signed by manager Willie MacFadyen from Elmwood Juniors. He made his first team debut on 2 October 1950, against Hamilton at Tannadice. David was picked to play in the Scottish Amateur side that met Wales in May 1951. In June 1951, United allowed him to tour Iceland with Middlesex Wanderers.

Alec Stuart, joined Dundee from Aberdeen East End in November 1958. He played in 215 games and scored 28 goals for Dundee. Alec was freed by the Dens Park side on 25 April 1969. Before signing for United, he played in a couple of trials with a Swiss outfit. The player signed for the club on 9 July 1969 and played in his first game on 2 August 1969, against Everton at Tannadice. The club wore their new tangerine strips for the first time. While he was with United Alex played in two League Cup games and scored one goal. Alec left United to become player-manager with Montrose on 27 November 1969.

G. E. Stuart, played for Dundee Hibs and during season 1921-22 he appeared for the club on 25 occasions and scored six goals.

Peter Stuart, signed by manager Jerry Kerr in March 1967 from Aberdeen Sunnybank. At the time of signing, the 17-year-old was working as an electrician.

Dirk Stulcken, played for Detroit cougars in the US Soccer League. When they folded, he joined German side FC St Pauli, a Second Division Hamburg side. Dirk went on trial with United in January 1969. However, after this trial period, the club decided to let him go on 23 January 1969.

Blair Sturrock, signed by manager Tommy McLean on 15 January 1997. The 15-year-old son of the present manager Paul, he was following in his father's footsteps.

Dave Sturrock, signed by manager Reggie Smith during the close season of 1956 and made his United first team debut on 14 January against Queen's Park at Hampden, before a crowd of 15,000. He played six games with United during season 1959-60. Dave was given a free transfer, and received an offer from Accrington Stanley on 17 May 1960. In 1962, Dave was playing for Bedford Town. Their manager was Reggie Smith.

Paul Sturrock, born on 10 October 1956 in Aberdeenshire but was raised in Pitlochry as a child. Paul was signed by Jim McLean as an apprentice 17-year-old player from Bankfoot Juniors. The manager was Chick McNaughton, who incidentally was also a scout for United. Paul soon realized what it meant to be an apprentice under the discipline and standards laid down by Jim McLean.

He made his first team debut in the European Cup Winners Cup against Jiul Petroseni (Rumania) in September 1974, United winning 3-2 on aggregate. His first goals for the Club came in April 1975 after scoring twice in the 2-2 draw against Rangers.

On 16 June 1979, Paul married Barbara Wilkie in Dundee. When Paul retired from playing at the end of season 1988-89, he had made 385 appearances and scored 109 league goals. Clearly an all-time United great. He has been capped 20 times at International level, winning his first honour against Wales in 1981. Jim McLean appointed Paul as club coach in June 1989. At the same time it was announced that the assistant manager would be Steve Murray.

On 17 November 1993, Paul left United to take over the manager's post at St Johnstone from John McClelland. He succeeded in taking the Club from the Scottish First Division to the Premier League on 19 April 1997, after beating East Fife by 3 goals to 2. Following an approach from Hibs, Paul signed a contract with St Johnstone. that would have kept him at McDiarmid Park until the year 2002.

But all that changed in September 1998 when he returned home to Tannadice as manager.

E. Stygal, hailed from Norway and played as a War guest for United on 30 September 1944 against Aberdeen at Pittodrie.

Chris Sulley, born in Camberwell on 3 December 1959 and signed for United on 28 June 1986 from Bournemouth. He had played in 206 games for them and scored three goals. Chris was not long with United, featuring in only seven league games during 1986-87. Later he went on loan to Blackburn Rovers.

Dom Sullivan, was freed by Celtic in the close season of 1983. Dom played for United reserves on 2 September 1983 in a game against Dundee reserves. However, on 9 September 1983, Sullivan turned down the offer of a short term contract and the club.

Sutherland, of Brora, made his debut for Dundee Hibs on 17 August 1910 against St Johnstone.

George Sutherland I, signed by Dundee Hibs manager Pat Reilly in October 1913. His previous club was Arbroath. It was quite some time before he made his club debut, on 1 January 1914 in the Northern-League game against Montrose. He made his Tannadice debut on 10 January in the 1-1 draw with Leith Athletic. While he was with the club, he featured in eight competitive games. In 1914 George left the club to enlist during the First World War.

George Sutherland II, played for Partick Thistle, and on 1 April 1943, United secured his services to play as a War guest. His debut was on 3 April against Raith Rovers at Stark's Park.

John Suttar, joined United for training in February 1983. The goalkeeper was invited back to train with the club during the Easter break of 1983.

John Sveenson, signed on amateur forms with United on 14 October 1944. John had made his debut for the club when he guested for them on 7 October 1944 against Raith Rovers at Tannadice. The player had also been capped for Norway at international level.

Jackie Swan, signed for United on 6 March 1953. He had previously played for Hamilton and Arbroath.

John Swan, signed for Dundee Hibs on 18 September 1923. The previous season the player had been with Clydebank. He made his club debut on 22 September 1923 against Arbroath. While he was with the club, he featured in 20 games.

Robert Swan, made his first team debut on 24 March 1951 against Alloa at Tannadice. Before signing for United, Robert had played for Alloa for two seasons. It was a memorable United debut for him as United won 10-1 that day. In May 1953, United freed the player.

W. Swan, of Arbroath, made his debut for Dundee Hibs on 17 August 1910 against St Johnstone. During season 1910-11 he featured in eight competitive games for Dundee Hibs and scored six goals.

Andy Tait, signed to the club in September 1953 from Dumbarton and made his first team debut on 19 September against St Johnstone at Tannadice.

Matt Tannahill, played in a trial match with the club on 11 August 1951, against Brechin City at Glebe Park.

Taylor, played for Dundee Hibs during the First World War. His first appearance for the club was on 20 April 1918 in the Penman Cup Final against Dundee at Dens Park.

Alec Taylor, was 19 years old when he signed on S-form with United from Blantyre St Joseph's in 1978. In June 1985 he failed to report to Tannadice during the close season of 1985-86. The player took up an accountancy course at a college in Hamilton in September 1985. He then played for Walsall and Falkirk. He made his Falkirk debut on 20 October 1990, in a game against Dundee at Dens Park.

Archie Taylor, played for United and Dundee in the 1920s, and was also a trainer with the club. In September 1926 he left United to become trainer at Huddersfield. On 6 July 1933, he was appointed trainer at Nottingham Forest. In May 1934, he was manager of the same club. Archie won an English League Cup medal with Barnsley in 1912.

Bill Taylor, signed for the club by manager Jimmy Brownlie in December 1927 from Slammannan Hearts. Bill made his United debut on 10 December 1927 against Ayr United at Tannadice. He also played in the 1929 promotion winning team. While he was with United Bill appeared in one 186 games and scored twice. The club later transferred Bill to St Johnstone on 16 March 1933. He played with them until season 1937-38.

James Taylor, played for Notts County, and played as a War guest for United on 5 August 1944 in a trial match at Tannadice.

H. Taylor, played in three competitive matches for Dundee Hibs during season 1911-12.

Bob Temple, signed for United by Sam Irving on 4 August 1938 from Aberdeen. Bob made his United debut on 13 August 1938 in the 5-4 victory over Montrose. While he was with United, he played in 34 league games and scored nine goals.

Jim Temple, signed by manager Willie MacFadyen in December 1952, from Dundonald Bluebell. Jim made his first team debut on 6 December 1952 in the 1-1 draw with Dunfermline at East End Park.

Thomas Tengstedt, born in Scandinavia in 1976. He was signed by manager Tommy McLean from Chang Aalborg in August 1997. Thomas played his first match for United on 15 August 1997 in a reserve match against Hibs. Failing to make the grade with United Thomas returned to Scandinavia on 30 December 1977.

James Tennant, signed for United on 15 March 1940 from St Johnstone. The club had granted the player a temporary move to Tannadice to play as a War guest. James had previously played for Kilwinning before he turned senior with the Muirton Park outfit.

N. Thain, played for Dundee Hibs and during season 1921-22 he played 15 times and scored once for the club.

Lewis Thom, joined the club from Aberdeen in May 1964. He made his first team debut against his old club on 9 May 1964. The final score that day was 4-1 for Dundee United. Lewis then moved to Shrewsbury on 15 September 1965. The player was freed by them on 10 May 1967.

Thomas, played for Swansea Town and was fixed up by United as a War guest. He made his debut for the club on 31 October 1942 against Hibs at Easter Road.

Billy Thomson, born in Linwood, and signed to Partick Thistle from Glasgow United. Then he signed for St Mirren. From there Billy signed for United on 28 June 1984 for a reported fee of 75,000. At the time of signing Billy had won seven full caps for Scotland. He played his first game in United colours in a friendly game in Germany in July 1984. United lost 4-0 to Viktoria Aschaffenburg. Billy made his Premier League debut at Tannadice on 11 August 1984 in a game against Hearts. A crowd of 10,027 saw United run out 2-0 winners that day. He was transferred to Motherwell on 10 July 1991, for a reported fee of £50,000. On 25 July 1994, Billy signed for Rangers. The keeper signed for Dundee in August 1996, after he was freed from the Ibrox club.

Bobby Thomson, was freed by Stenhousemuir in May 1951. On 14 June 1951, they invited him to Tannadice for a trial.

Charlie Thomson, joined United as a War guest on 30 November 1939. The player had previously played for Exeter City, and Falkirk. He made his United debut on 2 December 1939 in the 5-2 win over Dunfermline at Tannadice. Charlie was recruited into the Army on 20 June 1940. After active service he returned to United. However, he was freed by the club in April 1947.

George Thomson, signed by manager Jimmy Brownlie on 28 August 1929 from Clydebank. George made his United debut on 31 August 1929 against Dundee at Dens Park. While he was with United he played in 15 games and scored twice. The player joined Bo'ness in April 1932. However, George returned to Tannadice and played as War guest on 14 August 1943 against Hearts. George had been playing for Aberdeen, and left United on 30 November 1943.

Ian Thompson, provisionally signed by manager Jerry Kerr on 28 December 1966 from Valleyfield. Ian played in a trial game for the club reserves on 23 December 1966, against Stirling Albion. Ian was freed by the club in April 1968.

'Napper' Thomson, made his first appearance for Dundee Hibs on 1 September 1917 against Dunfermline Athletic. This match was played at North End Park in Dunfermline in the Eastern-League. His home debut was on 8 September 1917 in a 3-1 win over Armadale. Napper agreed to sign for Dundee FC on 12 August 1919.

Richard Thomson, born in Perth on 11 August 1977 and turned out for United reserves in 1998.

Scott Thomson, born in Edinburgh, was 17 years old when he signed for United. The keeper joined the club from Hutchison Vale Club in 1984. He was included in the United pool for the 24 November 1984 game against Hibs. Manager Jim McLean wanted to give the young lad a taste of big match atmosphere. Scott made his first team debut on 2 May 1987 in a 2-1 victory at Tannadice against Hibs. The crowd that day was 9,227. His last appearance in United's first team was against Dundee in August 1989, at Dens Park. Scott was signed by Forfar on 25 June 1991, by then manager Paul Hegarty. In September 1993, he was signed by Raith Rovers. After refusing to sign a new contract with Raith in June 1997, he signed on short term with St Johnstone. Later, Scott signed for Hull City. On 24 March 1998, Scott returned to Scotland on loan to Motherwell from Hull City.

Steven Thompson, born in Paisley on 14 October 1978. He began playing in United's Under-18 youth team before graduating to reserve football with the club. The player made his first team debut against Hearts in May 1997. Thompson was also chosen to represent his country at Under-21 level at the Toulon Tournament in May 1997.

Timmins, made his Second Division debut in goal for Dundee Hibs on 3 December 1910. This game ended 1-1 against Ayr United at Tannadice.

J. Timmons, signed by manager Willie MacFadyen in October 1952. On 11 October 1952, he made his first team debut against Stirling Albion at Tannadice.

Thomas Timmons, became the treasurer of Dundee Hibs in March 1909.

John Tivendale, signed by manager Willie MacFadyen on 29 June 1946 from Watford. John made his United debut on 14 August 1946 against Stenhousemuir.

Oskar Tomasson, was an Icelandic guest for the club in October 1975. The 19-year-old played in a reserve game on 4 October 1975 against Ayr United at Somerset Park. The reserves won that night 4-0, with the player scoring twice. Tomasson headed back home again on 17 October 1975.

Gordon Tosh, signed on a month's trial with the club in October 1958. Gordon played in United's first team on 11 October 1958 against Queen's Park at Hampden.

Jerry Tracey, played in a trial game for United on 13 December 1952 against Forfar at Tannadice. However, on 15 December 1952, the player signed for Ayr United.

Tommy Traynor, joined Hearts in 1962 from Dunipace Juniors. Tommy signed for United in the close season of 1970, in a deal that saw Wilson Wood's departure to Hearts.

Priti Trivedi, joined United in 1985, and she is currently the club's Company Secretary.

Willie Tullis, of Carnoustie Panmure, made his league debut for Dundee Hibs on 17 August 1910 against St Johnstone. This was the only competitive game he played for Dundee Hibs during season 1910-11. In season 1911-12 he featured in only two competitive games.

George Tulloch, the keeper played for Everton, signed to United, then played for St Johnstone and East Stirling.

Maxwell Turnball, played for Motherwell from October 1938, and signed to United as a War guest on 16 September 1942. Maxwell made his United debut on 26 September against Hearts at Tannadice.

Dario Ubrico, signed by Billy Kirkwood on 31 March 1995. Ubrico joined the club from Alto Peru, but he had been on loan to Rampla Juniors. He made his debut on 4 April 1995, in a reserve game against Kilmarnock at Tannadice. On 20 April 1995, he was allowed to return to South America. The player had struggled with the Scottish style of play.

Ronaldo Ugolini, started his career with Lochee Harp, and was then transferred to Swansea. He played for Celtic then transferred to Middlesborough spending ten years with them. The goalkeeper was signed from Wrexham in June 1960. Ronaldo made his debut in a friendly game against a United Black and White team against United Reds. This match was played on 6 August 1960, at Tannadice. While at Tannadice, he played in 34 League and cup games in 1960-61. Then in season 1961-62, he played in 18 games. The player was released by the club in May 1962. Two months later he was helping out in goal with Berwick Rangers and Cowdenbeath. However, on 13 September 1962 he announced his retirement from football. He planned to open a small business in Edinburgh.

George Ure, signed by manager Jimmy Brownlie on 25 June 1935 from junior side Stobswell. The 17-year-old player made only 12 league appearances for United, then he was freed in April 1938.

Jose Valeriani, played his first game for United on 18 July 1998 in a friendly match against St Mirren at Love Street. Jose was one of three South American players who were invited to Tannadice for a trial in July 1998. The player also left with the United squad when they toured Holland in July 1998.

Oscar Garcia Valle, was a trialist from Spain. United manager Tommy McLean had been impressed by the 24-year-old during training, and decided to try him out with the reserves. Oscar played in a reserve game against Dunfermline at East End Park on 31 March 1998. While Oscar was in Spain, he had played in over 200 games with Primera Division side's Athletico Madrid, Osasuna, and Villareal. Oscar made his first team debut on 18 April 1998 against Kilmarnock at Rugby Park.

Freddie Van Der Hoorn, the 25-year-old midfield player signed for the club on 31 July 1989 from Dutch club Den Bosch. Freddie cost United around £200,000. The player made his first team debut on 12 August 1989, in a game against Motherwell at Tannadice. The score was 1-1. In November 1990, he won the B&Q Superskills Award.

Guido Van De Kamp, born in 1964. He was signed for £40,000 from BVV Den Bosch (Holland) on 11 July 1991. Guido had also played for Nec Nijmegen. He made his Premier League debut on 13 August 1991, in a 4-1 victory over St Mirren at Tannadice. On his arrival he was a deputy to keeper Alan Main. However, he did not have to wait too long for the opportunity to make his mark as first team keeper. After an injury to Alan Main, Van De Kamp played in most of the first team games in season 1992-93. It was not until 1994 that Guido again took over the top position after another injury to Main. Guido played in the 1994, Scottish Cup Final and won a winner's medal. Following a dispute over a re-signing fee the player returned to Holland. In just over a year, Guido was back in Scotland having signed for Dunfermline on 21 January 1995. They had agreed to pay

United a nominal fee for the player's services. While with Dunfermline, Guido won a First Division Championship medal. In June 1997, he was given a free transfer and signed for Jimmy Nicholl's Raith Rovers. The goalkeeper made his first team appearance with them on 2 August 1997, against Stirling Albion.

Vannet, received permission from his club Arbroath to turn out as a War guest for United on 14 July 1941.

Gary Voy, signed for the club in October 1983. Gary played his first game for the club in a reserve match played on 24 October 1983 against Arbroath reserves. In August 1984, the player nearly ripped off his toe after an accident in the shower room. On 9 May 1985, he was given a free transfer. He signed for Raith Rovers in July of that year.

Dave Walker, signed by manager Jimmy Brownlie on 16 July 1925 from St Johnstone, for a reported fee of £100. Dave made his United debut on 15 August 1925 against Raith Rovers. From seasons 1925-1929, Dave made 112 appearances for United and scored 18 goals. The player was freed by United in April 1929.

Eric Walker, born in Bathgate, and joined the RAF at the age of 19. He signed for the club in January 1960, from Alloa. Eric made his debut on 9 January 1960, against Stranraer. United won 3-0. He made his home debut on 16 January 1960, against Stenhousemuir. The game ended in a 2-1 victory for Stenhousemuir. While he was playing for the club, Eric worked as a costing clerk with West Lothian County Council.

J. Walker, was an ex-player with Dundee FC when he made his club debut for United. This took place on 3 November 1923 against St Bernard's at Tannadice. The player scored one of the goals in the 3-2 victory.

Jason Walker, signed by the club on 6 January 1975 from St Mirren. A small fee was involved. His debut in United colours was on 7 January 1975 in a reserve game against Motherwell.

Jimmy Walker, signed for the club in August 1925 from Third Lanark. United had also tried to sign his brother Frank who was an accomplished forward. The player made his United debut on 15 August 1925 against Raith Rovers. Jimmy captained the first United side to beat Celtic on 19 September 1925. The final score was United 1 Celtic 0.

Paul Walker, born in Kilwinning on 20 August 1977 and played in a couple of first team games during season 1997-98. Paul then signed a contract in May 1998 that would keep him at Tannadice until the year 2000.

Clive Wallace, played for Kirrie Thistle and played in a first team United trial game on 1 October 1956. This match was against Berwick Rangers at Tannadice. However, the player made his way across the road and became a Dundee player. Clive was freed by them during the close season of 1958, and then signed by manager Tommy Gray for United. He made his first team debut for United on 13 August 1958 against Cowdenbeath at Tannadice. The player signed for Montrose in January 1959.

Gordon Wallace I, first signed for Montrose in the 1960s before signing for Raith Rovers. In 1969, he won The Player of the Year Award. Gordon signed for Dundee FC on 16 September 1969, and scored the winning goal in the 1973 League Cup Final against Celtic. The player was freed on 29 April 1976 and went to play for the American club Seattle Sounders. On 30 August 1976, he signed for United. He left the club to join Raith Rovers as player-manager. He returned to Tannadice in July 1983 after being appointed coach by Jim McLean. On 20 February 1989, he left United to become manager of Dundee FC. His first game in charge was on 25 February 1989 against Celtic. Dundee lost 3-0 at Dens Park that day. He left Dundee to take up the post as assistant-manager at Dunfermline on 7 October 1991, joining up with Jocky Scott who had been appointed manager there. Gordon and Jocky were both sacked by Dunfermline on 19 May 1993. On 18 November 1993, Gordon returned to Tannadice again as a coach. This was after Paul Sturrock had taken up the manager's post with St Johnstone. In 1998, the coaching staff included Gordon, Maurice Malpas, Ian Campbell, and Graeme Liveston. Gordon Wallace resigned as coach on 4 September 1998 after the resignation of manager Tommy McLean.

Gordon Wallace II, signed by the club on 21 October 1977 from Raith Rovers for a fee of £12,000. Wallace made his first team debut at Tannadice on 22 October in a game against Celtic. United lost 2-1 in front of a crowd of 17,000. The player was transferred in season 1979-80 to Berwick Rangers for £5,000.

Jim Wallace I, of Perth YMCA played in a trial match for United on 30 December 1933 against Dumbarton at Tannadice.

Jim Wallace II, signed by manager Tommy Gray during the close season of 1958 from Aberdeen. He made his United first team debut on 9 August 1958 against St Johnstone at Muirton Park.

M. Wallace, played for Dundee Hibs in the 1920s.

Raymond Wallace, signed for United on 13 January 1939 from English North-Eastern side Consett Celtic. The player made his United debut on 14 January 1939 against Dunfermline at Tannadice.

Mark Walton, was freed by Norwich City, and came to United for a trial in February 1994.

Bert Wann, assisted United as a War guest. Bert played in games against Rangers and East Fife, and played against Raith Rovers at Tannadice on 28 March 1942. At the time Bert was a regular player in the juniors.

Noel Wannan, signed by United's assistant manager Ally Gallacher on 4 July 1956, after Montrose had freed him. United freed the player on 19 December 1956.

Jimmy Ward, signed to the club on 21 August 1953, after he received a free transfer from Blackburn Rovers in the close season. Jimmy made his United debut in the first team on 22 August 1953 in the 2-2 draw with Morton at Tannadice.

Joe Ward, was signed on a free transfer from Hibs. Ward was a former player with Clyde and Aston Villa. Made his debut with United on 2 August 1980 in a friendly against West Ham United.
    The player was transferred to Ayr United on 20 November 1981 for a reported fee of £8,000.

T. Waterston, played for Hearts before signing to Dundee Hibs by manager Pat Reilly. He made his club debut on 22 October 1910 in the 2-1 win over Port Glasgow at Clune Park. While he was with the club, he played in nine competitive games during season 1910-11 and scored three goals.

Alec Watson, signed by the club on 25 April 1938 from Brechin City. Alec made his first team debut as a signed player on 27 April 1938. This was in a Forfarshire Cup game with Dundee at Dens Park.

David Watson, played for United on 21 August 1937 against Raith Rovers at Stark's Park. The young keeper was signed up shortly after this game from his junior club Ashfield. While he was with United, he made five league appearances. David signed for East Stirling on 13 January 1939.

Fred Watson, goalkeeper, signed for United on 23 August 1948. Fred had previously played in two first team games against Dunfermline and St Johnstone. He was signed by manager Willie MacFadyen after the St Johnstone game. The player was freed by the club in May 1949.

George Watson, signed by manager Jimmy Brownlie in July 1929 from junior side North End. From seasons 1929-1933 George played in 61 competitive games for the club. On 20 October 1933 he left the city for an extended trial with Bradford City.

Joe Watson, signed by Jerry Kerr in March 1971. Watson was a former player with Nottingham Forest and was signed until the end of the season. In May 1973, he announced that he was emigrating to Australia.

Willie Watson, signed by manager Jimmy Brownlie on 20 January 1936 from Ayr United. Willie made his United debut on 25 January 1936 against Alloa at Tannadice. The player was given a free transfer from the club on 9 November 1936, and following spells with Lincoln City, New Allerton and Dundee, rejoined United on 15 July 1937. He made his debut on 14 August against St Bernard's at Tannadice.

Don Watt, signed by manager Reggie Smith in November 1956. Don made his United first team debut on 1 December 1956 in the 7-0 victory over Albion Rovers. The player was freed by United in April 1957 and signed for Dundee. He made his debut for them on 7 September 1957 against Hearts at Tynecastle.

Robert Watts, made his United debut on New Years Day 1945 against Arbroath. He was signed the following day from Crosshill Hearts.

Webster, he was in the Dundee Hibs side when they won the Forfarshire Cup against Dundee A on 1 May 1920.

Johnny Webster, played in goal for North End and had a trial with the club. On 18 April 1964 Johnny played in a reserve match at Tannadice against Aberdeen. Then on 20 April 1964, he played in a game against Hibs at Easter Road. At the time he was standing in for keeper Donald Mackay who was out injured.

Chick Weir, signed to United by manager Willie Reid on 7 September 1933, he had been with Dunfermline the previous season. The player made his United debut on 9 September 1933 against Morton at Tannadice.

James Weir, had been on a months trial with United during season 1932-33. However, the player was freed by United on 12 October 1933.

Robert Welch, played right-back for Whitburn Juniors, and was called up by manager Jerry Kerr on 16 July 1964. Robert was freed by the club in May 1965.

Brian Welsh, born in Edinburgh on 23 February 1969. Brian signed for the club in June 1985 from Tynecastle Boys Club. Welsh struggled to gain first team experience in his early days with the club. Although by the time United won the Scottish Cup in 1994, Brian was beginning to show promise as a first team player. He also gained a Scottish Cup winner's medal that year. It was Welch's last minute goal in the 1996 play off game against Partick Thistle that saved United from an embarrassing second season in Division One. On 6 August 1996, he was transferred to Hibernian following a contractual dispute with United. The reported fee was £195,000.

Jimmy Welsh, played for Aberdeen Lad's Club, and was called up by United manager Andy McCall on 19 March 1959. He made his first team debut on 28 March 1959 against Arbroath at Gayfield.

Willie Welsh, played for Hearts before joining United in October 1925. The player made his United debut on 10 October 1925 against Hamilton Accies at Tannadice. In May 1927 he was transferred to Charlton Athletic.

Willie Westwater, signed to the club on 6 August 1953. The player made his first team debut on 8 August 1953 against Morton at Cappielow. In January 1954, the player announced that he was leaving the UK to go to Canada.

Joe and Sandy White, were identical twins who played under manager's Kerr and McLean in the early 1970s. Sandy made his first team debut in October 1971. The twins appeared together in the first team on 18 December 1971, in a game against Aberdeen at Pittodrie which United lost 3-0.

John White, signed for the club in 1956 from Bonnyrigg Rose.

Willie White, signed for the club in August 1939 from Charlton Athletic. Willie made his United debut on 12 August 1939 in the 3-2 win over Edinburgh City. He played in a couple of games just before the outbreak of the Second World War.

Charles Whyte, signed for United on 8 June 1932 from Arbroath Ardenlea Juniors. While he was at Tannadice, he made 20 league appearances and scored three goals. Charles was freed by United in April 1933.

Sam Whyte, signed for Dundee Hibs in season 1912-13. On 14 December 1912, Sam was injured in a game against St Bernard's. This resulted in Sam having to quit playing for one year. Sam made 39 league appearances with the club and in 1914 he left the club to serve in the forces during the First World War.

Dave Whytock, signed by Jerry Kerr in December 1959, from Brechin. Dave made his debut in a game played on Boxing Day in 1959 against East Fife, and scored a hat-trick in the game. He was freed by United on 6 February 1961.

John Wightman, played for United as a War guest.

G. Wilkie, played for Dundee Hibs, and was in the side when they won the Forfarshire Cup against Dundee A on 1 May 1920. During season 1921-22 he played in seven games for the club.

Alex Will, signed by manager Reggie Smith in the close season of 1955. Alex made his United debut in a B. Division game against Brechin City at Glebe Park on 24 August 1955. The player was freed by United in April 1958.

Billy Williams, signed for United on 22 February 1977 for £14,000 from Aberdeen. Williams made his home debut on 26 February 1977 in a reserve game against Hearts. United won 4-0 with Williams scoring.

Horace Williams, signed for Dundee Hibs on 12 June 1921. Horace had previously played for St Johnstone and Edinburgh Hibs. The player made his club debut on 20 August 1921 against Bo'ness at Tannadice. This game ended in a 2-2 draw with Horace scoring. He played in 23 league games for Dundee Hibs and scored 13 goals in season 1921-22. The player was later transferred to Gillingham.

Billy Williamson, played for Aberdeen, United and Dundee. He left the UK in 1981 to play in Australia with the Brisbane Lions. Billy returned to Scotland in October 1984.

Tim Williamson, made his United debut on 23 August 1930 against his old club Stenhousemuir. Tim signed for Accrington Stanley in July 1931. Before he signed for United his previous clubs included Hearts, Hamilton, Clyde, Dunfermline, and Montrose.

J. H. Wilkinson, signed by manager Jimmy Brownlie on 1 July 1936. He had previously played for Hibs for eight seasons. The player made his United debut on 8 August 1936 in a 4-2 win over King's Park. In total the player made only eight league appearances for United and was freed in November 1936.

Davie Wilson, born on 10 January 1938. Wilson came to the club on 3 August 1967, with Wilson Wood, from Rangers in exchange for Orjan Persson. The player made his United debut on 5 August 1967, in a friendly at Tannadice against Sheffield United. Davie made his first United appearance in a League Cup game on 12 August 1967 against Celtic at Parkhead, which Dundee United lost 1-0. In 1974 Wilson was second coach with Dumbarton. They then appointed him manager in 1977. He left the club on 11 April 1980.

Jimmy Wilson, signed by manager Tommy Gray on 4 September 1957 from Duntocher Hibs. Jimmy made his United debut on 5 September 1957 against Arbroath at Gayfield. The player made his first team debut on 11 September 1957 against Cowdenbeath.

John Wilson, turned out for United on 7 August 1943 in a trial game for the club.

Willie Wilson, was a former player for Dundee Hibs who was transferred to St Johnstone in February 1923. In December 1926 he was playing for Hibs.

Lennart Wing, was born in 1935, and was signed by manager Jerry Kerr on 19 January 1965, from the club Orgryte. Before signing he had been working as a firefighter. The player had also been capped for Sweden with fellow player Orjan Persson. He made his first team debut on 23 January 1965, in the 2-0 win over St Mirren at Tannadice, before a crowd of 12,000. On 20 February 1967, it was announced through the media that the player had decided to return home at the end of the 1967 season. Wing played his last game for the club on 22 April 1967, in a game against Partick Thistle.

Robbie Winters, born in East Kilbride on 4 November 1974. After he left school he became a professional player and never thought about doing anything else. In November 1994, Ivan Golac signed the player. He played in his first match as a trialist in a friendly game against Partisan Belgrade. His Premier League debut was on 19 November 1994, in a 5-2 victory over Hearts at Tannadice. His football career took off under manager Tommy McLean who has

guided him since his arrival at the club. If he had not made it as a professional player, Robbie would have liked to have become a PE teacher. He recalls his first goal for United, which he scored against Kilmarnock with an overhead kick, as one of his best memories. Robbie was named as Scotland's young player of the year for the 1996 season. In his spare time he enjoys golf and the odd game of snooker.

Jonas Wirmola, signed by Tommy McLean on a short term contract from Malmo in January 1997. The player made his first team debut on 11 January 1997 when he came off the subs bench in a match against Dunfermline. The score at East End Park was Dunfermline 1 United 3. Jonas played his first game from the start on 18 January 1997 against Hearts in the 2-1 win for United at Tynecastle.

Witherspoon, played his first game for United as a War guest in the North-Eastern League game against St Bernard's. This match was played on 16 August 1941, and United won 4-1 that day.

George Wood, signed by Jerry Kerr in 1970, from West Calder United. The player was originally on Heart's books back in 1968. His brother Ian was signed to Dundee.

Wilson Wood, joined United on 3 August 1967, in a swap deal that brought Davie Wilson and himself to Tannadice from Rangers. He made his United debut on 5 August 1967 in a friendly game against Sheffield United at Tannadice. Wilson played in his first competitive game for the club on 12 August 1967. This was on the opening day of season 1967-68, in a League Cup tie game against Celtic at Parkhead. In 1970, the player joined Hearts, and was freed by them on 30 April 1973. Wood then joined Raith Rovers in August 1973.

Woods, played for Dunfermline, and guested for United on 4 May 1946 in the Forfarshire Cup game against Arbroath at Tannadice.

Jimmy Woodburn, played for Newcastle United and for Dundee United as a War guest. Jimmy turned out for United on 5 September 1942 against East Fife at Methil.

Horace Wooley, signed on a month's contract with United on 16 September 1938. Horace made his United debut the day after he signed against Dundee at Tannadice, and United won 3-0 that day. While he was with the club, he made three league appearances and scored two goals in the derby game with Dundee. His previous clubs included Partick Thistle and Blackburn Rovers. After he was freed by United in October 1938, he signed for Morton.

Jackie Wren, signed to the club in December 1962, by manager Jerry Kerr from Hibs. The keeper made his United debut on 14 December 1962, in a reserve game against Hearts at Tannadice. Jackie was released by United on 11 January 1963.

Wright, signed by manager Willie MacFadyen from Clyde in October 1947. He made his United debut in a reserve match against Arbroath at Gayfield.

Bob Wylie, joined United from Monifieth Tayside in September 1949, and he was a former goalkeeper with the club when Willie MacFadyen was boss. Bob made his debut as a United player on 10 September 1949 against East Fife reserves at Bayview in a C-Division game. The player made his first league debut for United on 19 November 1949 against Morton at Cappielow. Bob was transferred to Blackpool in May 1953. Then on 3 May 1956, he was transferred to West Ham. He was later transferred to Mansfield and was freed by them on 12 May 1962.

Thomas Wyllie, signed by manager Willie MacFadyen on 9 October 1946 from Arbroath Vics. Tom went on loan to Arbroath, and played for them on 15 October 1949 against St Johnstone at Muirton.

Ron Yeats, born in Aberdeen in 1937, and signed by manager Tommy Gray in December 1957. He played his first team debut for United on 22 December 1957 in the 3-1 victory over East Stirling at Tannadice. Ron was one of the key United players when the club was promoted to Division One in season 1959-60. Ron scored only one goal for the club in a game against East Stirling. On 24 July 1961, he was transferred to Liverpool for a fee of £30,000. Ron made his 100th appearance in the English League on 14 December 1963. On 15 February 1969, he made his 300th League appearance against Notts County at Anfield. After he left Liverpool on 30 December 1971, he became a player with Tranmere Rovers. He would later become manager of the side. On leaving Liverpool, their manager Bill Shankly said, 'No player in the history of the Liverpool club has given greater service than Yeats.' Ron was capped for his country on two occasions, winning his first cap in 1965 in a match against Wales. His second cap came in 1966, in a game against Italy. On 4 April 1975, Ron was sacked as manager of Tranmere Rovers.

Bobby Yorke, was signed by manager Willie Brownlie on 7 August 1934. The player made his United debut on 11 August 1934 against Forfar at Station Park. During his first spell with United he made 33 league appearances and scored nine goals. Bobby left the club, but returned in September 1937 for a second spell. His comeback game was on 11 September 1937 in the 5-2 win over Edinburgh City at Tannadice. During season 1937-38 he played in 30 league games and scored one goal. In 1939 he was playing for Montrose when the Second World War began. In March 1940, he guested for Edinburgh side St Bernard's.

Benny Yorston, played for Aberdeen and Middlesborough. Benny guested for United on 24 November 1945 against Albion Rovers at Tannadice.

Andy Young, signed by manager Tommy Gray on 25 August 1958 from Kirkintilloch Rob Roy.

Bobby Young, signed by manager Jerry Kerr in March 1964, after he was freed by Celtic. The player was freed by United on 19 December 1964.

Duncan Young, signed from Butterburn Youth Club by manager Reggie Smith in February 1956. Duncan made his first team debut on 25 February 1956 against Alloa. The player was freed by the club in April 1959.

J. Young, transferred from Celtic to Dundee Hibs during the close season of 1911. The player made his debut for the club on 19 August 1911 against East Stirlingshire at Bainsford. He played in three games for Dundee Hibs in season 1911-12.

P. Yule, played in seven competitive matches for Dundee Hibs during season 1910-11 and scored one goal for the club.

Lars Zetterland, born in Harnosant, Sweden on 11 February 1964. Lars signed for the club in 1996 from Orebro S.K. Sweden. The former Swedish Under-21 Internationalist previously played for I.F.K. Gothenburg and A.I.K. Stockholm. Zetterland was also part of the I.F.K. set up when they defeated United in the 1987 UEFA Cup Final. Lars arrived at Tannadice on 29 October 1996. He had signed a short term contract with United and made his first team debut on 2 November 1996 against Motherwell.

– 2 –
THE MANAGERS

Jimmy Allan, was manager of Dundee United shortly after the Second World War began. Jimmy was well known in the city as he owned a barber's shop in Lochee. In July 1940 he took United to the final of the Emergency War Cup, which they played at Hampden Park. The tie was against Glasgow Rangers, and attracted a crowd of 90,000. Rangers won by one goal to nil that day. Jimmy resigned his manager's post in July 1940 after the club had decided that it did not want to compete in the season 1940-41. However, they appointed Jimmy, trainer with United on 7 October 1942. His former clubs included Falkirk and Cowdenbeath.

Jimmy Brownlie, born in Blantyre on 15 May 1885. Formerly with Third Lanark who honoured him with a benefit game in 1913, between 1923 and 1939, Jimmy held several posts within United. These ranged from player-secretary-manager-and director-manager. The talented goalkeeper made 16 appearances in a Scotland jersey, and was always popular with the supporters. On 25 April 1931, Jimmy announced that he was leaving Tannadice. The odd thing about this announcement was the fact that United had just gained promotion to Division One the same day. There were no reasons given as to his decision. In February 1934, after a group of wealthy businesspeople had saved the club from bankruptcy, the new board again invested in his wealth of experience. On his return to the club his first game in charge was on 3 March 1934 against Kings Park. The United board officially announced that Jimmy was manager on 17 July 1934. However, in October 1936 they again showed him the door. In June 1938 a new set of directors took over, and this time the board included Jimmy. With the outbreak of the Second World War, Jimmy again left Tannadice. This finally ended his illustrious career there. Jimmy was still seen regularly supporting the club from the 1940s until the 1960's. Jimmy died on 29 December 1973, aged 83.

Arthur Cram, United's manager from 1941-1944, stepped down from manager's role, but became club secretary. He resigned as United's Secretary on 10 October 1945, this was due to his outside business pressure. However, he did remain on the United board.

Herbert Dainty, was born in England in 1879. The centre-half won a Scottish Cup medal with rivals Dundee in 1910. He signed for Ayr United on 30 October 1913. On 6 May 1914 he became manager of the club. Herbert left Ayr and was signed for Dundee Hibs on 20 April 1915 by manager Pat Reilly. His club debut was made on 24 April 1915 in the 1-0 win over Forfar Athletic at Tannadice in the Northern-League. He retired from the game in 1918, but was eventually invited to become involved with the everyday affairs of running Dundee Hibs. Eventually in 1922 he became club chairman. However, he did not hold onto the position for long. This was due to severe financial difficulties that besotted the club then. Towards the end of 1922 a group of prosperous businesspeople entered the game and saved the club from financial ruin. They turned the club into a limited company, and Dainty found that he was surplus to requirements, and had to go. Herbert Dainty died in 1961.

Ally Gallacher, born in 1909, and held the manager's post for a mere seven weeks. He joined the club in November 1954 after United manager Reggie Smith asked if he would like to be his assistant at the club. Smith eventually resigned as manager to take up a similar post with Falkirk. The United directors put Gallacher in the hot seat for a temporary period. In what was a disastrous month for him, a series of poor results followed, and Gallacher was no longer manager at the club. However, Ally did remain with the club as an employee of Taypools. He died in 1964.

Ivan Golac, born in 1950. Dundee United Vice-chairman Doug Smith made the announcement of Ivan's pending arrival on 5 July 1993. He did not officially arrive at Tannadice until 9 July 1993. As a player Ivan played for Partisan Belgrade, and turned out in more than 350 occasions with them. In 1978 he signed for Southampton for a fee of £50,000. From there he moved to Bournemouth. Ivan had also played at international level with Yugoslavia. He was the former manager of Partizan Belgrade, arriving at United with glowing credentials. However, problems were soon to develop with Golac's easy style and lack of staff discipline. On 21 May 1994 Golac made United history when they lifted the Scottish Cup for the first time. The club had previously been runners-up in the competition on six previous occasions. A crowd of 38,000 saw United win 1-0 against Rangers that day. However, the honeymoon period was soon over. On the opening day of the season, United lost 5-0 to Hibs on 13 August 1994. After this game Golac fined the 12 players and himself £100. The following season, after a series of defeats, the United board had to take the decision to remove Golac. On 14 March 1995 Dundee United chairman Jim McLean announced that Golac had left the club. Jim said that he had 'left by mutual agreement and in accordance with his contract.' Ivan Golac made it clear that he felt no bitterness to the club. He said: 'things have not worked out as I'd hoped, but I wish the players all the best.' Stories circulating in the media claimed that the board had sacked Golac. Whether or not you agreed with Ivan Golac, the fans will always remember Golac as a character. His carefree attitude was different, and we will best remember him for burying the Hampden hoodoo, and bringing United the Scottish Cup in May 1994.

Tommy Gray, born in 1926, and appointed club manager on 26 March 1957. The former Dundee FC player became United's third manager in the space of eight weeks. Before joining the club he had been manager of Arbroath. He worked on a part-time basis, and carried on with his well paid secure day job. His first game in charge with United was on 30 March 1957 against Albion Rovers. In 1958 after a year and a half in the position Tommy Gray resigned from the post. On 22 June 1967, he joined the Rangers as a part-time scout. Tommy died in 1989.

George Greig, was born in 1871, and became one of the club's greatest saviours. The Conservative councillor on Dundee Corporation saved United from bankruptcy on 26 February 1934. George and William McIntosh put the required finance into the club and persuaded the Scottish League that the club was to continue. George eventually persuaded the other directors at the club to resign after he had given personal assurances to creditors that he would pay of all their debts. Later, George's power base was in full flight. First, he sacked manager Jimmy Brownlie, and having no football background, he took on the role as director-manager. For 18 months he selected the team each week and left all the tactics to trainer Johnny Hart. However, toward the end of the season 1938-39 Greig decided that he had enough of the club and sold his shares. The wealthy tobacconist died in 1940.

Sam Irving, born in Belfast 1893, returned to Scotland when he was three months old. Sam played for Dundee in 1925 and he was a member of their Scottish Cup Final team. He joined Cardiff City and was a member of their FA Cup winning side. In 1938, along with several prominent businesspeople, they bought out wealthy businessperson George Greig's share at Tannadice. Sam joined the United board on 5 July 1938. He was also joint United manager with Jimmy Brownlie from July 1938 until June 1939. He remained at the club for two years before leaving in 1940 after the club was close to bankruptcy. Sam was on the Board at Tannadice when the club reached the War Cup Final in 1940. As a player Sam won 18 caps for Northern Ireland. He gained ten caps while he was at Dens, six caps with Cardiff, and two with Chelsea. On 24 June 1941, Sam was re-elected to the United Board of Directors. After retiring from the game he opened a newsagent's shop in Monifieth. Sam died in 1969.

Jerry Kerr, born in 1912, will best be remembered as the manager who put in place the structure for the future of United. Following spells with Alloa Athletic, Motherwell, St. Bernards and Rangers Jerry was signed for United by Bobby McKay in 1939 and released in 1940.

After service in the forces Jerry managed Peebles Rovers before joining Berwick Rangers. There followed a period as manager of Alloa Athletic.

On 7 July 1959 Jerry returned to Tannadice as Manager and within a year of his appointment had led the club from Division Two to Division One. In the 1960s Jerry recognised that Scandinavian players would come to Scotland at very little cost to the club and he signed Orjan Persson and Leonart Wing from Sweden and from Denmark Finn Dossing, Mogens Berg and Finn Seaman. Perhaps the highlight of his career came in 1966 when he led the club to home and away wins over Barcelona. In 1971 Jerry was moved to a General Managerial role within the club which he did not enjoy and quit in 1973. His contribution to the club, however, will be long remembered. From 1974 to 1976 Jerry was manager of Forfar Athletic.

Billy Kirkwood, born in 1958, was signed by manager Jim McLean in 1976. Dundee United included Kirkwood in the pool to play in a friendly against St Johnstone on 31 July 1976. The following year he broke through the reserve ranks and became a member of the first team. In May of 1986 Billy left the club to pursue his career with Hibs. Also included in this departure was Stewart Beedie.

On 31 December 1986 within six months of leaving United he was back at Tannadice. The reported fee was in the region of £50,000. In September 1987 he was transferred to East End Park home of Dunfermline where he teamed up with old club mate John

Holt. The reported signing fee was £50,000. In April 1988 he was back in the city again, this time he had signed for rivals Dundee. By 1991 he had gained the required knowledge to sign on as a coach with Walter Smith's Rangers. Four years later on 28 March 1995, he was again back at Tannadice, this time he was manager at the club. The club was going through a tough patch that ultimately led to them being relegated to the First Division. Within a year United were back in the Premier Division after a tough play off game against Partick Thistle which went to extra time (at Tannadice) after a dramatic equaliser from Brian Welsh of United in the 89th minute. On 10 September 1996 the club sacked Billy after a series of poor results. However, the board offered Billy to stay on as an assistant-manager. Billy decided not to accept the offer and left. On 8 January 1997 he took up a coaching job in Hong Kong with Instant Dict. Later he returned to the United Kingdom to take up the post of assistant-manager with Hull City in July 1997. New manager at Hull was ex-Rangers player Mark Hateley, and he appointed Billy as his assistant. Billy made more than 400 appearances with United, and was also a member of the UEFA Cup Final side of 1987.

Jimmy Littlejohn, born in Glasgow in 1910, was a product of St Anthony's Club. After spells with St Johnstone and Cowdenbeath the centre-half joined United in 1939. Jimmy appeared in the Emergency War Cup at Hampden Park in 1940 against Rangers. In 1944, he took up the post of manager at the club. Managing the club from August to November, then he took up the offer of a directorship the club. Throughout the 1950s, Jimmy played an integral part of the club's setup. Along with his fellow directors, Jimmy was instrumental at initiating the club's financial scheme of Taypools. Jimmy remained on the board of director's right up to his death on 24 August 1989.

Willie MacFadyen, born in 1904, and appointed secretary-manager at the club on 30 October 1945. During his playing career he joined Motherwell in the 1930s, and Huddersfield Town. He was club manager for nine years, and stayed with the club until 24 August 1954. Willie resigned from the club, and the parties parted on the best of terms. Willie MacFadyen died in 1971.

Andy McCall, born in 1908, and became manager of United on 29 October 1958, before resigning after only six months in the job, on 23 May 1959.

His playing career had began with Cumnock Juniors before playing for Ayr United from 1928 until 1936. He then joined, in turn, St Johnstone, Huddersfield Town, Nottingham Forrest and then a coaching appointment with Dundee at Dens Park. Andy McCall died in 1979.

Charlie McGillivary, born in 1912, and signed for United on 28 October 1943 and made his debut for the club on 30 October against an RAF Select side. The club invited him to be manager in November 1944 after the resignation of Jimmy Littlejohn. As manager his job was short lived, he asked the directors to free him on 16 October 1945 and he left at the end of that month to be succeeded by Willie MacFadyen. Charlie McGillivary died in 1986.

Bobby McKay, was appointed manager of the club in July 1939. In his early days he had been a player with Morton, and had been part of their Scottish Cup winning side of 1921. Other clubs he played for included Rangers and Newcastle United, and had been capped for Scotland several times. One of his signings for United included Jerry Kerr, who would later manage the club from 1959 until 1971. Following the abandonment of league football in September 1939, the club terminated Bobby McKay's contract after just 12 weeks as manager. However, the club did resume playing football throughout the War, but Bobby was not in their plans. Bobby had seen only five competitive games played at the club before leaving. The former manager died in 1977.

James McLean, brought up in Ashgill by parents who appreciated family values, respect for hard work and honesty. Jim joined Hamilton Accies from Larkhall Thistle in 1956, before moving to Clyde in 1961. Clyde transferred him to Dundee in September 1965 for a fee of £10,000. He was one of Dundee manager Bobby Ancell's first signings, but after three years he joined Kilmarnock in August 1968. His last game as a player was on the 18 April 1970 when Killie drew 1-1 with St Johnstone.

His managerial career started with a move to Dundee as first team coach under manager John Prentice. However, in December 1971, Jim moved across the road to Tannadice to become United's new manager. Present day Dundee United history was now in the making, with a new approach to developing football skills and a youth policy that would later yield enormous benefits. He also helped out Scotland by agreeing to be Jock Stein's assistant in 1979 in a match against Peru. The assignment lasted nearly four years.

By now other clubs had recognized Jim's special talents and he had offers to manage Hearts in 1981, Motherwell, Hibs, Wolves, Chelsea and West Ham. A more difficult opportunity to turn down was the attractive package offered by Rangers in November 1983. Within 24 hours he had decided to stay with United because of his loyalty to United Chairman Johnstone Grant and the other members of the Board.

The club rewarded him for his loyalty with a testimonial game on 8 August 1984 against Brian Clough's Nottingham Forest. In May 1987 Jim collected the Scottish Brewers Personality Manager of the year award.

In 1989 he became Managing Director and Chairman, combining these roles with that of manager.

Probably the highlight of Jim McLean's career was the Wednesday evening of 20 May 1987, at Tannadice, when United played IFK Gothenburg in the EUFA Cup Final, played before 20,911 spectators. In an emotional game, drawn 1-1, United lost on aggregate, having lost the away game.

Jim faced his brother Tommy, manager of Motherwell in the Scottish Cup Final of 1991, which Motherwell won in a thrilling match by 4 goals to 3. The game was marred when the brothers' father died just hours before the match.

Jim McLean was honoured by the city when he became a Freeman of the City of Dundee at a ceremony held in the Caird Hall on Sunday 29 August 1993. He was to celebrate 25 years with the club on the 6 of December 1996.

Tommy McLean, began his professional footballing career with Kilmarnock, signing for Willie Waddell, and playing mostly as a winger. Tommy's father had persuaded him to sign for Killie, turning down an approach from Scot Symon of Rangers. He did eventually join Rangers, by that time managed by the same Willie Waddell. Chelsea were also interested in signing him. At Ibrox he won three championship badges and a European Winners Cup medal in 1972 after defeating Moscow Dynamo.

His first step on the managerial ladder was when he became first team coach and then assistant manager at Ibrox. On 25 November 1983 he joined Morton as manager, leading them to a First Division Championship. He repeated this success with Motherwell, winning the First Division Championship in 1985 and a Scottish Cup win in 1991. He left Motherwell after a disagreement and after a short time joined Hearts as manager in June 1994. His stay was short as he joined Raith Rovers on 3 September 1996, only to leave them and join Dundee United on the 10 September of the same year, replacing Billy Kirkwood. For the third time, Tommy won the Bell's Manager of the Month award in March 1997. His biggest success was when he took United to the Coca Cola Cup final in November 1997, only to lose 3 goals to 0 to Celtic.

Tommy gained six caps for his country winning the first one in 1969 against Denmark.

Tommy McLean, left Tannadice by mutual consent on Friday 4 September 1998, after a series of poor results since the November 1997 Coca Cola Cup Final defeat. This meant that one of Scotland's finest managers paid the ultimate price in today's modern game. In an interview with the *Evening Telegraph*, Tommy said: 'I spoke to the board and told them if they were of the opinion that a change was needed, I would stand down. It's disappointing but, in the end, you have to stand up and be judged by your results and ours have not been good enough. I accept that. I would like to stress I am leaving on good terms with the board and they have my best wishes.'

Peter O'Rourke, was born in Ayrshire 1874, and as a player he was with Celtic, Lincoln City, Burnley, Bradford City and Third Lanark. He was appointed manager of Dundee Hibs on 6 December 1922, and was with the club until March 1923. At that time the club was playing in the Scottish Alliance League, and a new board had taken over at Tannadice. Over the years there have been various arguments and debates as to the real intentions of the board in appointing O'Rourke. Some believed that they did not give him enough money to buy players. Others said it was that the club had wanted to drop the Irish connection. Whatever the reason, O'Rourke had one of the shortest spells ever as manager of the club. Peter O'Rourke died in 1956.

Willie Reid I, was 49 years old when appointed manager of United on 1 June 1931. As a player Reid spent three seasons with Greenock Morton and one season with Third Lanark. He also played for Motherwell and had a spell with Portsmouth. In April 1909 he joined Rangers, and gained nine International caps. His first cap was in 1911 in a game against England, which ended in a 1-1 draw. His last cap was won in 1914. With Rangers he scored 220 goals. Reid joined Albion Rovers in 1920 as player-manager, retiring from the playing side in 1922 when he took up the position of secretary-manager before joining United. The United board had interviewed only two candidates for the job. One was Willie, and the other was ex-United player Johnny Hart, at that time Johnny was with Ross County. A financial crisis at Tannadice did not help Reid in his role as manager. He signed Willie Logie from Portsmouth and George Radcliffe from Albion Rovers on free transfers. A goalkeeper, Chic McIntosh, was signed from junior side Logie. Willie Reid was manager until 1934.

Patrick Reilly, born in Ireland in 1874, and was founder of Dundee Hibs. The family arrived in Dundee in the 1870s and his father worked in a jute factory in the city.

Having improved his financial position, Pat soon took an interest in football and working within the Irish community and Catholic church was the chief instigator of securing Clepington Park for Dundee Hibs. Within a year the club had gained access to the Scottish League and Pat had become responsible for running the club's affairs. After the First World War, Dundee Hibs were under financial pressure and the club was sold to new owners in December 1922, Pat Reilly standing down. The new owners soon gave the club a new strip and a new name of Dundee United.

It was reported in the media on 5 April 1937 that Pat Reilly was critically ill in Dundee Royal Infirmary. He died the following day aged 63. On 10 April in the match against St Bernards at Tannadice, the flag was flown at half mast and 3000 spectators, players and officials observed a minute's silence.

Reggie Smith, appointed United manager in September 1954 replacing Willie MacFadyen. Earlier in his career Reggie had signed for Dundee in 1946, staying eight years at Dens. In 1957 he left United for the manager's post at Falkirk. Within three months of joining them Falkirk had won the Scottish Cup, beating Kilmarnock 2-1 after extra time. He joined Millwall as manager in July 1959 and later joined Bedford Town, leaving in November 1963. In 1966 he was manager of Cape Town, South Africa.

Paul Sturrock, became manager of Dundee United on 4 September 1998 after the resignation of manager Tommy McLean.

LEAGUE POSITIONS

Northern League 1909-1910

		P	W	D	L	PTS
1.	Dundee A.	9	7	1	1	15
2.	Brechin City	11	6	1	4	13
3.	DUNDEE HIBS	11	4	3	4	11
4.	Montrose	9	3	3	3	9
5.	Forfar Ath.	12	3	3	6	9
6.	Dundee Wand.	8	1	4	3	6
7.	Aberdeen A.	6	1	1	4	3

Scottish League Division Two 1910-1911

		P	W	D	L	PTS
1.	Dumbarton	22	15	1	6	31
2.	Ayr United	22	12	3	7	27
3.	Albion Rovers	22	10	5	7	25
4.	Leith Athletic	22	9	6	7	24
5.	Cowdenbeath	22	9	5	8	23
6.	St Bernard's	22	10	2	10	22
7.	East Stirling	22	7	6	9	20
8.	Port Glasgow	22	8	3	11	19
9.	DUNDEE HIBS	22	7	5	10	19
10.	Arthurlie	22	7	5	10	19
11.	Abercorn	22	9	1	12	19
12.	Vale of Leven	22	4	8	10	16

Scottish League Division Two 1911-12

		P	W	D	L	PTS
1.	Ayr United	22	16	3	3	35
2.	Abercorn	22	13	4	5	30
3.	Dumbarton	22	13	1	8	27
4.	Cowdenbeath	22	12	2	8	26
5.	St Johnstone	22	10	4	8	24
6.	St Bernard's	22	9	5	8	23
7.	Leith Athletic	22	9	4	9	22
8.	Arthurlie	22	7	5	10	19
9.	East Stirling	22	7	3	12	17
10.	DUNDEE HIBS	22	5	5	12	15
11.	Albion Rovers	22	6	1	15	13
12.	Vale of Leven	22	6	1	15	13

Division Two 1912-1913

		P	W	D	L	PTS
1.	Ayr United	26	13	8	5	34
2.	Dunfermline Ath.	26	13	7	6	33
3.	East Stirling	26	12	8	6	32
4.	Abercorn	26	12	7	7	31
5.	Cowdenbeath	26	12	6	8	30
6.	Dumbarton	26	12	5	9	29
7.	St Bernard's	26	12	3	11	27
8.	Johnstone	26	9	6	11	24
9.	Albion Rovers	26	10	3	13	23
10.	DUNDEE HIBS	26	6	10	10	22
11.	St Johnstone	26	7	7	12	21
12.	Vale of Leven	26	8	5	13	21
13.	Arthurlie	26	7	5	14	19
14.	Leith Athletic	26	5	8	13	18

Division Two 1913-1914

		P	W	D	L	PTS
1.	Cowdenbeath	22	13	5	4	31
2.	Albion Rovers	22	10	7	5	27
3.	Dunfermline Ath.	22	11	4	7	26
4.	DUNDEE HIBS	22	11	4	7	26
5.	St Johnstone	22	9	5	8	23
6.	Abercorn	22	10	3	9	23
7.	St Bernard's	22	8	6	8	22
8.	East Stirling	22	7	8	7	22
9.	Arthurlie	22	8	4	10	20
10.	Leith Athletic	22	5	9	8	19
11.	Vale of Leven	22	5	3	14	13
12.	Johnstone	22	4	4	14	12

B Division 1914-1915

		P	W	D	L	PTS
1.	Cowdenbeath	26	16	5	5	37
2.	Leith Athletic	26	15	7	4	37
3.	St Bernard's	26	18	1	7	37
4.	East Stirling	26	13	5	8	31
5.	Clydebank	26	13	4	9	30
6.	Dunfermline Ath.	26	13	2	11	28
7.	Johnstone	26	11	5	10	27
8.	St Johnstone	26	10	6	10	26
9.	Albion Rovers	26	9	7	10	25
10.	Lochgelly United	26	9	3	14	21
11.	DUNDEE HIBS	26	8	3	15	19
12.	Abercorn	26	5	7	14	17
13.	Arthurlie	26	6	4	16	16
14.	Vale of Leven	26	4	5	17	13

Eastern League 1915-1916

		P	W	D	L	PTS
1.	Armadale	21	17	2	2	36
2.	St Bernard's	22	16	1	5	33
3.	Cowdenbeath	22	12	3	7	27
4.	Bathgate	22	12	2	8	26
5.	East Fife	22	8	6	8	22
6.	Broxburn United	22	9	4	9	22
7.	East Stirling	22	10	2	10	22
8.	Leith Athletic	20	7	4	9	18
9.	Lochgelly United	21	7	4	10	18
10.	DUNDEE HIBS	22	7	1	14	15
11.	Dunfermline Ath.	20	5	4	11	14
12.	Kirkcaldy United	22	2	1	19	5

In this season the remaining fixtures were not completed due to the First World War

Eastern League 1916-1917

		P	W	D	L	PTS
1.	Cowdenbeath	18	11	5	2	27
2.	East Fife	14	7	5	2	23
3.	St Bernard's	18	10	2	6	22
4.	Armadale	17	7	6	4	20
5.	DUNDEE HIBS	17	6	3	8	15
6.	Dunfermline Ath.	16	7	1	8	15
7.	East Stirling	15	5	4	6	14
8.	Broxburn United	14	5	2	7	12
9.	Bathgate	16	3	2	11	8
10.	Lochgelly United	15	4	0	11	8

Eastern League 1917-1918

		P	W	D	L	PTS
1.	Cowdenbeath	24	15	3	6	33
2.	Dundee	24	15	3	6	33
3.	Raith Rovers	22	11	5	6	27
4.	Armadale	20	7	5	8	19
5.	*DUNDEE HIBS	24	7	5	12	19
6.	Dunfermline Ath.	24	6	3	15	15
7.	East Fife	22	5	4	13	14

* During season 1918-1919 Dundee Hibs only played in friendly games.

Eastern League 1919-1920

		P	W	D	L	PTS
1.	DUNDEE HIBS	18	13	2	3	28
2.	Dundee A.	18	10	5	3	25
3.	Cowdenbeath	18	10	4	4	24
4.	St Johnstone	18	8	4	6	20
5.	Arbroath	18	9	2	7	20
6.	Forfar Athletic	18	8	2	8	18
7.	Lochgelly United	18	6	4	8	16
8.	Raith Rovers A.	18	7	0	11	14
9.	Montrose	18	4	2	12	10
10.	Brechin City	18	1	3	14	5

Central League 1920-1921

		P	W	D	L	PTS
1.	Bo'ness	34	21	7	6	49
2.	Hearts A.	34	22	4	8	48
3.	Cowdenbeath	34	20	6	8	46
4.	Dunfermline Ath	34	16	7	11	39
5.	East Fife	34	13	12	9	38
6.	Bathgate	34	13	11	10	37
7.	St Bernard's	34	11	12	11	34
8.	Stenhousemuir	34	15	4	15	34
9.	Alloa Athletic	34	9	15	10	33
10.	St Johnstone	34	13	6	15	32
11.	Falkirk A.	34	10	10	14	30
12.	Broxburn United	34	12	5	17	29
13.	Clackmannan	34	13	3	18	29
14.	East Stirling	34	10	8	16	28
15.	Armadale	34	10	7	17	27
16.	King's Park	34	9	9	16	27
17.	DUNDEE HIBS	34	10	7	17	27
18.	Lochgelly United	34	11	5	18	27

Division Two 1921-1922

		P	W	D	L	PTS
1.	Alloa Athletic	38	26	8	4	60
2.	Cowdenbeath	38	19	9	10	47
3.	Armadale	38	20	5	13	45
4.	Vale of Leven	38	17	10	11	44
5.	Bathgate	38	16	11	11	43
6.	Bo'ness	38	16	7	15	39
7.	Broxburn United	38	14	11	13	39
8.	Dunfermline Ath.	38	14	10	14	38
9.	St Bernard's	38	15	8	15	38
10.	Stenhousemuir	38	14	10	14	38
11.	Johnstone	38	14	10	14	38
12.	East Fife	38	14	10	14	38
13.	St Johnstone	38	12	11	15	35
14.	Forfar Athletic	38	11	12	15	34
15.	East Stirling	38	12	10	16	34
16.	Arbroath	38	11	11	16	33
17.	King's Park	38	10	12	16	32
18.	Lochgelly United	38	11	9	18	31
19.	DUNDEE HIBS	38	10	8	20	28
20.	Clackmannan	38	9	8	21	26

Scottish Alliance 1922-1923

		P	W	D	L	PTS
1.	Airdrie	26	16	6	4	38
2.	St Mirren A.	26	14	6	6	34
3.	Hearts A.	26	13	6	7	32
4.	Aberdeen A.	26	11	9	6	31
5.	Queen's Park Str.	26	12	6	8	30
6.	Rangers A.	26	12	6	8	30
7.	Dundee A.	26	11	5	10	27
8.	Partick Thistle A.	26	10	5	11	25
9.	Raith Rovers A.	26	8	9	9	25
10.	Kilmarnock A.	26	7	10	9	24
11.	Albion Rovers A.	26	7	6	13	20
12.	DUNDEE HIBS	26	5	7	14	17
13.	Ayr United A.	26	7	2	17	16
14.	Third Lanark A.	26	4	7	15	15

Division Two 1923-1924

		P	W	D	L	PTS
1.	St Johnstone	38	22	12	4	56
2.	Cowdenbeath	38	23	9	6	55
3.	Bathgate	38	16	12	10	44
4.	Stenhousemuir	38	16	11	11	43
5.	Albion Rovers	38	15	12	11	42
6.	King's Park	38	16	10	12	42
7.	Dunfermline Ath.	38	14	11	13	39
8.	Johnstone	38	16	7	15	39
9.	DUNDEE UNITED	38	12	15	11	39
10.	Dumbarton	38	17	5	16	39
11.	Armadale	38	16	6	16	38
12.	East Fife	38	14	9	15	37
13.	Bo'ness	38	13	11	14	37
14.	Forfar Ath.	38	14	7	17	35
15.	Alloa Ath.	38	14	6	18	34
16.	Vale of Leven	38	12	9	17	33
17.	Arbroath	38	12	8	18	32
18.	St Bernard's	38	11	10	17	32
19.	Broxburn United	38	12	8	18	32
20.	Lochgelly United	38	4	4	30	12

Division Two Season 1924-1925

		P	W	D	L	PTS
1.	DUNDEE UNITED	38	20	10	8	50
2.	Clydebank	38	20	8	10	48
3.	Clyde	38	20	7	11	47
4.	Alloa Ath.	38	17	11	10	45
5.	Arbroath	38	16	10	12	42
6.	Bo'ness	38	16	9	13	41
7.	Broxburn United	38	16	9	13	41
8.	Dumbarton	38	15	10	13	40
9.	East Fife	38	17	5	16	39
10.	King's Park	38	15	8	15	38
11.	Stenhousemuir	38	15	7	16	37
12.	Arthurlie	38	14	8	16	36
13.	Dunfermline Ath.	38	14	7	17	35
14.	Armadale	38	15	5	18	35
15.	Albion Rovers	38	15	5	18	35
16.	Bathgate	38	12	10	16	34
17.	St Bernard's	38	14	4	20	32
18.	East Stirling	38	11	8	19	30
19.	Johnstone	38	12	4	22	28
20.	Forfar Ath.	38	10	7	21	27

Division One Season 1925-1926

		P	W	D	L	PTS
1.	Celtic	38	25	8	5	58
2.	Airdrie	38	23	4	11	50
3.	Hearts	38	21	8	9	50
4.	St Mirren	38	20	7	11	47
5.	Motherwell	38	19	8	11	46
6.	Rangers	38	19	6	13	44
7.	Cowdenbeath	38	18	6	14	42
8.	Falkirk	38	14	14	10	42
9.	Kilmarnock	38	17	7	14	41
10.	Dundee	38	14	9	15	37
11.	Aberdeen	38	13	10	15	36
12.	Hamilton Accies	38	13	9	16	35
13.	Queen's Park	38	15	4	19	34
14.	Partick Thistle	38	10	13	15	33
15.	Morton	38	12	7	19	31
16.	Hibs	38	12	6	20	30
17.	DUNDEE UNITED	38	11	6	21	28
18.	St Johnstone	38	9	10	19	28
19.	Raith Rovers	38	7	8	23	22

Division One Season 1926-1927

		P	W	D	L	PTS
1.	Rangers	38	23	10	5	56
2.	Motherwell	38	23	5	10	51
3.	Celtic	38	21	7	10	49
4.	Airdrie	38	18	9	11	45
5.	Dundee	38	17	9	12	43
6.	Falkirk	38	16	19	12	42
7.	Cowdenbeath	38	18	6	14	42
8.	Aberdeen	38	13	14	11	40
9.	Hibs	38	16	7	15	39
10.	St Mirren	38	16	5	17	37
11.	Partick Thistle	38	15	6	17	36
12.	Queen's Park	38	15	6	17	36
13.	Hearts	38	12	11	15	35
14.	St Johnstone	38	13	9	16	35
15.	Hamilton Accies	38	13	9	16	35
16.	Kilmarnock	38	12	8	18	32
17.	Clyde	38	10	9	19	29
18.	Dunfermline Ath.	38	10	8	20	28
19.	Morton	38	12	4	22	28
20.	DUNDEE UNITED	38	7	8	23	22

Division Two Season 1927-1928

		P	W	D	L	PTS
1.	Ayr United	38	24	6	8	54
2.	Third Lanark	38	18	9	11	45
3.	King's Park	38	16	12	10	44
4.	East Fife	38	18	7	13	43
5.	Forfar Ath.	38	18	7	13	43
6.	DUNDEE UNITED	38	17	9	12	43
7.	Arthurlie	38	18	4	16	40
8.	Albion Rovers	38	17	4	17	38
9.	East Stirling	38	14	10	14	38
10.	Arbroath	38	16	4	18	36
11.	Dumbarton	38	16	4	18	36
12.	Queen of the South	38	15	6	17	36
13.	Leith Ath.	38	13	9	16	35
14.	Clydebank	38	16	3	19	35
15.	Alloa Ath.	38	12	11	15	35
16.	Stenhousemuir	38	15	5	18	35
17.	St Bernard's	38	15	5	18	35
18.	Morton	38	13	8	17	34
19.	Bathgate	38	10	11	17	31
20.	Armadale	38	8	8	22	24

Division Two Season 1928-1929

		P	W	D	L	PTS
1.	DUNDEE UNITED	36	23	4	9	51
2.	Morton	36	21	8	7	50
3.	Arbroath	36	18	9	8	47
4.	Albion Rovers	36	18	8	10	44
5.	Leith Ath.	36	18	7	11	43
6.	St Bernard's	36	16	9	11	41
7.	Forfar Ath.	36	14	10	11	38
8.	East Fife	36	15	6	14	36
9.	Queen of the South	36	16	4	16	36
10.	Bo'ness	36	15	5	15	35
11.	Dunfermline Ath.	36	13	7	16	33
12.	East Stirling	36	14	4	18	32
13.	Alloa Ath.	36	12	7	17	31
14.	Dumbarton	36	11	9	16	31
15.	King's Park	36	8	13	15	29
16.	Clydebank	36	11	5	20	27
17.	Arthurlie	36	9	7	16	25
18.	Stenhousemuir	36	9	6	20	24
19.	Armadale	36	8	7	21	23

Division One Season 1929-1930

		P	W	D	L	PTS
1.	Rangers	38	28	4	6	60
2.	Motherwell	38	25	5	8	55
3.	Aberdeen	38	23	7	8	53
4.	Celtic	38	22	5	11	49
5.	St Mirren	38	18	5	15	41
6.	Partick Thistle	38	16	9	13	41
7.	Falkirk	38	16	9	13	41
8.	Kilmarnock	38	15	9	14	39
9.	Ayr United	38	16	6	16	38
10.	Hearts	38	14	9	15	37
11.	Clyde	38	13	11	14	37
12.	Airdrie	38	16	4	18	36
13.	Hamilton Accies	38	14	7	17	35
14.	Dundee	38	14	6	18	34
15.	Queen's Park	38	15	4	19	34
16.	Cowdenbeath	38	13	7	18	33
17.	Hibs	38	9	11	18	29
18.	Morton	38	10	7	21	27
19.	DUNDEE UNITED	38	7	8	23	22
20.	St Johnstone	38	6	7	25	19

Division Two Season 1930-1931

		P	W	D	L	PTS
1.	Third Lanark	38	27	7	4	61
2.	DUNDEE UNITED	38	21	8	9	50
3.	Dunfermline Ath	38	20	7	11	47
4.	Raith Rovers	38	20	6	12	46
5.	St Johnstone	38	19	6	13	44
6.	Queen of the South	38	18	6	14	42
7.	East Stirling	38	17	7	14	41
8.	Montrose	38	19	3	16	41
9.	Albion Rovers	38	14	11	13	39
10.	Dumbarton	38	15	8	15	38
11.	St Bernard's	38	14	9	15	37
12.	Forfar Ath.	38	15	6	17	36
13.	Alloa Ath.	38	15	5	18	35
14.	King's Park	38	14	6	18	34
15.	Arbroath	38	15	4	19	34
16.	Brechin City	38	13	7	18	33
17.	Stenhousemuir	38	12	6	20	30
18.	Armadale	38	13	2	23	28
19.	Clydebank	38	10	2	26	22
20.	Bo'ness	38	9	4	25	22

Division One Season 1931-1932

		P	W	D	L	PTS
1.	Motherwell	38	30	6	2	66
2.	Rangers	38	28	5	5	61
3.	Celtic	38	20	8	10	48
4.	Third Lanark	38	21	4	13	46
5.	St Mirren	38	20	4	14	44
6.	Partick Thistle	38	19	4	15	42
7.	Aberdeen	38	16	9	13	41
8.	Hearts	38	17	5	16	39
9.	Kilmarnock	38	16	7	15	39
10.	Hamilton Accies	38	16	6	16	38
11.	Dundee	38	14	10	14	38
12.	Cowdenbeath	38	15	8	15	38
13.	Clyde	38	13	9	16	35
14.	Airdrie	38	13	6	19	32
15.	Morton	38	12	7	19	31
16.	Queen's Park	38	13	5	20	31
17.	Ayr United	38	11	7	20	29
18.	Falkirk	38	11	5	22	27
19.	DUNDEE UNITED	38	6	4	25	19
20.	Leith Ath.	38	6	4	28	16

Division Two Season 1932-1933

		P	W	D	L	PTS
1.	Hibs	34	25	4	5	54
2.	Queen of the South	34	20	9	5	49
3.	Dunfermline Ath	34	20	7	7	47
4.	Stenhousemuir	34	18	6	10	42
5.	Albion Rovers	34	19	2	13	40
6.	Raith Rovers	34	16	4	14	36
7.	East Fife	34	15	4	15	34
8.	King's Park	34	13	8	13	34
9.	Dumbarton	34	14	6	14	34
10.	Arbroath	34	14	5	15	33
11.	Alloa Ath	34	14	5	15	33
12.	St Bernard's	34	13	6	15	32
13.	DUNDEE UNITED	34	14	4	16	32
14.	Forfar Ath	34	12	4	18	28
15.	Brechin City	34	11	4	19	26
16.	Leith Ath	34	10	5	19	25
17.	Montrose	34	8	5	21	21
18.	Edinburgh City	34	4	4	26	12

Division Two Season 1933-1934

		P	W	D	L	PTS
1.	Albion Rovers	34	20	5	9	45
2.	Dunfermline Ath	34	20	4	10	44
3.	Arbroath	34	20	4	10	44
4.	Stenhousemuir	34	18	4	12	40
5.	Morton	34	17	5	12	39
6.	Dumbarton	34	17	3	14	37
7.	King's Park	34	14	8	12	36
8.	Raith Rovers	34	15	5	14	35
9.	East Stirling	34	14	7	13	35
10.	St Bernard's	34	15	4	15	34
11.	Forfar Ath	34	13	7	14	33
12.	Leith Ath	34	12	8	14	32
13.	East Fife	34	12	8	14	32
14.	Brechin City	34	13	5	16	31
15.	Alloa Ath	34	11	9	14	31
16.	Montrose	34	11	4	19	26
17.	DUNDEE UNITED	34	10	4	20	24
18.	Edinburgh City	34	4	6	24	14

Division Two Season 1934-1935

		P	W	D	L	Pts
1.	Third Lanark	34	23	6	5	52
2.	Arbroath	34	23	4	7	50
3.	St Bernard's	34	20	7	7	47
4.	DUNDEE UNITED	34	18	6	10	42
5.	Stenhousemuir	34	17	5	12	39
6.	Morton	34	17	4	13	38
7.	King's Park	34	18	2	14	38
8.	Leith Ath	34	16	5	13	37
9.	East Fife	34	16	3	15	35
10.	Alloa Ath	34	12	10	12	34
11.	Forfar Ath	34	13	8	13	34
12.	Cowdenbeath	34	13	6	15	32
13.	Raith Rovers	34	13	3	18	29
14.	East Stirling	34	11	7	16	29
15.	Brechin City	34	10	6	18	26
16.	Dumbarton	34	9	4	21	22
17.	Montrose	34	7	6	21	20
18.	Edinburgh City	34	3	2	29	8

Division Two Season 1935-1936

		P	W	D	L	PTS
1.	Falkirk	34	28	3	3	59
2.	St Mirren	34	25	2	7	52
3.	Morton	34	21	6	7	48
4.	Alloa Ath	34	19	6	9	44
5.	St Bernard's	34	18	4	12	40
6.	East Fife	34	16	6	12	38
7.	DUNDEE UNITED	34	16	5	13	37
8.	East Stirling	34	13	8	13	34
9.	Leith Ath	34	15	3	16	33
10.	Cowdenbeath	34	13	5	16	31
11.	Stenhousemuir	34	13	3	18	29
12.	Montrose	34	13	3	18	29
13.	Forfar Ath	34	10	7	17	27
14.	King's Park	34	11	5	18	27
15.	Edinburgh City	34	8	9	17	25
16.	Brechin City	34	8	6	20	22
17.	Raith Rovers	34	9	3	22	21
18.	Dumbarton	34	5	6	23	16

Division Two Season 1936-1937

		P	W	D	L	PTS
1.	Ayr United	34	25	4	5	54
2.	Morton	34	23	5	6	51
3.	St Bernard's	34	22	4	8	48
4.	Airdrie	34	18	8	8	44
5.	East Fife	34	15	8	11	38
6.	Cowdenbeath	34	14	10	10	38
7.	East Stirling	34	18	2	14	38
8.	Raith Rovers	34	16	4	14	36
9.	Alloa Ath	34	13	7	14	33
10.	Stenhousemuir	34	14	4	16	32
11.	Leith Ath	34	13	5	16	31
12.	Forfar Ath	34	11	8	15	30
13.	Montrose	34	11	6	17	28
14.	DUNDEE UNITED	34	9	9	16	27
15.	Dumbarton	34	11	5	18	27
16.	Brechin City	34	8	9	17	25
17.	King's Park	34	11	3	20	25
18.	Edinburgh City	34	2	3	29	7

Division Two Season 1937-1938

		P	W	D	L	Pts
1.	Raith Rovers	34	27	5	2	59
2.	Albion Rovers	34	20	8	6	48
3.	Airdrie	34	21	5	8	47
4.	St Bernard's	34	20	5	9	45
5.	East Fife	34	19	5	10	43
6.	Cowdenbeath	34	17	9	8	43
7.	Dumbarton	34	17	5	12	39
8.	Stenhousemuir	34	17	5	12	39
9.	Dunfermline Ath	34	17	5	12	39
10.	Leith Ath	34	16	5	13	37
11.	Alloa Ath	34	11	4	19	26
12.	King's Park	34	11	4	19	26
13.	East Stirling	34	9	7	18	25
14.	DUNDEE UNITED	34	9	5	20	23
15.	Forfar Ath	34	8	6	20	22
16.	Montrose	34	7	8	19	22
17.	Edinburgh City	34	7	3	24	17
18.	Brechin City	34	5	2	27	12

Division Two Season 1938-1939

		P	W	D	L	Pts
1.	Cowdenbeath	34	28	4	2	60
2.	Alloa Ath	34	22	4	8	48
3.	East Fife	34	21	6	7	48
4.	Airdrie	34	21	5	8	47
5.	Dunfermline Ath	34	18	5	11	41
6.	Dundee	34	15	7	12	37
7.	St Bernard's	34	15	6	13	36
8.	Stenhousemuir	34	15	5	14	35
9.	DUNDEE UNITED	34	15	3	16	33
10.	Brechin City	34	11	9	14	31
11.	Dumbarton	34	9	12	13	30
12.	Morton	34	11	6	17	28
13.	King's Park	34	12	2	20	26
14.	Montrose	34	10	5	19	25
15.	Forfar Ath	34	11	3	20	25
16.	Leith Ath	34	10	4	20	24
17.	East Stirling	34	9	4	21	22
18.	Edinburgh City	34	6	4	24	16

Eastern Regional League Season 1939-1940

		P	W	D	L	PTS
1.	Falkirk	29	20	5	4	45
2.	Hearts	29	18	4	7	40
3.	Dunfermline Ath	29	19	2	8	40
4.	Aberdeen	29	16	4	9	36
5.	St Johnstone	29	13	8	8	34
6.	Dundee	29	11	8	10	30
7.	Alloa Ath	29	13	4	12	30
8.	Hibs	29	12	5	12	29
9.	DUNDEE UNITED	29	12	2	15	26
10.	East Fife	29	11	3	15	25
11.	Raith Rovers	29	10	3	16	23
12.	King's Park	29	9	4	16	22
13.	St Bernard's	29	8	5	16	21
14.	Stenhousemuir	29	7	3	19	17
15.	Arbroath	29	6	5	18	17

*Due to the start of World War Two the Scottish League closed in June 1940.

North Eastern League 1941-1942

First Series		P	W	D	L	PTS
1.	Rangers	14	10	2	2	22
2.	East Fife	14	8	5	1	21
3.	Aberdeen	14	8	3	3	19
4.	Dunfermline Ath	14	6	3	5	15
5.	St Bernard's	14	5	3	6	13
6.	DUNDEE UNITED	14	3	4	7	10
7.	Raith Rovers	14	3	1	10	7
8.	Leith Ath	14	2	1	11	5
Second Series						
1.	Aberdeen	14	9	2	3	26
2.	Rangers	14	10	1	3	26
3.	East Fife	14	8	2	4	22
4.	DUNDEE UNITED	14	7	3	4	21
5.	Raith Rovers	14	6	2	6	17
6.	Dunfermline Ath	14	4	2	8	12
7.	Leith Ath	14	3	2	9	9
8.	St Bernard's	14	1	2	11	4

North Eastern League 1942-1943

First Series	P	W	D	L	PTS
1. Aberdeen	14	11	1	2	23
2. Dunfermline	14	10	0	4	20
3. East Fife	14	8	1	5	17
4. Rangers	14	6	0	8	12
5. Hearts	14	6	0	8	12
6. DUNDEE UNITED	14	5	0	9	10
7. Hibs	14	4	1	9	9
8. Raith Rovers	14	4	1	9	9
Second Series					
1. Aberdeen	14	10	2	2	29
2. East Fife	14	9	2	3	25
3. Raith Rovers	14	9	1	4	23
4. Dunfermline Ath	14	6	3	5	18
5. Rangers	14	5	2	7	15
6. Hearts	14	4	3	7	13
7. DUNDEE UNITED	14	5	1	8	13
8. Hibs	14	1	0	13	2

North Eastern League 1943-1944

First Series	P	W	D	L	PTS
1. Raith Rovers	14	11	0	3	22
2. Hearts	14	9	1	4	19
3. Aberdeen	14	7	3	4	17
4. Dunfermline Ath	14	8	1	5	17
5. DUNDEE UNITED	14	7	0	7	14
6. Rangers	14	4	1	9	9
7. East Fife	14	4	1	9	9
8. Falkirk	14	2	1	11	5
Second Series					
1. Aberdeen	14	9	2	3	24
2. Rangers	14	9	2	3	24
3. East Fife	14	6	3	5	18
4. DUNDEE UNITED	14	6	1	7	15
5. Hearts	14	5	2	7	14
6. Dunfermline Ath	14	5	1	8	13
7. Raith Rovers	14	4	3	7	13
8. Falkirk	14	4	2	8	12

North Eastern League 1944-1945

First Series		P	W	D	L	PTS
1.	Dundee	18	13	2	3	28
2.	Aberdeen	18	13	1	4	27
3.	Raith Rovers	18	10	2	6	22
4.	Dunfermline Ath	18	8	5	5	21
5.	Rangers	18	7	2	9	16
6.	East Fife	18	6	4	8	16
7.	Arbroath	18	6	4	8	16
8.	DUNDEE UNITED	18	5	3	10	13
9.	Hearts	18	5	2	11	12
10.	Falkirk	18	3	3	12	9
Second Series						
1.	Aberdeen	18	11	3	4	31
2.	East Fife	18	10	3	5	28
3.	Rangers	18	10	3	5	27
4.	Dundee	18	10	0	8	24
5.	Dunfermline Ath	18	9	3	6	24
6.	DUNDEE UNITED	18	7	2	9	19
7.	Arbroath	18	5	4	9	18
8.	Raith Rovers	18	7	1	10	18
9.	Hearts	18	5	4	9	18
10.	Falkirk	18	4	1	13	11

Southern League 'B' Division Season 1945-1946

		P	W	D	L	PTS
1.	Dundee	26	21	2	3	44
2.	East Fife	26	15	4	7	34
3.	Ayr United	26	15	4	7	34
4.	Airdrie	26	14	5	7	33
5.	St Johnstone	26	12	6	8	30
6.	Albion Rovers	26	14	2	10	30
7.	Alloa Ath	26	12	4	10	28
8.	Dumbarton	26	11	4	11	26
9.	Dunfermline Ath	26	10	4	12	24
10.	Cowdenbeath	26	8	5	13	21
11.	Stenhousemuir	26	6	5	15	17
12.	DUNDEE UNITED	26	6	3	17	15
13.	Raith Rovers	26	6	2	18	14
14.	Arbroath	26	6	2	18	14

'B' Division Season 1946-1947

		P	W	D	L	PTS
1.	Dundee	26	21	3	2	45
2.	Airdrie	26	19	4	3	42
3.	East Fife	26	12	7	7	31
4.	Albion Rovers	26	10	7	9	27
5.	Alloa Ath	26	11	5	10	27
6.	Raith Rovers	26	10	6	10	26
7.	Stenhousemuir	26	8	7	11	23
8.	Dunfermline Ath	26	10	3	13	23
9.	St Johnstone	26	9	4	13	22
10.	DUNDEE UNITED	26	9	4	13	22
11.	Ayr United	26	9	2	15	20
12.	Arbroath	26	7	6	13	20
13.	Dumbarton	26	7	4	15	18
14.	Cowdenbeath	26	6	6	14	18

'B' Division Season 1947-1948

		P	W	D	L	PTS
1.	East Fife	30	25	3	2	53
2.	Albion Rovers	30	19	4	7	42
3.	Hamilton Accies	30	17	6	7	40
4.	Raith Rovers	30	14	6	10	34
5.	Cowdenbeath	30	12	8	10	32
6.	Kilmarnock	30	13	4	13	30
7.	Dunfermline Ath	30	13	3	14	29
8.	Stirling Albion	30	11	6	13	28
9.	St Johnstone	30	11	5	14	27
10.	Ayr United	30	9	9	12	27
11.	Dumbarton	30	9	7	14	25
12.	Alloa Ath	30	10	6	14	24*
13.	Arbroath	30	10	3	17	23
14.	Stenhousemuir	30	6	11	13	23
15.	DUNDEE UNITED	30	10	2	18	22
16.	Leith Ath	30	6	7	17	19

*Alloa Athletic had two points deducted from their league points for fielding unregistered players in this season.

'B' Division Season 1948-1949

		P	W	D	L	PTS
1.	Raith Rovers	30	20	2	8	42
2.	Stirling Albion	30	20	2	8	42
3.	Airdrie	30	16	9	5	41
4.	Dunfermline Ath	30	16	9	5	41
5.	Queen's Park	30	14	7	9	35
6.	St Johnstone	30	14	4	12	32
7.	Arbroath	30	12	8	10	32
8.	DUNDEE UNITED	30	10	7	13	27
9.	Ayr United	30	10	7	13	27
10.	Hamilton Accies	30	9	8	13	26
11.	Kilmarnock	30	9	7	14	25
12.	Stenhousemuir	30	8	8	14	24
13.	Cowdenbeath	30	9	5	16	23
14.	Alloa Ath	30	10	3	17	23
15.	Dumbarton	30	8	6	16	22
16.	East Stirling	30	6	6	18	18

'B' Division Season 1949-1950

		P	W	D	L	PTS
1.	Morton	30	20	7	3	47
2.	Airdrie	30	19	6	5	44
3.	Dunfermline Ath	30	16	4	10	36
4.	St Johnstone	30	15	6	9	36
5.	Cowdenbeath	30	16	3	11	35
6.	Hamilton Accies	30	14	6	10	34
7.	DUNDEE UNITED	30	14	5	11	33
8.	Kilmarnock	30	14	5	11	33
9.	Queen's Park	30	12	7	11	33
10.	Forfar Ath	30	11	8	11	30
11.	Albion Rovers	30	10	7	13	27
12.	Stenhousemuir	30	8	8	14	24
13.	Ayr United	30	8	6	16	22
14.	Arbroath	30	5	9	16	19
15.	Dumbarton	30	6	4	20	16
16.	Alloa Ath	30	5	3	22	13

'B' Division Season 1950-1951

		P	W	D	L	PTS
1.	Queen of the South	30	21	3	6	45
2.	Stirling Albion	30	21	3	6	45
3.	Ayr United	30	15	6	9	36
4.	DUNDEE UNITED	30	16	4	10	36
5.	St Johnstone	30	14	5	11	33
6.	Queen's Park	30	13	7	10	33
7.	Hamilton Accies	30	12	8	10	32
8.	Albion Rovers	30	14	4	12	32
9.	Dumbarton	30	12	5	13	29
10.	Dunfermline Ath	30	12	4	14	28
11.	Cowdenbeath	30	12	3	15	27
12.	Kilmarnock	30	8	8	14	24
13.	Arbroath	30	8	5	17	21
14.	Forfar Ath	30	9	3	18	21
15.	Stenhousemuir	30	9	2	19	20
16.	Alloa Athletic	30	7	4	19	18

'B' Division Season 1951-1952

		P	W	D	L	PTS
1.	Clyde	30	19	6	5	44
2.	Falkirk	30	18	7	5	43
3.	Ayr United	30	17	5	8	39
4.	DUNDEE UNITED	30	16	5	9	37
5.	Kilmarnock	30	16	2	12	34
6.	Dunfermline Ath	30	15	2	13	32
7.	Alloa Ath	30	13	6	11	32
8.	Cowdenbeath	30	12	8	10	32
9.	Hamilton Accies	30	12	6	12	30
10.	Dumbarton	30	10	8	12	28
11.	St Johnstone	30	9	7	14	25
12.	Forfar Ath	30	10	4	16	24
13.	Stenhousemuir	30	8	6	16	22
14.	Albion Rovers	30	6	10	14	22
15.	Queen's Park	30	8	4	18	20
16.	Arbroath	30	6	4	20	16

'B' Division Season 1952-1953

		P	W	D	L	PTS
1.	Stirling Albion	30	20	4	6	44
2.	Hamilton Accies	30	20	3	7	43
3.	Queen's Park	30	15	7	8	37
4.	Kilmarnock	30	17	2	11	36
5.	Ayr United	30	17	2	11	36
6.	Morton	30	15	3	12	33
7.	Arbroath	30	13	7	10	33
8.	DUNDEE UNITED	30	12	5	13	29
9.	Alloa Ath	30	12	5	13	29
10.	Dumbarton	30	11	6	13	28
11.	Dunfermline Ath	30	9	9	12	27
12.	Stenhousemuir	30	10	6	14	26
13.	Cowdenbeath	30	8	7	15	23
14.	St Johnstone	30	8	6	16	22
15.	Forfar Ath	30	8	4	18	20
16.	Albion Rovers	30	5	4	21	14

'B' Division Season 1953-1954

		P	W	D	L	PTS
1.	Motherwell	30	21	3	6	45
2.	Kilmarnock	30	19	4	7	42
3.	Third Lanark	30	13	10	7	36
4.	Stenhousemuir	30	14	8	8	36
5.	Morton	30	15	3	12	33
6.	St Johnstone	30	14	3	13	31
7.	Albion Rovers	30	12	7	11	31
8.	Dunfermline Ath	30	11	9	10	31
9.	Ayr United	30	11	8	11	30
10.	Queen's Park	30	9	9	12	27
11.	Alloa Ath	30	7	10	13	24
12.	Forfar Ath	30	10	4	16	24
13.	Cowdenbeath	30	9	5	16	23
14.	Arbroath	30	8	7	15	23
15.	DUNDEE UNITED	30	8	6	16	22
16.	Dumbarton	30	7	8	15	22

'B' Division Season 1954-1955

		P	W	D	L	PTS
1.	Airdrie	30	18	10	2	46
2.	Dunfermline Ath	30	19	4	7	42
3.	Hamilton Accies	30	17	5	8	39
4.	Queen's Park	30	15	5	10	35
5.	Third Lanark	30	13	7	10	33
6.	Stenhousemuir	30	12	8	10	32
7.	St Johnstone	30	15	2	13	32
8.	Ayr United	30	14	4	12	32
9.	Morton	30	12	5	13	29
10.	Forfar Ath	30	11	6	13	28
11.	Albion Rovers	30	8	10	12	26
12.	Arbroath	30	8	8	14	24
13.	DUNDEE UNITED	30	8	6	16	22
14.	Cowdenbeath	30	8	5	17	21
15.	Alloa Ath	30	7	6	17	20
16.	Brechin City	30	8	3	19	19

'B' Division Season 1955-1956

		P	W	D	L	PTS
1.	Queen's park	36	23	8	5	54
2.	Ayr United	36	24	3	9	51
3.	St Johnstone	36	21	7	8	49
4.	Dumbarton	36	21	5	10	47
5.	Stenhousemuir	36	20	4	12	44
6.	Brechin City	36	18	6	12	42
7.	Cowdenbeath	36	16	7	13	39
8.	DUNDEE UNITED	36	12	14	10	38
9.	Morton	36	15	6	15	36
10.	Third Lanark	36	16	3	17	35
11.	Hamilton Accies	36	13	7	16	33
12.	Stranraer	36	14	5	17	33
13.	Alloa Ath	36	12	7	17	31
14.	Berwick Rangers	36	11	9	16	31
15.	Forfar Ath	36	10	9	17	29
16.	East Stirling	36	9	10	17	28
17.	Albion Rovers	36	8	11	17	27
18.	Arbroath	36	10	6	20	26
19.	Montrose	36	4	3	29	11

Division Two Season 1956-1957

		P	W	D	L	PTS
1.	Clyde	36	29	6	1	64
2.	Third Lanark	36	24	3	9	51
3.	Cowdenbeath	36	20	5	11	45
4.	Morton	36	18	7	11	43
5.	Albion Rovers	36	18	6	12	42
6.	Brechin City	36	15	10	11	40
7.	Stranraer	36	15	10	11	40
8.	Stirling Albion	36	17	5	14	39
9.	Dumbarton	36	17	4	15	38
10.	Arbroath	36	17	4	15	38
11.	Hamilton Accies	36	14	8	14	36
12.	St Johnstone	36	14	6	16	34
13.	DUNDEE UNITED	36	14	6	16	34
14.	Stenhousemuir	36	13	6	17	32
15.	Alloa Ath	36	11	5	20	27
16.	Forfar Ath	36	9	5	22	23
17.	Montrose	36	7	7	22	21
18.	Berwick Rangers	36	7	6	23	20
19.	East Stirling	36	5	7	24	17

Division Two Season 1957-1958

		P	W	D	L	PTS
1.	Stirling Albion	36	25	5	6	55
2.	Dunfermline Ath	36	24	5	7	53
3.	Arbroath	36	21	5	10	47
4.	Dumbarton	36	20	4	12	44
5.	Ayr United	36	18	6	12	42
6.	Cowdenbeath	36	17	8	11	42
7.	Brechin City	36	16	8	12	40
8.	Alloa Ath	36	15	9	12	39
9.	DUNDEE UNITED	36	12	9	15	33
10.	Hamilton Accies	36	12	9	15	33
11.	St Johnstone	36	12	9	15	33
12.	Forfar Ath	36	13	6	17	32
13.	Morton	36	12	8	16	32
14.	Montrose	36	13	6	17	32
15.	East Stirling	36	12	5	19	29
16.	Stenhousemuir	36	12	5	19	29
17.	Albion Rovers	36	12	5	19	29
18.	Stranraer	36	9	7	20	25
19.	Berwick Rangers	36	5	5	26	15

Division Two Season 1958-1959

		P	W	D	L	PTS
1.	Ayr United	36	28	4	4	60
2.	Arbroath	36	23	5	8	51
3.	Stenhousemuir	36	20	6	10	46
4.	Dumbarton	36	19	7	10	45
5.	Brechin City	36	16	10	10	42
6.	St Johnstone	36	15	10	11	40
7.	Hamilton Accies	36	15	8	13	38
8.	East Fife	36	15	8	13	38
9.	Berwick Rangers	36	16	6	14	38
10.	Albion Rovers	36	14	7	15	35
11.	Morton	36	13	8	15	34
12.	Forfar Ath	36	12	9	15	33
13.	Alloa Ath	36	12	7	17	31
14.	Cowdenbeath	36	13	5	18	31
15.	East Stirling	36	10	8	18	28
16.	Stranraer	36	8	11	17	27
17.	DUNDEE UNITED	36	9	7	20	25
18.	Queen's Park	36	9	6	21	24
19.	Montrose	36	6	6	24	18

Division Two Season 1959-1960

		P	W	D	L	PTS
1.	St Johnstone	36	24	5	7	53
2.	DUNDEE UNITED	36	22	6	8	50
3.	Queen of the South	36	21	7	8	49
4.	Hamilton Accies	36	21	6	9	48
5.	Stenhousemuir	36	20	4	12	44
6.	Dumbarton	36	18	7	11	43
7.	Montrose	36	19	5	12	43
8.	Falkirk	36	15	9	12	39
9.	Berwick Rangers	36	16	5	15	37
10.	Albion Rovers	36	14	8	14	36
11.	Queen's Park	36	17	2	17	36
12.	Brechin City	36	14	6	16	34
13.	Alloa Ath	36	13	5	18	31
14.	Morton	36	10	8	18	28
15.	East Stirling	36	10	8	18	28
16.	Forfar Ath	36	10	8	18	28
17.	Stranraer	36	10	3	23	23
18.	East Fife	36	7	6	23	20
19.	Cowdenbeath	36	6	2	28	14

Scottish Division One Season 1960-1961

		P	W	D	L	PTS
1.	Rangers	34	23	5	6	51
2.	Kilmarnock	34	21	8	5	50
3.	Third Lanark	34	20	2	12	42
4.	Celtic	34	15	9	10	39
5.	Motherwell	34	15	8	11	38
6.	Aberdeen	34	14	8	13	34
7.	Hearts	34	13	8	13	34
8.	Hibs	34	15	4	15	34
9.	DUNDEE UNITED	34	13	7	14	33
10.	Dundee	34	13	6	15	32
11.	Partick Thistle	34	13	6	15	32
12.	Dunfermline Ath	34	12	7	15	31
13.	Airdrie	34	10	10	14	30
14.	St Mirren	34	11	7	16	29
15.	St Johnstone	34	10	9	15	29
16.	Raith Rovers	34	10	7	17	27
17.	Clyde	34	6	11	17	23
18.	Ayr United	34	5	12	17	22

Scottish Division One Season 1961-1962

		P	W	D	L	PTS
1.	Dundee	34	25	4	5	54
2.	Rangers	34	22	7	5	51
3.	Celtic	34	19	8	7	46
4.	Dunfermline Ath	34	19	5	10	43
5.	Kilmarnock	34	16	10	8	42
6.	Hearts	34	16	6	12	38
7.	Partick Thistle	34	16	3	15	35
8.	Hibs	34	14	5	15	33
9.	Motherwell	34	13	6	15	32
10.	DUNDEE UNITED	34	13	6	15	32
11.	Third Lanark	34	13	5	16	31
12.	Aberdeen	34	10	9	15	29
13.	Raith Rovers	34	10	7	17	27
14.	Falkirk	34	11	4	19	26
15.	Airdrie	34	9	7	18	25
16.	St Mirren	34	10	5	19	25
17.	St Johnstone	34	9	7	18	25
18.	Stirling Albion	34	6	6	22	18

Scottish Division One Season 1962-1963

		P	W	D	L	PTS
1.	Rangers	34	25	7	2	57
2.	Kilmarnock	34	20	8	6	48
3.	Partick Thistle	34	20	6	8	46
4.	Celtic	34	19	6	9	44
5.	Hearts	34	17	9	8	43
6.	Aberdeen	34	17	7	10	41
7.	DUNDEE UNITED	34	15	11	8	41
8.	Dunfermline Ath	34	13	8	13	34
9.	Dundee	34	12	9	13	33
10.	Motherwell	34	10	11	13	31
11.	Airdrie	34	14	2	18	30
12.	St Mirren	34	10	8	16	28
13.	Falkirk	34	12	3	19	27
14.	Third Lanark	34	9	8	17	26
15.	Queen of the South	34	10	6	18	26
16.	Hibs	34	8	9	17	25
17.	Clyde	34	9	5	20	23
18.	Raith Rovers	34	2	5	27	9

Scottish Division One Season 1963-1964

		P	W	D	L	PTS
1.	Rangers	34	25	5	4	55
2.	Kilmarnock	34	22	5	7	49
3.	Celtic	34	19	9	6	47
4.	Hearts	34	19	9	6	47
5.	Dunfermline Ath	34	18	9	7	45
6.	Dundee	34	20	5	9	45
7.	Partick Thistle	34	15	5	14	35
8.	DUNDEE UNITED	34	13	8	13	34
9.	Aberdeen	34	12	8	14	32
10.	Hibs	34	12	6	16	30
11.	Motherwell	34	9	11	14	29
12.	St Mirren	34	12	5	17	29
13.	St Johnstone	34	11	6	17	28
14.	Falkirk	34	11	6	17	28
15.	Airdrie	34	11	4	19	26
16.	Third Lanark	34	9	7	18	25
17.	Queen of the South	34	5	6	23	16
18.	East Stirling	34	5	2	27	12

Scottish Division One Season 1964-1965

		P	W	D	L	PTS
1.	Kilmarnock	34	22	6	6	50
2.	Hearts	34	22	6	6	50
3.	Dunfermline Ath	34	22	5	7	49
4.	Hibs	34	21	4	9	46
5.	Rangers	34	18	8	8	44
6.	Dundee	34	15	10	9	40
7.	Clyde	34	17	6	11	40
8.	Celtic	34	16	5	13	37
9.	DUNDEE UNITED	34	15	6	13	36
10.	Morton	34	13	7	14	33
11.	Partick Thistle	34	11	10	13	32
12.	Aberdeen	34	12	8	14	32
13.	St Johnstone	34	9	11	14	29
14.	Motherwell	34	10	8	16	28
15.	St Mirren	34	9	6	19	24
16.	Falkirk	34	7	7	20	21
17.	Airdrie	34	5	4	25	14
18.	Third Lanark	34	3	1	30	7

Scottish Division One Season 1965-1966

		P	W	D	L	PTS
1.	Celtic	34	27	3	4	57
2.	Rangers	34	25	5	4	55
3.	Kilmarnock	34	20	5	9	45
4.	Dunfermline Ath	34	19	6	9	44
5.	DUNDEE UNITED	34	19	5	10	43
6.	Hibs	34	16	6	12	38
7.	Hearts	34	13	12	9	38
8.	Aberdeen	34	15	6	13	36
9.	Dundee	34	14	6	14	34
10.	Falkirk	34	15	1	18	31
11.	Clyde	34	13	4	17	30
12.	Partick Thistle	34	10	10	14	30
13.	Motherwell	34	12	4	18	28
14.	St Johnstone	34	9	8	17	26
15.	Stirling Albion	34	9	8	17	26
16.	St Mirren	34	9	4	21	22
17.	Morton	34	8	5	21	21
18.	Hamilton Accies	34	3	2	29	8

Scottish Division One Season 1966-1967

		P	W	D	L	PTS
1.	Celtic	34	26	6	2	58
2.	Rangers	34	24	7	3	55
3.	Clyde	34	20	6	8	46
4.	Aberdeen	34	17	8	9	42
5.	Hibs	34	19	4	11	42
6.	Dundee	34	16	9	9	41
7.	Kilmarnock	34	16	8	10	40
8.	Dunfermline Ath	34	14	10	10	38
9.	DUNDEE UNITED	34	14	9	11	37
10.	Motherwell	34	10	11	13	31
11.	Hearts	34	11	8	15	30
12.	Partick Thistle	34	9	12	13	30
13.	Airdrie	34	11	6	17	28
14.	Falkirk	34	11	4	19	26
15.	St Johnstone	34	10	5	19	25
16.	Stirling Albion	34	5	9	20	19
17.	St Mirren	34	4	7	23	15
18.	Ayr United	34	1	7	26	9

Scottish Division One Season 1967-1968

		P	W	D	L	PTS
1.	Celtic	34	30	3	1	63
2.	Rangers	34	28	5	1	61
3.	Hibs	34	20	5	9	45
4.	Dunfermline Ath	34	17	5	12	39
5.	Aberdeen	34	16	5	13	37
6.	Morton	34	15	6	13	36
7.	Kilmarnock	34	13	8	13	34
8.	Clyde	34	15	4	15	34
9.	Dundee	34	13	7	14	33
10.	Partick Thistle	34	12	7	15	31
11.	DUNDEE UNITED	34	10	11	13	31
12.	Hearts	34	13	4	17	30
13.	Airdrie	34	10	9	15	29
14.	St Johnstone	34	10	7	17	27
15.	Falkirk	34	7	12	15	26
16.	Raith Rovers	34	9	7	18	25
17.	Motherwell	34	6	7	21	19
18.	Stirling Albion	34	4	4	26	12

Scottish Division One Season 1968-1969

		P	W	D	L	PTS
1.	Celtic	34	23	8	3	54
2.	Rangers	34	21	7	6	49
3.	Dunfermline Ath	34	19	7	8	45
4.	Kilmarnock	34	15	4	5	44
5.	DUNDEE UNITED	34	17	9	8	43
6.	St Johnstone	34	16	5	13	37
7.	Airdrie	34	13	11	10	37
8.	Hearts	34	14	8	12	36
9.	Dundee	34	10	12	12	32
10.	Morton	34	12	8	14	32
11.	St Mirren	34	11	10	13	32
12.	Hibs	34	12	7	15	31
13.	Clyde	34	9	13	12	31
14.	Partick Thistle	34	9	10	15	28
15.	Aberdeen	34	9	8	17	26
16.	Raith Rovers	34	8	5	21	21
17.	Falkirk	34	5	8	21	18
18.	Arbroath	34	5	6	23	16

Scottish Division One Season 1969-1970

		P	W	D	L	PTS
1.	Celtic	34	27	3	4	57
2.	Rangers	34	19	7	8	45
3.	Hibs	34	19	6	9	44
4.	Hearts	34	13	12	9	38
5.	DUNDEE UNITED	34	16	6	12	38
6.	Dundee	34	15	6	13	36
7.	Kilmarnock	34	13	10	11	36
8.	Aberdeen	34	14	7	13	35
9.	Dunfermline Ath	34	15	5	14	35
10.	Morton	34	13	9	12	35
11.	Motherwell	34	11	10	13	32
12.	Airdrie	34	12	8	14	32
13.	St Johnstone	34	11	9	14	31
14.	Ayr United	34	12	6	16	30
15.	St Mirren	34	8	9	17	25
16.	Clyde	34	9	7	18	25
17.	Raith Rovers	34	5	11	18	21
18.	Partick Thistle	34	5	7	22	17

Scottish Division One Season 1970-1971

		P	W	D	L	PTS
1.	Celtic	34	25	6	3	56
2.	Aberdeen	34	24	6	4	54
3.	St Johnstone	34	19	6	9	44
4.	Rangers	34	16	9	9	41
5.	Dundee	34	14	10	10	38
6.	DUNDEE UNITED	34	14	8	12	36
7.	Falkirk	34	13	9	12	35
8.	Morton	34	13	8	13	34
9.	Airdrie	34	13	8	13	34
10.	Motherwell	34	13	8	13	34
11.	Hearts	34	13	7	14	33
12.	Hibs	34	10	10	14	30
13.	Kilmarnock	34	10	8	16	28
14.	Ayr United	34	9	8	17	26
15.	Clyde	34	8	10	16	26
16.	Dunfermline Ath	34	6	11	17	23
17.	St Mirren	34	7	9	18	23
18.	Cowdenbeath	34	7	3	24	17

Scottish Division One Season 1971-1972

		P	W	D	L	PTS
1.	Celtic	34	28	4	2	60
2.	Aberdeen	34	21	8	5	50
3.	Rangers	34	21	2	11	44
4.	Hibs	34	19	6	9	44
5.	Dundee	34	14	13	7	41
6.	Hearts	34	13	13	8	39
7.	Partick Thistle	34	12	10	12	34
8.	St Johnstone	34	12	8	14	32
9.	DUNDEE UNITED	34	12	7	15	31
10.	Motherwell	34	11	7	16	29
11.	Kilmarnock	34	11	6	17	28
12.	Ayr United	34	9	10	15	28
13.	Morton	34	10	7	17	27
14.	Falkirk	34	10	7	17	27
15.	Airdrie	34	7	12	15	26
16.	East Fife	34	5	15	14	25
17.	Clyde	34	7	10	17	24
18.	Dunfermline Ath	34	7	9	18	23

Scottish Division One Season 1972-1973

		P	W	D	L	PTS
1.	Celtic	34	26	5	3	57
2.	Rangers	34	26	4	4	56
3.	Hibs	34	19	7	8	45
4.	Aberdeen	34	16	11	7	43
5.	Dundee	34	17	9	8	43
6.	Ayr United	34	16	8	10	40
7.	DUNDEE UNITED	34	17	5	12	39
8.	Motherwell	34	11	9	14	31
9.	East Fife	34	11	8	15	30
10.	Hearts	34	12	6	16	30
11.	St Johnstone	34	10	9	15	29
12.	Morton	34	10	8	16	28
13.	Partick Thistle	34	10	8	16	28
14.	Falkirk	34	7	12	15	26
15.	Arbroath	34	9	8	17	26
16.	Dumbarton	34	6	11	17	23
17.	Kilmarnock	34	7	8	19	22
18.	Airdrie	34	4	8	22	16

Scottish Division One Season 1973-1974

		P	W	D	L	PTS
1.	Celtic	34	23	7	4	53
2.	Hibs	34	20	9	5	49
3.	Rangers	34	21	6	7	48
4.	Aberdeen	34	13	16	5	42
5.	Dundee	34	16	7	11	39
6.	Hearts	34	14	10	10	38
7.	Ayr United	34	15	8	11	38
8.	DUNDEE UNITED	34	15	7	12	37
9.	Motherwell	34	14	7	13	35
10.	Dumbarton	34	11	7	16	29
11.	Partick Thistle	34	9	10	15	28
12.	St Johnstone	34	9	10	15	28
13.	Arbroath	34	10	7	17	27
14.	Morton	34	8	10	16	26
15.	Clyde	34	8	9	17	25
16.	Dunfermline Ath	34	8	8	18	24
17.	East Fife	34	9	6	19	24
18.	Falkirk	34	4	14	16	22

Scottish Division One Season 1974-1975

		P	W	D	L	PTS
1.	Rangers	34	25	6	3	56
2.	Hibs	34	20	9	5	49
3.	Celtic	34	20	5	9	45
4.	DUNDEE UNITED	34	19	7	8	45
5.	Aberdeen	34	16	9	9	41
6.	Dundee	34	16	6	12	38
7.	Ayr United	34	14	8	12	36
8.	Hearts	34	11	13	10	35
9.	St Johnstone	34	11	12	11	34
10.	Motherwell	34	14	5	15	33
11.	Airdrie	34	11	9	14	31
12.	Kilmarnock	34	8	15	11	31
13.	Partick Thistle	34	10	10	14	30
14.	Dumbarton	34	7	10	17	24
15.	Dunfermline Ath	34	7	9	18	23
16.	Clyde	34	6	10	18	22
17.	Morton	34	6	10	18	22
18.	Arbroath	34	5	7	22	17

Scottish Premier Division 1975-1976

		P	W	D	L	PTS
1.	Rangers	36	23	8	5	54
2.	Celtic	36	21	6	9	48
3.	Hibs	36	18	7	11	43
4.	Motherwell	36	16	8	12	40
5.	Hearts	36	13	9	14	35
6.	Ayr United	36	14	5	17	33
7.	Aberdeen	36	11	10	15	32
8.	DUNDEE UNITED	36	12	8	16	32
9.	Dundee	36	11	10	15	32
10.	St Johnstone	36	3	5	28	11

Scottish Premier Division Season 1976-1977

		P	W	D	L	PTS
1.	Celtic	36	23	9	4	55
2.	Rangers	36	18	10	8	46
3.	Aberdeen	36	16	11	9	43
4.	DUNDEE UNITED	36	16	9	11	41
5.	Partick Thistle	36	11	13	12	35
6.	Hibs	36	8	18	10	34
7.	Motherwell	36	10	12	14	32
8.	Ayr United	36	11	8	17	30
9.	Hearts	36	7	13	16	27
10.	Kilmarnock	36	4	9	23	17

Scottish Premier Division Season 1977-1978

		P	W	D	L	PTS
1.	Rangers	36	24	7	5	55
2.	Aberdeen	36	22	9	5	53
3.	DUNDEE UNITED	36	16	8	12	40
4.	Hibs	36	15	7	14	37
5.	Celtic	36	15	6	15	36
6.	Motherwell	36	13	7	16	33
7.	Partick Thistle	36	14	5	17	33
8.	St Mirren	36	11	8	17	30
9.	Ayr United	36	9	6	21	24
10.	Clydebank	36	6	7	23	19

Scottish Premier Division Season 1978-1979

		P	W	D	L	PTS
1.	Celtic	36	21	6	9	48
2.	Rangers	36	18	9	9	45
3.	DUNDEE UNITED	36	18	8	10	44
4.	Aberdeen	36	13	14	9	40
5.	Hibs	36	12	13	11	37
6.	St Mirren	36	15	6	15	36
7.	Morton	36	12	12	12	36
8.	Partick Thistle	36	13	8	15	34
9.	Hearts	36	8	7	21	23
10.	Motherwell	36	5	7	24	17

Scottish Premier Division Season 1979-1980

		P	W	D	L	PTS
1.	Aberdeen	36	19	10	7	48
2.	Celtic	36	18	11	7	47
3.	St Mirren	36	15	12	9	42
4.	DUNDEE UNITED	36	12	13	11	37
5.	Rangers	36	15	7	14	37
6.	Morton	36	14	8	14	36
7.	Partick Thistle	36	11	14	11	36
8.	Kilmarnock	36	11	11	14	33
9.	Dundee	36	10	6	20	26
10.	Hibs	36	6	6	24	18

Scottish Premier Division Season 1980-1981

		P	W	D	L	PTS
1.	Celtic	36	26	4	6	56
2.	Aberdeen	36	19	11	6	49
3.	Rangers	36	16	12	8	44
4.	St Mirren	36	18	8	10	44
5.	DUNDEE UNITED	36	17	9	10	43
6.	Partick Thistle	36	10	10	16	30
7.	Airdrie	36	10	9	17	29
8.	Morton	36	10	8	18	28
9.	Kilmarnock	36	5	9	22	19
10.	Hearts	36	6	6	24	18

Scottish Premier Division Season 1981-1982

		P	W	D	L	PTS
1.	Celtic	36	24	7	5	55
2.	Aberdeen	36	23	7	6	53
3.	Rangers	36	16	11	9	43
4.	DUNDEE UNITED	36	15	10	11	40
5.	St Mirren	36	14	9	13	37
6.	Hibs	36	11	14	11	36
7.	Morton	36	9	12	15	30
8.	Dundee	36	11	4	21	26
9.	Partick Thistle	36	6	10	20	22
10.	Airdrie	36	5	8	23	18

Scottish Premier Division Season 1982-1983

		P	W	D	L	PTS
1.	DUNDEE UNITED	36	24	8	4	56
2.	Celtic	36	25	5	6	55
3.	Aberdeen	36	25	5	6	55
4.	Rangers	36	13	12	11	38
5.	St Mirren	36	11	12	13	34
6.	Dundee	36	9	11	16	29
7.	Hibs	36	7	15	14	29
8.	Motherwell	36	11	5	20	27
9.	Morton	36	6	8	22	20
10.	Kilmarnock	36	3	11	22	17

Scottish Premier Division Season 1983-1984

		P	W	D	L	PTS
1.	Aberdeen	36	25	7	4	57
2.	Celtic	36	21	8	7	50
3.	DUNDEE UNITED	36	18	11	7	47
4.	Rangers	36	15	12	9	42
5.	Hearts	36	10	16	10	36
6.	St Mirren	36	9	14	13	32
7.	Hibs	36	12	7	17	31
8.	Dundee	36	11	5	20	27
9.	St Johnstone	36	10	3	23	23
10.	Motherwell	36	4	7	25	15

Scottish Premier Division Season 1984-1985

		P	W	D	L	PTS
1.	Aberdeen	36	27	5	4	59
2.	Celtic	36	22	8	6	52
3.	DUNDEE UNITED	36	20	7	9	47
4.	Rangers	36	13	12	11	38
5.	St Mirren	36	17	4	15	38
6.	Dundee	36	15	7	14	37
7.	Hearts	36	13	5	18	31
8.	Hibs	36	10	7	19	27
9.	Dumbarton	36	6	7	23	19
10.	Morton	36	5	2	29	12

Scottish Premier Division Season 1985-1986

		P	W	D	L	PTS
1.	Celtic	36	20	10	6	50
2.	Hearts	36	20	10	6	50
3.	DUNDEE UNITED	36	18	11	7	47
4.	Aberdeen	36	16	12	8	44
5.	Rangers	36	13	9	14	35
6.	Dundee	36	14	7	15	35
7.	St Mirren	36	13	5	18	31
8.	Hibs	36	11	6	19	28
9.	Motherwell	36	7	6	23	20
10.	Clydebank	36	6	8	22	20

Scottish Premier Division Season 1986-1987

		P	W	D	L	PTS
1.	Rangers	44	31	7	6	69
2.	Celtic	44	27	9	8	63
3.	DUNDEE UNITED	44	24	12	8	60
4.	Aberdeen	44	21	16	7	58
5.	Hearts	44	21	14	9	56
6.	Dundee	44	18	12	14	48
7.	St Mirren	44	12	12	20	36
8.	Motherwell	44	11	12	21	34
9.	Hibs	44	10	13	21	33
10.	Falkirk	44	8	10	26	26
11.	Clydebank	44	6	12	26	24
12.	Hamilton Accies	44	6	9	29	21

Scottish Premier Division Season 1987-1988

		P	W	D	L	PTS
1.	Celtic	44	31	10	3	72
2.	Hearts	44	23	16	5	62
3.	Rangers	44	26	8	10	60
4.	Aberdeen	44	21	17	6	59
5.	DUNDEE UNITED	44	16	15	13	47
6.	Hibs	44	12	19	13	43
7.	Dundee	44	17	7	20	41
8.	Motherwell	44	13	10	21	36
9.	St Mirren	44	10	15	19	35
10.	Falkirk	44	10	11	23	31
11.	Dunfermline Ath	44	8	10	26	26
12.	Morton	44	3	10	31	16

Scottish Premier Divison Season 1988-1989

		P	W	D	L	PTS
1.	Rangers	36	26	4	6	56
2.	Aberdeen	36	18	14	4	50
3.	Celtic	36	21	4	11	46
4.	DUNDEE UNITED	36	16	12	8	44
5.	Hibs	36	13	9	14	35
6.	Hearts	36	9	13	14	31
7.	St Mirren	36	11	7	18	29
8.	Dundee	36	9	10	17	28
9.	Motherwell	36	7	13	16	27
10.	Hamilton Accies	36	6	2	28	14

Scottish Premier Division Season 1989-1990

		P	W	D	L	PTS
1.	Rangers	36	20	11	5	51
2.	Aberdeen	36	17	10	9	44
3.	Hearts	36	16	12	8	44
4.	DUNDEE UNITED	36	11	13	12	35
5.	Celtic	36	10	14	12	34
6.	Motherwell	36	11	12	13	34
7.	Hibs	36	12	10	14	34
8.	Dunfermline Ath	36	11	8	17	30
9.	St Mirren	36	10	10	16	30
10.	Dundee	36	5	14	17	24

Scottish Premier Division Season 1990-1991

		P	W	D	L	PTS
1.	Rangers	36	24	5	7	55
2.	Aberdeen	36	22	5	9	53
3.	Celtic	36	17	7	12	41
4.	DUNDEE UNITED	36	17	7	12	41
5.	Hearts	36	14	7	15	35
6.	Motherwell	36	12	9	15	33
7.	St Johnstone	36	11	9	16	31
8.	Dunfermline Ath	36	8	11	17	27
9.	Hibs	36	6	13	17	25
10.	St Mirren	36	5	9	22	19

Scottish Premier Division Season 1991-1992

		P	W	D	L	PTS
1.	Rangers	44	33	6	5	72
2.	Hearts	44	27	9	8	63
3.	Celtic	44	26	10	8	62
4.	DUNDEE UNITED	44	19	13	12	51
5.	Hibs	44	16	17	11	49
6.	Aberdeen	44	17	14	13	48
7.	Airdrie	44	13	10	21	36
8.	St Johnstone	44	13	10	21	36
9.	Falkirk	44	12	11	21	35
10.	Motherwell	44	10	14	20	34
11.	St Mirren	44	6	12	26	24
12.	Dunfermline Ath	44	4	10	30	18

Scottish Premier Division Season 1992-1993

		P	W	D	L	PTS
1.	Rangers	44	33	7	4	73
2.	Aberdeen	44	27	10	7	64
3.	Celtic	44	24	12	8	60
4.	DUNDEE UNITED	44	19	9	16	47
5.	Hearts	44	15	14	15	44
6.	St Johnstone	44	10	20	14	40
7.	Hibs	44	12	13	19	37
8.	Partick Thistle	44	12	12	20	36
9.	Motherwell	44	11	13	20	35
10.	Dundee	44	11	12	21	34
11.	Falkirk	44	11	7	26	29
12.	Airdrie	44	6	17	21	29

Scottish Premier Division Season 1993-1994

		P	W	D	L	PTS
1.	Rangers	44	22	14	8	58
2.	Aberdeen	44	17	21	6	55
3.	Motherwell	44	20	14	10	54
4.	Celtic	44	15	20	9	50
5.	Hibs	44	16	15	13	47
6.	DUNDEE UNITED	44	11	20	13	42
7.	Hearts	44	11	20	13	42
8.	Kilmarnock	44	12	16	16	40
9.	Partick Thistle	44	12	16	16	40
10.	St Johnstone	44	10	20	14	40
11.	Raith Rovers	44	6	19	19	31
12.	Dundee	44	8	13	23	29

Scottish Premier Division Season 1994-1995

		P	W	D	L	PTS
1.	Rangers	36	20	9	7	69
2.	Motherwell	36	14	12	10	54
3.	Hibs	36	12	17	7	53
4.	Celtic	36	11	18	7	51
5.	Falkirk	36	12	12	12	48
6.	Hearts	36	12	7	17	43
7.	Kilmarnock	36	11	10	15	43
8.	Partick Thistle	36	10	13	13	43
9.	Aberdeen	36	10	11	15	41
10.	DUNDEE UNITED	36	9	9	18	36

Scottish First Division Season 1995-1996

		P	W	D	L	PTS
1.	Dunfermline Ath	36	21	8	7	71
2.	*DUNDEE UNITED	36	19	10	7	67
3.	Morton	36	20	7	9	67
4.	St Johnstone	36	19	8	9	65
5.	Dundee	36	15	12	9	57
6.	St Mirren	36	13	8	15	47
7.	Clydebank	36	10	10	16	40
8.	Airdrie	36	9	11	16	38
9.	Hamilton Accies	36	10	6	20	36
10.	Dumbarton	36	3	2	31	11

*Dundee United returned to the Premier Division after two play off games with Premier side Partick Thistle. The first game was played on Sunday 12 May 1996 and the return leg was played at Tannadice on Thursday 16 May 1996.

Scottish Premier Division Season 1996-1997

		P	W	D	L	PTS
1.	Rangers	36	25	5	6	80
2.	Celtic	36	23	6	7	75
3.	DUNDEE UNITED	36	17	9	10	60
4.	Hearts	36	14	10	12	52
5.	Dunfermline Ath	36	12	9	15	45
6.	Aberdeen	36	10	14	12	44
7.	Kilmarnock	36	11	6	19	39
8.	Motherwell	36	9	11	16	38
9.	Hibs	36	9	11	16	38
10.	Raith Rovers	36	6	7	23	25

Scottish Premier Division Season 1997-1998

		P	W	D	L	PTS
1.	Celtic	36	22	8	6	74
2.	Rangers	36	21	9	6	72
3.	Hearts	36	19	10	7	67
4.	Kilmarnock	36	13	11	12	50
5.	St Johnstone	36	13	9	14	48
6.	Aberdeen	36	9	12	15	39
7.	DUNDEE UNITED	36	8	13	15	37
8.	Dunfermline Ath	36	8	13	15	37
9.	Motherwell	36	9	7	20	34
10.	Hibs	36	6	12	18	30

BIBLIOGRAPHY

Jousting With Giants, Jim McLean with Ken Gallacher, Edinburgh, Mainstream Publishing, 1987.

Across the Great Divide, Jim Wilkie, Edinburgh, Mainstream Publishing, 1984.

Rags to Riches, Mike Watson, Dundee, David Winters and Sons, 1985 edition.

The Paul Sturrock Story, Paul Sturrock, with Charlie Duddy, and Peter Rondo, Edinburgh, Mainstream Publishers, 1989.

Dundee United Through the Years, Simmath Press, Dundee, 1947.

The Irish in Scotland, J.E. Handley, Glasgow, J.S. Burns Publishers, 1964.

Scotland the Team, Andrew Ward, Derby, The Breeding Book Publishing Company Ltd, 1987.

Other Sources from D.C. Thompson Publications:

The Dundee Courier & Advertiser

The Dundee Evening Telegraph

The Sporting Post

The People's Journal

The Saturday Evening Post

The Sunday Post

Other Newspaper Sources,

The Daily Record

The Sunday Mail

Scotland on Sunday

The News of the World

The Sunday People

TRIVIA

Dundee United beat Rangers 8-1 in the North Eastern League on 18 April 1942. Scorers that day were Juliussen (2), Gardiner, Morgan, Nevins, Low, and Glassey (2).

By January 1970, Dennis Gillespie had scored 126 goals for the club.

Also by January 1970, Ian Mitchell had scored 106 goals for the club.

Season 1970-71. Admission prices for First Division were announced. A rise of 1s, up to 6s for an adult. Boys and OAP's prices were up to 3s. The price of a season ticket at Tannadice was £7 5s for the stand, and £5 for a ground ticket.

In 1970 Dundee United's home gate record was 26,500, United v. Barcelona. The away record was 75,000, Rangers v. United at Hampden Park in the 1940 War Cup Final.

United's record crowd for a derby was in 1938 when 38,000 turned up at Dens Park for a Scottish Cup game. The score was Dundee 2 United 2 on 27 January 1951.

United's stand was used for the first time in a public trial match on 4 August 1962. The first official match was on 11 August 1962 when United beat Dundee 3-2. The floodlights were first switched on 10 November 1962 when United beat Rangers 2-1.

Dundee United were the first Scottish club to win a European tie in Spain when they beat Barcelona 2-1 on 25 August 1966 in the Fairs Cup.

On 9 October 1972, General Manager Jerry Kerr announced that the club was to close down the player's hostel in Seafield Road Broughty Ferry. The reason given was that it had become .an uneconomic proposition'.

A list of United managers since the beginning: Jimmy Brownlie was first from 1923-32. Willie Reid took over until 1934, then Jimmy Brownlie again became manager. Bailie George Greig was manager from 193 5-3 8. Then Brownlie and Sam Irving, both directors at the club, then became joint managers for one year. Bobby McKay took over in 1939, and lasted only two months due to the Second World

War. Arthur Gray and Charlie McGillivary were in charge during the War years. The post War managers were Willie MacFadyen, Reggie Smith, Ally Gallacher, Tommy Gray, Andy McCall, Jerry Kerr from 1959-71, Jim McLean, Ivan Golac, Billy Kirkwood, Tommy McLean and Paul Sturrock.

There was a delay in renaming Dundee United from Dundee Hibs. This was caused by Dundee FC protesting about the name. The first game played as United was against Dumbarton away from home on 27 October 1923 which United lost 3-0. The team was Brownlie; Kay, Stirling, Swan, Richards, Gilfeather, McEwan, O'Kane, Mackie, Cottingham, Gilmour.

United's first home league game was played on 3 November 1923. The score was United 3 St. Bernard's 2.

In January 1974, the United directors offered to return 25p to their season ticket holders who were against the introduction of games being played on a Sunday.

United season ticket prices in 1975-76: Stand: £18 for adults, £12 for OAPs and Juveniles £9. For the Ground: £11.50 for adults, OAPs £9, and juveniles £6.

United's lowest gate for a Division One match was 300 when the club lost 5-0 to Hamilton. They played the match on 16 April 1932. The lowest recorded gate for a Second Division match was 100. This was in a game against Edinburgh City on 18 November 1938. United were comfortable winners that day by 9 goals to 3.

In 1909, Dundee Hibs bought Clepington Park from Dundee Wanderers. They changed the name to Tannadice Park. The first game played there was on 18 August 1909 when Dundee Hibs took on Edinburgh Hibs. The score that day ended 1-1.

In 1981, a United programme cost 20 pence.

United changed to the tangerine strips in season 1969-70. Their first competitive match wearing the colours was on 9 September 1969 in a game against Hearts in the League Cup. Unfortunately the strips did not bring luck that day as United lost 3-2 at Tynecastle.

United season tickets for season 1982-83, Stand for adults was £50, £30 for OAPs, and £25 for Juveniles. Season tickets for the ground were £30, £20 and £15 respectively.

On 1 January 1941, Tannadice Park was used as a venue for boxing. Boxer Jim Brady beat Kid Tanner for the Empire Bantamweight Title.

On 30 April 1983 over 5,000 United supporters travelled through to Cappielow to cheer on the club in an important match. United were close to winning their first Premier League title and the club's directors paid the fans' entrance fee. It certainly did the trick as United beat Morton 4-0. They also won the Premier League too.

Under soil heating was installed at Tannadice during the close season of 1985-86. Dundee United launched their new look strips on 22 June 1989. The strips had been manufactured by Adidas for 12 years. However the club switched to a Japanese company called Asics.

United opened a new club shop in the Forum Centre in November 1989.

On 4 October 1990, United launched a new video entitled *Dundee United, The Jim McLean Years*. As part of the promotional launch a United supporters' rally was held in the Caird Hall that night.

The George Fox Stand was officially opened on 8 August 1992. The game played that day was against Hearts. The score was 1-1, and the crowd 9,500.

On 21 October 1993, the announcement was made that home supporters could no longer stand in The Shed from start of season 1994-95. The estimated cost of seating and improvements was put at £200,000.

When United lost to Hearts on 17 February 1968, a crowd of 9,000 turned out. The official receipts that day were a staggering £1,949!

In season 1934-35 you could purchase your season ticket for 25 shillings.

The Dundee Hibs side that secured the Eastern League Flag for the club on 13 March 1920 was: Miller, Stalker, Mulholland, Wilkie, Hughes, Stirling, Heron, D.S. Miller, Wilson Murray, and Cargill.

On 11 July 1913 season tickets for Dundee Hibs went on sale, the cost – 5 shillings.